Israel The Chosen

Israel The Chosen

HER IDENTITY, LAND, ENEMIES,
RELIGION AND MESSIAH

Quinton Everest, Jr.

Unless otherwise noted, the Scripture quotations contained herein are from the New Revised Standard Version Bible, copyright 1989, Division of Christian Education of the National Council of the Churches of Christ in the U.S.A. Used by permission. All rights reserved.

Front cover image: Hurva Synagogue in Jerusalem. A historic synagogue in the Jewish Quarter of the Old City of Jerusalem. Shutterstock/Fat Jackey

ISBN: 1539874842
ISBN 13: 9781539874843
Library of Congress Control Number: 2016918332
CreateSpace Independent Publishing Platform
North Charleston, South Carolina

Contents

Preface

THE RESEARCH FOR THIS BOOK began with an effort to see through the controversy surrounding the Jewish people and the State of Israel. To my dismay, some of my friends and relatives were making disparaging remarks about both that made my presynaptic neurons quiver.

I came to realize that such remarks are not uncommon.

"The Jews are now acting like the Nazis." Was I living in the United States or Syria? Even among men in a church setting (I hate to admit it), I heard this: "The Jews. Someone ought to put them on a piece of land far from civilization." And then there was this one, said by leftist Jews and Gentiles alike as they weighed in on the State of Israel being formed in our modern era: "It was a bold experiment, but it has failed."

Have these speakers no heads and no hearts? Have they neither? Don't they know anything about the agony of pre-twentieth-century Jewry, let alone the European anti-Semitism of the twentieth? Or the whole history of the crushing treatment of the Jews in lands other than their own—where they were seen as "the wandering Jew" and where their allegiance to their adopted land was always questioned because it was adopted and not native? I wonder if they know how discreetly the Israelis go about defending themselves. Case in point: they—the Israelis and their government—tolerated the launching of four thousand missiles from Gaza into Israel before the Israel Defense Force

(IDF) went into serious action! And before the IDF did bomb, they dropped flyers so the population could seek cover.

I had to get into the historical details. So I decided to do a little digging.

Now I have one hundred and fifty books in the Israel-Jewish-Arab section of my library, I subscribe to Jewish periodicals, and I read favorite Jewish bloggers and talk to Jewish people. And yes, I read the literature of Palestinians and left-wing Israelis. My previous instincts have been reinforced. Now I am convinced that the Jewish people are a gift to the nations—not a bother. This book outlines the evidence in rudimentary form. Because it would be less than honest to imply otherwise, I'll let you know this up front without your having to leaf through this book: I am pro-Israeli, and I respect the Jewish people. I belong to the little Facebook group called "Jews Who Love Christians Who Love Jews (and the Christians Who Love Them)." I'm there in the parentheses.

When, as a reader, I leaped into various streams of Zionism (see Glossary if necessary), I wanted to get the feel of each one. The deeply felt need of persecuted and traumatized European Jewry to escape is one aspect of Zionism—a continuing one, as we see in the twenty-first century. Secondly, the ages-long yearning to return to their land of promise, to re-establish their kingdom and re-build their temple is deep-seated in the religious Jew. Thirdly, those Jews desiring their culture to continue, yes even to be revived, were vocal in calling for the revival of the Hebrew language and promotion of Jewish literature and music. Some were calling for Jerusalem to be a cultural center. Then the issue of political Zionism concerned not only the form of government but the question of how one ethnic population can move in on another or alongside another. Palestine, to which the Jewish immigrants of the late nineteenth century bravely immigrated, was *literally* a quagmire, full of swamps and neglected land. Yet the resident Arab Muslim and Christian populations were immediately enraged by the Jews' arrival.

I examined that clash between the new Jewish pioneers and the Arabs. Why were the Arabs belligerent? Did the behavior of the Jewish settlers provoke them? I analyzed the mind-set of the Middle East Arabs—their false claims of landownership when most of the land before the Israeli state was not in private hands—their fraudulent narrative of ancient history, denying, for example, the existence of Solomon's temple, the Israelite monarchy and the very existence of the Jewish people as a nation—and their ferocious hatred of and cruelty towards the Jews through most of Islamic history as documented by recent histories of dhimmitude (the placement of the Jews in second and third class citizenry with no judicial rights). Focusing on this intensity became depressing. When I reached that point, I knew I had to put distance between myself and that subject. Distance—that was what I needed. I threw it all to one side for a year. Then I walked back into the mess, knowing the book would have to take a different direction.

I saw then that I could not allow the Arab-Israeli controversy to dominate the book, and I needed to cover other vital topics—to wit, the religion of the Jewish people and Judaism's evolution from the destruction of Jerusalem to the present. This would require delving into the Torah, the Talmud, and rabbinical studies. Oh, but that was only the beginning. For that would, in turn, direct me toward the deep-seated and ages-long Jewish expectation of the Messiah. Making that turn moved me to focus more on the scriptures and Jewish tradition. There I beheld not just the Chosen People but the figure of the Messiah, the Chosen *One.*

I wanted to see what the Jewish rabbis—ancient, medieval, and modern—wrote about this figure, who was so exquisitely portrayed in one of most beautifully written ancient works of literature to ever grace ancient scrolls: the prophecy of Isaiah. I saw how important it was not to linger on Arab "rejectionism," as the historians call it, but rather on the "Comfort ye my people" aspect of Isaianic prophecy.

I engrossed myself in the Zionist movement and discovered that there were various approaches to it, the three most important being political, cultural, and Messianic. Some Jewish philosophers insist that Messianic Zionism underlays all other forms. They assert that the Messianic Age will outshine all the other ages when it appears in the world, and the very expectation of it motivates observant Jews. As they carefully observe their holy days and pray, they yearn for their *Mashiach* (Hebrew for "Messiah") and His age of blessedness. Many of the Orthodox believe that, with the land back in their possession, the days of redemption have begun.

In taking the turn toward the Messianic expectation, I came into view of Isaiah's revelation of two servants. The first servant is Israel. And—glory, glory, glory—the Second Servant is the Suffering One, who is the perfect reflection of the gracious God.

So my turn toward grace was made by paying no heed to the object of my peripheral vision, the stubborn intransigence and rejectionism found in Palestine. I instead looked straight at—with awe and wonder—the redemption for both the Jews and the nations. I began working on this book with *joy*! The message of the prophets—Isaiah especially, Zechariah secondarily, and others as well—became the focus.

So what began as an effort to sort out the issues of a Middle East conflict came to include the religion of the Jewish people, ancient to modern. My attention easily and eventually moved to the rabbis and their literature (the Talmud), the prophets, and the marching of history toward the end—yes, the culmination of all things historical. That necessarily included looking at the Servant of the Lord, who upended history and will finally close it out with the inauguration of His Kingdom.

Upon making the finishing touches to this book, I realized that I had neither grown tired of this subject nor become depressed with negativity— nor could I be finished with it yet, though the book itself was complete. The subject continues to fascinate me because I see the finger of God guiding His people, because I see the hand of God weakening Gentile nations while reaching out to help people of faith—both Jew and Gentile—in their time of confusion and pain.

"The Lord is near." Behold the Chosen One. See this Servant and conquering King who I firmly believe will gradually make known His love to the Chosen People as they walk where He walked, and who—in the denouement—will appear to them in His glory.

I present this book with the hope and prayer that it will be the means of reflecting positively on the goodness of the God of Abraham, Isaac, and Jacob—on the sovereignty and grace of *Hashem* (the Name), *Adonai* (the Lord), and His self-revelation and providence.

Glory and power be to Him!

Please note the usage in this book for the names for "God." I do not use the common English transliteration from the four Latin letters *YHWH*, which is called the Tetragrammaton. Placing vowels in it gives us "Yahweh." Its derivation may be from a verb meaning "to be." Many Jewish people believe it to be too sacred to utter or put into writing. I use, in its stead, the English "Lord." Likewise, some traditional Jews use the term "Hashem," meaning "The Name" in referring to God to avoid speaking His name. I have chosen to use that term in some places.

This book developed one step at a time. That wasn't because I didn't wish to plan ahead. I could wish it, but it wouldn't have worked with this project. I was ordered to look only at the present task. When I needed an editor, I didn't know how to choose from the editors I found. But *voilà*! You might say that my editor found me. Before setting afoot with my wife to walk down our block and dine at a neighbor's home, I decided to take the hard copy of the chapter called "The Land" and present it to our hostess. After dinner I asked her if she might want to read it. (Caution to first time authors: don't do this unless you are prepared to be humiliated by a disinterested recipient.) Little did I know that she was an editor! Her background was in the legal profession, but she was currently editing books. She asked me if I would mind if she edited that one chapter. "Oh no," I said, surprised by the offer. And that's how Carole Gold was "chosen."

When we were halfway through the project, we agreed that this was good and that perhaps it was God as well, and together we rejoiced in the fact that God is good. Her brief residence on the block where my wife and I live was a godsend. She introduced me to Word 2013 and expressions or contexts that might be offensive to her people and could be better rephrased or reworded. While I admit that I was not a totally obedient student, Carole gave me exactly what I needed during the editing process. Our friendship endures.

My wife has been my primary "editor" by always being willing to review my work while, so to speak, the ink was still wet. As she read the work in progress, I was there to look at her face and inquire, "Is the product worth the labor and agony?" Always supportive, she would reply, "This is what the world is in need of." That was not exactly how she said it, for she was an English teacher. She was actually a cheerleader way back when, and I am blessed to be the recipient of her expressions of encouragement. Yes, without her I would have thought there was no winning, or end to, this authorial game.

I want to give special thanks to authors of biblical commentaries that aided my understanding of certain books of the *Tenakh*/Old Testament. (See Glossary if necessary.) Thank you, J. Alec Motyer, author of *The Prophecy of Isaiah*; Christopher Wright, author of *The New International Commentary on*

Deuteronomy; and the late David Baron, author of *Zechariah: A Commentary on His Visions and Prophecies*.

Unless otherwise noted, the Bible translation used throughout is the New Revised Standard Version (NRSV). Where the Hebrew title of a book of the Torah/Pentateuch differs from the English, both will be used with a forward slash separating the two, as I have done in this sentence.

Introduction

But now, thus says the Lord,
He who created you, O Jacob,
He who formed you, O Israel:
Do not fear, for I have redeemed you,
I have called you by name,
You are mine.

—Isaiah 43:1

ON THE NIGHT OF NOVEMBER 9, 1938, throughout all of Germany, the destruction of Jewish property was a public spectacle. It was Kristallnacht—the Night of Broken Glass, when men with sledgehammers and axes smashed windows, set fire to buildings, and took Jewish males prisoner. Fourteen hundred synagogues were either set on fire or demolished; stores, schools, homes, and hospitals were destroyed. The perpetrators were instructed to wreak havoc only on Jewish buildings; those owned by Gentiles were spared in order to demonstrate that German Jewry was the target. The Nazi spotlights were on the Jews.

Kristallnacht was also a Hebrew Bible-burning eve. In Frankfurt Jews were forced to shred the Torah scrolls and burn them. In Berlin people carried the scrolls from the Fasanen Street Synagogue to Wittenberg Square and set fire to them. As Torah scrolls burned in the yard of a synagogue in Dusseldorf,

German men, some wearing the robes of rabbis and cantors, danced around the fire. The carefully preserved scrolls were "touched, carried, rolled out, trampled on, biked and walked over, tied to the backs of Jews, thrown into rivers, torn apart, set ablaze."[1]

This high-handed crime proved that the anti-Semitism in Germany was more than just a racial reaction; it was also religious. In fact, it was an attack on the very foundation of the Western world's Judeo-Christian civilization. Specifically, it was aimed at the monotheism of the Hebrew religion, the Ten Commandments, and God's covenants with Israel. Further evidence of this was the fact that Nazi leaders were working with National Socialist Party sympathizers in the German church to discard the use of the Old Testament. On Kristallnacht they went further: they used their hands to profanely handle, tear, and set fire to the very pages on which the Mosaic law and prophets were memorialized.

The Nazi leadership believed that after once disposing of the despised biblical foundation, they could replace it with their cherished new philosophies of pan-Germanism and social Darwinism. George Bernard Shaw, distinguished twentieth-century playwright, excused the Nazis by saying they were "merely imitating the Jews' doctrine of chosenness" with their own doctrine of racial superiority and their own sacred land—the völkisch German fatherland.[2]

Why should the Nazis be concerned with a people so small in numbers, when they clearly had their eyes on all of Europe? The answer lies in the profound influence the Hebrew religion had throughout the world, due in part to its position as the precursor of Christianity. Europe was then known as Christian Europe, but Nazism was building a radically different structure. Once disposed of the old, they could establish a fascist government for the Germanic peoples and other conquered nations.

In a subtle and somewhat mysterious way, Israel is a check on tyranny. Despite their flaws, the Jewish people have been representatives of the law, righteousness, and the worship of the one true and living God. Chapter 2 elaborates on this, aiming to show that another benefit of Judaism has been the development of a republican form of democracy. In seventeenth-century England, the *Tenakh* (Jewish term for what Christians know as the Old Testament) and the Talmud (to a lesser degree) were influential in the formation of the political philosophies of John Locke, Thomas Hobbes, John Milton, and John Selden. Especially since the Puritan era, the Hebrew Torah and Prophets have been a threat to tyrants and a sourcebook for good government.

However, the Jews have been disliked by the masses too, and it has been so from the beginning, as we discover when reading the Old Testament. The Seder ritual at every Passover acknowledges it: "In each and every generation they rise up against us to destroy us. And the Holy One, blessed be He, rescues us from their hands." The reason for anti-Semitism has been explored by many commentators, but the most basic answer that touches the depth of this hatred is, as stated above, the calling of Israel to be the chosen and separate people and recipients of the law. To attribute anti-Semitism to Jewish affluence alone is myopic; masses of poor Jews have also been the objects of harassment and massacre.

Most nations in Europe and Asia that have been home to Jews of the dispersion have, at one time or another, expelled them. The list of countries is long: "England in 1290, France in 1306 and 1394, Hungary between 1349 and 1360, Austria in 1421, numerous localities in Germany between the fourteenth and sixteenth centuries, Lithuania in 1445 and 1495, Spain in 1492, Portugal in 1497, and Bohemia and Moravia in 1744–45. Between the fifteenth century and 1772, Jews were not allowed into Russia; when finally admitted, they were restricted to one area, the Pale of Settlement. Between 1948 and 1967, nearly all the Jews of Algeria, Egypt, Iraq, Syria and Yemen fled these countries, fearing for their lives."[3] When expelled or harassed, Jews fled to countries that would suffer them. Again and again they would establish themselves and generally thrive in fields such as finance, medicine, law, education, and the arts.

Notwithstanding their unsettled history, the Jews have been a blessing to their host nations. In chapter 2 we will see some of the ways Jewish presence has been beneficial, proving that Gentiles have an obligation to give thanks for the benefits that accrue from Jewish existence. The one obvious good which Jewry presents to the world is that it bears the message of salvation history. There are many lesser but still important ways that point to the wisdom of God in choosing such a special people.

Obviously, not all people have been appreciative of a Jewish presence. The malignant and contagious disease of anti-Semitism still threatens the Diaspora as well as the State of Israel. The perennial question in the minds of many people, particularly in Europe, North Africa, and the Middle East, is, "What should we do with the Jews?" Saying that we should give thanks for them would invite derision. Herein, however, we reject hatred and intolerance of the Jews and instead list reasons for gratitude.

Chapter 3 probes the matter of Israel's election. At heart this is a theological question and, therefore, difficult for the worldly journalist or politician to discuss, since the categories of those discussions are political in nature. It also can become an embarrassing subject to the secular Jew who rejects the idea of a God who involves Himself so closely with us, as well as to the liberal Jew who tends to adapt his thinking to current cultural trends.

According to historical analyses, Israel should not exist today. Other ancient nations have lost their identity but not Israel—and this author believes that she has been preserved through the ages for a purpose. The great ingathering of Jews to the reestablished State of Israel within the past century is a sign of the sovereignty of God in human history and the fulfillment of the observant Jew's perennial dream.

The land that ancient Israel occupied, though a gift, was not there for the taking. To displace the corrupt Canaanites, Israel was required to engage in military battles, a dismay-inducing mission for many Bible readers. Chapter

4, "The Land," will discuss the issue of Israel's title as well as her intimate attachment to it even throughout her long exile. The condition of the land while in the possession of other peoples is also deserving of examination. The final chapter, "The Denouement," will look at the prophetic promises concerning the final ingathering when the fortunes of Israel will be restored.

The contemporary scene presents the modern movement of Zionism—the return to what was British Palestine and the development of Israeli statehood. That return resulted in an instantaneous clash with the resident Arab population. Examination of the fierce early and continuing resistance to Jewish immigrants will occupy chapters 5 and 6. Ancient examples of the absolute rejection of the Jewish people in Palestine, as well as a discussion of the reasons for this rejection, will help link Israel's past with her present. Finally, the book will consider the response of the Yishuv (the Jewish community in Palestine) and the attempts of the British to neutralize Arab violence.

As alluded to previously, there is the curious issue of Jewish unbelief. Many Jews are atheist or agnostic, and among the others, spirituality is lacking even if tradition is closely held. In Western countries the various branches of Judaism, excepting Orthodoxy, have been weakening for many decades. This is acknowledged by many rabbinical authorities, some quoted in chapters 10 and 11, "The Crisis of Judaism, Parts I and II." This diminishing belief and wavering commitment must be seen as a crisis. The biblical narratives are considered "sacred myth," so the study of the Tanakh is rare. The Talmud, ossified with innumerable laws and traditions, is used selectively by some and never by most. Membership and attendance of services is in decline. When pressed, some Western Jews will profess "a rational faith" with perhaps a belief in a "supreme being." When they attend their temple or synagogue, the emphasis is likely to be on a liberal set of ethics and the way to self-fulfillment.

One of the pillars of traditional Judaism has been belief in the coming Messiah. Following the Roman destruction of Jerusalem in AD 70, the great hope of the Jews was that he would lead the restoration of their homeland

and the great ingathering of the Diaspora—all in fulfillment of the prophetic promises. Israel would then be the blessing to the world it was called to be, and the Gentile nations would come to accept this glorious new epoch. In chapter 12 we will examine false messiahs who have made appearances and some modern conceptions of the coming Messianic Age.

Chapters 13 and 14 present an exposition of certain sections in the second part of the prophecy of Isaiah regarding the servants of the Lord. These texts must be interpreted responsibly, for they are of paramount importance to both Jews and Christians. Some of the sections are usually thought to refer to the Messiah; others clearly speak of Israel. What did the ancient rabbis believe about these Servant Sections, and how do modern scholars of Judaism, with their liberal readings of the Tanakh, interpret these vivid prophecies? The personal sections (some call them "the Servant Songs") are descriptive of the Righteous One, who suffers vicariously for all the people. How can the rabbis reject the notion that this One is the Messiah? Indeed, the ancient ones did view it as messianic, while most modern rabbis reject it. How does the church today interpret it? Although the contemporary church does not speak with one voice, I am confident that the Spirit will guide into truth those who believe in the possibility and authority of the Word.

Many ask, what will the end of the Middle East conflict be like? The prophets paint a dramatic picture of the culmination of the struggle between Israel and the other nations. In the final chapter, the end of the story will be told through the Hebrew prophets. Can their picture of the return of the Jewish people really be what we are seeing today? This author believes so and supporting evidence given here should bear this out.

Many friends and acquaintances ask me why I have an interest in the Jewish people. The core of the matter is simple: the Bible is Jewish. The biblical narrative is set, for the most part, in a Jewish land, and its characters are mostly

Jewish—examples of faith and obedience on the one hand and skepticism and rebellion on the other. When our family moved from a small town to the city, I discovered that the Jewish people still lived. When I was twelve years old, I learned of the birth of the new nation of Israel—a subject of great interest to my father, for whom the event was a fulfillment of biblical promises. His interest became mine.

Later in my life, the Jewish-Arab conflict became a compelling interest. As the "peace process" became a newsworthy focus, I began reading about the history of the conflict in earnest. I saw the modern Middle East conflict partly in terms of the ancient Hebrews' existence in the shadow of the Near Eastern nations and empires. I now believe that one cannot understand the present mind-set of Jews and Arabs, as well as the Israeli nation's place in history, without immersion in biblical history. I am well aware that, with the birth of Islam, another element was added to the mix; however, in the ancient Near East, the conflict was already in place long before the appearance of Mohammed. I will go no further than that here, as the reader will discover more of my convictions as the argument proceeds and examines the Chosen People.

I would like to contribute to an appreciation for the presence of the Chosen People in our world and describe what would be missing if they were absent. Sharing enthusiasm about the new life of the Jewish nation—the dry bones being reconnected and coming to life—is a personal passion. The Spirit of the Lord breathes the breath of life into those bones, so I have hoped and prayed that the same Spirit would assist me in writing this book. Can we and do we believe in the resurrection? It is promised: "Thus says the Lord God: I am going to open your graves, and bring you up from your graves, O my people; and I will bring you back to the land of Israel…And I will put my Spirit within you, and you shall live." (Ezekiel 37:12–14)

So now consider the ongoing restoration of this people who were scattered throughout more than one hundred nations a century ago and whose very existence continues to be threatened—a people who still experience this world's reluctantly given gratitude for its genius and its contributions to humanity.

§

1. Alon Confino, "Why the Nazis Burned the Hebrew Bible," *Commentary*, June 2014, 30–34.
2. Dennis Prager and Joseph Telushkin, *Why the Jews?* (New York: Simon and Schuster, 2003), 27.
3. Ibid., 4.
4. Arthur Hertzberg, *The Zionist Idea.* (Philadelphia: The Jewish Publication Society, 1997), 243.

CHAPTER 1

Jewish Identity

You are a people holy to the Lord your God;
The Lord your God has chosen you out of all the peoples on earth
To be his people, his treasured possession.

—DEVARIM/DEUTERONOMY 7:6

As the first bearers of the promise—and thus as the people in whom
the great foundational phase of biblical history took place—they are
doubtless at the center of world history. One might think that such
a small people couldn't really be so important. But I believe there
is something special about this people and that the great decisions
of world history are almost always connected to them somehow.[1]

—JOSEPH CARDINAL RATZINGER

THE STATE OF ISRAEL IS diminutive among the family of nations, and
her people are few. During the reign of Herod the Great, her population
numbered about 8 million. Today, worldwide, the Jews number 13.7 million. During the long stretches of their dispersion, they constituted a small

minority in their host countries. Yet this nation has always exerted an impressive influence.

In antiquity, she was positioned between the two major empires of Egypt and Babylon, both of which were located in fertile valleys irrigated by great rivers—the Nile, the Tigris, and Euphrates. Both civilizations were imbued with high cultures based on advances in scientific knowledge and writing. Israel existed in a state of tension between these two. Her small size and central position might have seemed a liability. Some call it a "topographical weakness."[2] But there were compensating features. Her location put her at the crossroads of three major continents in the middle of global trade routes. She also had the linguistic advantage of being located where the earliest forms of writing—cuneiform and hieroglyphics—were developed.

The first printed mention of Israel was on the Merneptah Stele—an ancient inscription on a stone slab written about 1220 BC. Merneptah was an Egyptian king who, it seems certain, was falsely claiming to have destroyed Israel. This was his boast:

> *Israel is wasted, its seed is not;*
> *And Hurru is become a widow because of Egypt.*

Hurru is a term for Syria/Palestine. This inscription provides strong evidence that Israel was an established people at the time of Merneptah's reign, undercutting the position of skeptics to the contrary.[3] The Egyptian king could boast of destroying her regardless of the dishonesty of his claim (typical of the monarchs of that era) because, generally, news did not travel.

In modern times another strongman of Egypt, Gamal Abdel Nasser, shouted the mania of the Arab peoples before the Six-Day War of 1967:

> *We aim at the destruction if the State of Israel! The immediate aim: perfection of Arab military might. The national aim: the eradication of Israel.*[4]

A gap of three millennia separated the two Egyptian leaders, although they were united in their goal. While both would have liked to destroy Israel, it was beyond their power.

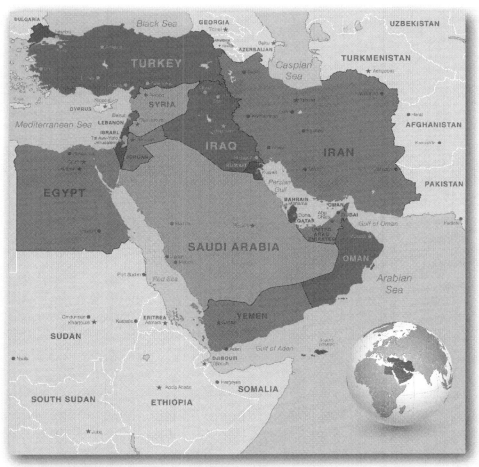

Shutterstock/Pingebat
"Map of the Middle East Zone"

A Vulnerable Nation

Israel was (and is) surrounded on every side by nations that despised her very existence, declared Israel to be illegal, and made her annihilation a prime objective. In the modern era, on the day following Israel's declaration as a state, the country was invaded by five neighboring Arab armies. In the Book of Psalms, there is one striking reference to Israel's vulnerability. The biblical author speaks as a representative of Israel:

> All nations surrounded me;
> In the name of the Lord I cut them off!...
> They surrounded me like bees;
> They blazed like a fire of thorns. (Psalms 118:10, 12)

After being dispersed to other nations, the Jews were vulnerable there as well. In those circumstances they were devoid of national leadership that could plead for them in their foreign residences. They were homeless—guests everywhere but at home nowhere, as the Zionists (those advocating a return to the Land) put it. Politically powerless and subject to the whims of kings and prejudices of the populace, they were collectively known as "the wandering Jew."

Periodically, eruptions of anti-Semitism occurred in a presumably Christian Europe, resulting, at times, in nationwide expulsions of the Jewish population. Then came the Nazi genocide. Approximately two-thirds of all the Jews living in Europe were exterminated.[5] Since then, Arab nations and Muslim terrorists of the Middle East have conspired to finish the work of the Nazis, waging war in an effort to annihilate the new nation and plotting the extermination of as many Jews worldwide as possible. Thus, the apt biblical metaphor for the Jews is nothing as imposing as a great tree; instead it's a mere scrub bush, such as the one seen by Moses on Mount Horeb—ablaze with the fires of affliction yet not consumed.

This paradox of a tiny nation wielding such an enduring influence in the world fits exactly with the biblical perspective on influence and power, which is this: *God utilizes what, on the face of it, is of little consequence in order to accomplish His saving purpose.* Due to the numerical insignificance or relative weakness of His agents, the divine influence is at first hardly perceptible; but eventually, like leaven, it acts as a pervasive change agent. In the case of this small nation, Israel, we have the advantage of the long view of world history from which to assess the impact of the Chosen People who have been dispersed throughout the nations. Her people have borne witness to the mighty acts of God, even in eras of national disgrace. And in bearing that witness so conspicuously, she has been regarded as a national phenomenon throughout her long history.

A Separate People

Contributing to her vulnerability, Israel has always been unique and set apart. The Jewish use of the classification "kosher" is indicative of Israel's own singularity. Kosher food is select food, fit and proper for eating. The Chosen People themselves are "kosher" in that they are separate from the rest of humanity, striving to be ritually fit for their unique vocation. Indeed, the clean-food laws of the Torah did provide, as one of their purposes, a sign of the separateness of the Hebrews from their pagan neighbors. The Jewish people are in the midst of the nations but are different. A key word here is *sanctification* (*kadosh* in Hebrew), meaning "set apart," or "declared to be holy." The Sabbath too is set apart in time from other days of the week for rest and replenishment of the soul, something the ancient world could not fathom. One of the nineteen blessings prayed in the Jewish service acknowledges this national separateness. The term used in the Havdalah ceremony at the conclusion of the Sabbath is the Hebrew word *l'havdil*, meaning "to differentiate." One version of the prayer (the Kiddush) reads in part,

> Blessed art thou, O Lord our God, King of the Universe, who hast made a distinction between holy and profane, between light and darkness, between Israel and other peoples, between the seventh day and the six days of work. Thou hast set a distinction between the holiness of the Sabbath and the holiness of the Festival, and hast hallowed the seventh day above the six days of work; thou hast distinguished and sanctified thy people Israel by thy holiness. Blessed art thou, O Lord, who hast made a distinction between holy and holy.[6]

The observance of the Sabbath distinguished ancient Israel from neighboring nations, just as the Sabbath day was set apart from the rest of the week. It was a reminder that Israel was to be the Lord's. "For you are a people holy to the Lord your God" (Devarim/Deuteronomy 7:6a). Persons of other tribes and cultures could join the Israelites but only if they kept the laws of the Torah. There was to be no assimilation.

In the covenant established at Mount Sinai, God made Himself known as a jealous God who would not tolerate rivalry. This stipulation in the covenant made Israel unlikable to the other nations because it left no room for even casual deference to their gods. Therefore, in Israel's associations with neighboring people, tension was built in because little Israel was to be nonconformist—intolerant of all the family and national gods that were worshipped by surrounding nations. Unless people understand this, they will not understand the enmity that has existed between Israel and other peoples throughout history.

So thoroughly did the Hebrews wish to renounce the ways of the people they originally replaced in the Promised Land that they were commanded to break down their altars, make no treaty with them, and not intermarry. This was to make certain that no disloyalty would be shown to Yahweh (the Lord) and no social bonding would be made with pagan people (Devarim/Deuteronomy 7:3–6). This is how the Jewish nation was founded. A midrash (commentary) on the Jewish Talmud contains this well-known question and answer: "Why are the Jews like the fruit of the olive tree? Because as all liquids mix with each other but the oil of the olive does not, so Israel does not mix with the Gentiles. As the olive does not yield its oil unless it is crushed, so Israel does not return to God unless it is crushed by affliction."

Throughout Jewish history but especially in the modern era, issues of separateness and integration have provoked much debate among thoughtful Jews. We will explore this further in this chapter and chapter 3, "Israel's Election." But there is yet another pressing, closely related question.

A CHOSEN PEOPLE

In the Tanakh it is made clear that Israel did not choose the Lord: *He* chose *them*. "The Lord set his heart on you and chose you" (Devarim/Deuteronomy 7:6). Throughout the Tanakh the writers use metaphors that represent this relationship between the Lord and Israel: the Lord as the male who woos the woman, the potter who forms the vessel, the farmer who plants and tends the vine.

It is made plain to her that she was chosen not because she was a numerous people; she was not numerous (Devarim/Deuteronomy 7:7–8). She wasn't chosen because she was good; she had proven to be a stiff-necked and unbelieving people (Devarim/Deuteronomy 9:4–6). She could not boast of her power and fruitfulness; this would come from Yahweh. "It is he who gives you power to get wealth, so that he may confirm his covenant" (Devarim/Deuteronomy 8:17). Thus Israel, the Chosen, was left without any reason for boasting of her position and achievements.

In contemporary Judaism another of the most widely used benedictions from the prayer book has the affirmation of this doctrine, a prayer that most rabbis insist be used before any reading from the Torah: "Blessed are You, God, King of the universe, Who has chosen us from all peoples, and has given us His Torah."

But do these statements about Israel's chosenness still pertain to the people we call the Jews of today? And do the Jewish people favor this view of their identity, or are they averse to it? We will explore the second question first.

SKEPTICISM AND AMBIVALENCE

Jews living in Western democracies are more likely to have an aversion to the concepts of chosenness and separateness, sensing that these are at variance with progressive thought that favors the view that every culture is equally interesting and every religion equally deserving of acceptance. For Jews to take the position that their people are uniquely related to God's purposes would likely be provocative. Therefore, not willing to give up the gains of assimilation into Gentile society, many Jews have discarded distinguishing features of these biblical concepts.

The emancipation of Jews in nineteenth-century Europe created a huge divide among them politically and religiously. This term, *emancipation*, one that is associated in the American mind with the freeing of slaves, is used to denote the laws in Europe in the eighteenth and nineteenth centuries that extended civil rights to the Jews, who were emerging from the ghettos. The hiring practices, voting rights, and societal structures were being liberalized for the Jews, and a major portion of the Jewish population was eagerly responding. At this point many European Jews cut themselves loose from the strictures of Judaism, although the Orthodox of Eastern Europe remained firm in their traditional doctrines. The German Jewish intellectual community contended that Jewish nationhood was defunct and had been for two millennia. In their view, there was nothing in Jewish teaching and tradition that *could* be preserved or was *worthy* of preservation. It was no use talking about a renewal of Judaism, a Messianic Age, or an ingathering of Jews to their ancient land. It was over. At this same time, Jewish social theorists determined that "if national identity was a real problem to reckon with, the Jews were not a nation but rather a fossil, and rather than espousing the fantasies of Zionism, Jews should cast off the aegis of chosenness and particularity, finally allowing their kernels as species-beings to shine through."[7] This meant that their identities should be defined as German, European, or even Universalist—belonging not to an ancient people but to the world and living as humanists.

These German Jewish intellectuals believed it was time to recognize the superiority of European culture, especially that of the German fatherland. For these thinkers the only Judaism worth retaining was a system of universal ethics that could satisfy all free-thinking people. One of these intellectuals eloquently opined, "A Jew that preferred a nonexistent state and nation (Israel) to Germany ought to be put under police protection not because his views were dangerous but because he was obviously insane."[8] If this idea had been adopted by the whole of Jewry, it would have buried Judaism and eventually the nation. But with the convulsions of the twentieth century and the establishment of the State of Israel, this view has certainly been challenged, if not eradicated.

Today some American rabbis bemoan the erosion of the "chosen" identity among their people and are calling Jews to revive stronger religious convictions and identities. One of these leaders is Jack Wertheimer, professor of American Jewish history at the Jewish Theological Seminary, who cites with a jaundiced eye the modern aspirations of his people to achieve inclusion and equality. He asks, "How could Jews argue for admission [into Gentile society] as equals on the grounds that they are *no different from their neighbors and [yet] simultaneously maintain a strong sense of distinctiveness?*"[9] (this author's emphasis) Some Jewish religious movements have removed offending passages from the Jewish liturgy in order to neutralize the claim of chosenness. Some have sought to reformulate their religious lives to deemphasize the ideas of separateness and chosenness. Wertheimer observes that "there is a sharp dissonance between traditional Jewish perspective and the prevailing cultural outlook within American society" but that "generations of American Jews have been taught that the Jewish and Western aspects of their identities mesh neatly rather than produce powerful—perhaps irreconcilable—dissonances." Wertheimer doesn't believe they mesh. "No revitalization of Judaism," he says, "is possible unless the Jewish community confronts this dilemma."[9]

We now live in a time when many peoples, especially western Europeans, see the nation-state as outdated. France, Belgium, Italy, and all the other European countries have lived out their time. For now the European Union constitutes the necessary political union, and they see a one-world government on the horizon. Therefore, they see no reason to help the Jewish people remain as one. So if the Jews are to remain a distinct people, they must consider the opposing forces and all the present demands they impose. If Jews remain complacent, it will be the thriving ultra-Orthodox Jews who will form the identity and be representative of Judaism. As David Singer, director of research for the American Jewish Committee, put it in his testimony concerning his Jewish beliefs, "Separatism is anathema to the vast majority of American Jews (meaning the liberal majority), but it remains a fact that without a heavy dose of it there can be no Jewish survival."[10] No lines of separation, no survival. Beyond that, it means no fulfillment of Israel's mission in the world.

One might then observe these Jews in Western nations to see whether they will choose to be a part of a declining Western culture or return to their roots, stand with their historic position, and affirm the position of distinctiveness as outlined in the Torah and their common liturgy.

It is easy to find modern Jews with a serious involvement in Judaism who, even so, are unconvinced of their people's position as God's chosen. Richard L. Rubenstein, PhD, a well-known educator, rabbi, author, and graduate of Hebrew Union College and Harvard University, says that "in no sense do I believe that Jews or any other people are the chosen of God, nor do I believe the Jewish people has a more distinctive role in the world than any other." Yet in the same article, he testifies, "Nevertheless, I regularly utter Hebrew prayers praising God for having chosen Israel, for there is no way to excise references to the election of Israel from the prayer book without destroying its integrity and authenticity." There is, in fact, a liberal branch of American Judaism that has removed "chosen" from its prayer book, but Rabbi Rubenstein prefers to keep it in. Using his term *excise*, it seems that though in one part of his mind, he rejects what seems to him a retrograde idea, with another part—the part that, perhaps, was built into his DNA—he just cannot *excise* this idea of chosenness.[11]

Some liberal rabbis have made a modification of this doctrine, in which the focus is switched from the Jews being a chosen people to their having a special *vocation*—one that will promote and exercise justice and compassion. Being chosen is too undemocratic, for, in their minds, it places them above the rest of humanity. However, claiming a special vocation, they believe, is more acceptable. The biblical support they garner for this special vocation is a phrase (favorite to them) from the prophecy of Isaiah: "Light to the nations." From the founders of Zionism to the present, this slogan has been used to lift up the higher and more benevolent ways of life, ideally the ethic of their own people. We will look at this phrase in the chapter entitled "The Servants," and we will ask, to whom does the designation "light to the nations" refer? It is surely an important question, since the prophet holds it up so very high and liberal Judaism is using it in an attempt to remove the "chosen" idea and level the field in the interest of the principle of equality.

Within the borders of Israel, the issue of "identity as chosen" is not quite the same as it is in Western countries. There the land tends to mold a more definitive identity. Yet even there, there is weakness. A survey was taken in 1991, 1999, and again in 2009, on the beliefs, observance, and values of Israeli Jews, and a representative sample of the Jewish adult population participated. The results showed that 67 percent of the respondents believed—or believed but sometimes had doubts—that the Jews are the Chosen People.[12] So what about that sizeable minority who live and breathe Jewish culture in the Zionist State and yet deny altogether their traditional position as the Chosen People of God? It is no secret that many Jews, even in Israel, have limited firmly held religious convictions.

CONNECTION AND CONTINUITY

Thus far in this introductory discussion of the identity of world of Jewry, we have assumed that the Israel of the Bible is the Israel of today. Obviously, the modern composition of world Jewry is different because of limited intermarriage and conversions. But the pertinent question is whether this people group in general constitutes the descendants of those who came forth from the barren womb of Sarah. In the corporate body of Jews, is there a common ethnic origin with a common ancestral homeland? Essentially, is this the Israel of Hebrew scripture?

Many people would say, "Well, of course. Who would deny that it is the same nation as the biblical Israel?" Let me name some of the people who would say that.

Some authors and scholars have been gaining notoriety of late by arguing that the modern State of Israel has co-opted its name. One prime example is Shlomo Sand, professor of contemporary history (not ancient history) at the University of Tel Aviv in 2008, who authored the book *The Invention of the Jewish People*.[13] This Israeli professor contends that modern Jews are not the descendants of the ancient Hebrew people. To the contrary, they have no common ethnic origin and national heritage, as has been widely accepted. He says that this is a national mythology consisting of fabrications taught by Zionists and disenchanted Jewish historians. The Jewish people of today, he contends, are a mishmash of ethnic groups, a major one being the Khazars of medieval Eurasia. Therefore, he contends that the Jews who have immigrated to the modern State of Israel are not returning to their homeland. It is the homeland of the Arab Palestinians, not the Jews. Sand is representative of a group of Israeli intellectuals that have their roots in radical philosophies and are embarrassed that their new nation is characterized as a Jewish state.

Sand's book, first published in Israel, was many months on the best-seller list. When translated into French, it was awarded the prestigious Aujourd'hui Award of the Association of French Journalists. Its publication in English brought wide recognition and numerous reviews in major publications and journals. Yet many reviewers of the book dismissed its conclusions as far-fetched. Hillel Halkin, American-born literary critic and novelist living in Jerusalem, writes in *The New Republic*, "What...shall we say of an age in which a book so intellectually shoddy that once, not very long ago, it would have been flunked as an undergraduate thesis by any self-respecting professor of history?" In the same article, Halkin cites the vast Jewish literary and rabbinical-law output from time immemorial when he states, "In all the enormous corpus of pre-nineteenth-century Jewish literature (from which, for understandable reasons, Sand does not quote), Jewish peoplehood is never treated as anything but an unchallenged and unchallengeable fact."[14]

Until recent times tradition has been a strong bulwark for the retention of Jewish community and the continuity of Jewish life. If there is one thing Jewish rabbis and scholars are noted for, it is the preservation of their history—a history bound up in and articulated by scripture, prayers, feasts, rituals, and customs, continually renewing the consciousness of peoplehood.

Historically, the strict insistence on marrying within the ethnic group stood firm. The ferocity with which Jewish parents have severed relationships with their children who married Gentile partners—and the grief they traditionally showed by saying the *Kaddish*/Mourner's Prayer for offspring who married Gentiles—has been, until recently, a major preserver of Jewish genealogy.

It is worth noting that recent DNA studies have given strong evidence of the Jewish people's retention of core genetic identity. An article in the *Jerusalem Post* written by a scientist from Columbia University sums this up as follows:

> More studies have been carried out on the genetic history of the Jews than on most ethnic groups, perhaps because there are so many Jewish doctors to take advantage of the fabled willingness of Jews to participate in research. These studies not only show that almost all Jewish populations have origins in the Middle East, but that the DNA of Jews from almost every corner of the Diaspora is more similar to that of other Jews than to any other population.[15]

The ethnic identity has remained strong. The connections between the Jews of today with their ancestors are many, and the evidence is convincing of a sense of ages-long peoplehood. The Israel of today is surely the Israel of history.

MUSLIM FABRICATION

There is yet another source of Jewish people's denial of connection to their history: it is Arab historians. Many contend that Jews now populating the State of Israel are not descendants of the ancient Hebrews and have no right to maintain a Jewish State in Palestine. The ancient Canaanites and Philistines were Arabs, they say, and it is the Arabs who ruled Palestine. Their concocted versions, of course, differ according to the audiences they are addressing, some saying that David and Solomon were kings but the only monarchs in Jerusalem's history. The chief judge of the Palestinian Authority, Sheikh Tayseer Rajab Tamimi, declared, as reported in the *Jerusalem Post* in 2009, that "there was no evidence to back up claims that Jews had ever lived in Jerusalem or that the temple ever existed. Tamimi claimed that Israeli archeologists had 'admitted' that Jerusalem was never inhabited by Jews...'Jerusalem is an Arab and Islamic city and it always has been so.'"[16]

The motive behind this fabrication is obvious: Arab professors and leaders are attempting to discredit Jewish history, and with it, they are hoping to deny all Jewish rights to govern any part of present-day Palestine. But as Samuel Katz says,

The city [of Jerusalem] never played any part in the Arabs' political life. While in turn Damascus, Baghdad, and Cairo glittered with the luster of an imperial capital, Jerusalem stagnated as a remote provincial townlet. It never served even as a provincial capital (an honor reserved for Remlah). No less significantly, it was never a Moslem cultural center...To the Moslems, Jerusalem, though the site of a Holy Place, was a backwater. Nor did the Arabs attach any importance to living in Jerusalem. Even when the Moslems ruled, for long periods, the majority of the population was Christian. After the middle of the nineteenth century, soon after modern Jewish reconstruction began, the Jews attained a majority, which they have never relinquished.[17]

This has been a sticking point in the Middle East peace process. Yasser Arafat, former chairman of the Palestine Liberation Organization, always insisted that there was no historical connection between the Jews and the land of Palestine. Therefore, they had no claim upon the land—none whatsoever. During the Camp David talks in July 2000, Arafat angered President Clinton by asserting that there had never been a Hebrew temple on the Temple Mount in Jerusalem— neither Solomon's Temple nor the postexilic Temple nor Herod's Temple.[18] Therefore, the Temple Mount in Jerusalem is of sacred significance only because of the Al Aksa Mosque and the Dome of the Rock, which sit on it today.

Shutterstock/Joshua Haviv
"Temple Mount in Jerusalem"

These views are echoed in the Middle East Muslim Arab press and the textbooks of Muslim children, which teach that Jewish people do not have their beginnings in the land of Israel. Arab scholars, clergy, and politicians join in propagating this fiction in order to break the connection between the Jews and the land of Palestine, thus undermining the legitimacy of the State of Israel in the eyes of their people.

The Koran describes the lives of some Old Testament figures, but their stories are changed almost beyond recognition. The Muslim claim for truth is that the Koran was composed in heaven, where the original is still in place, and that because the Tanakh versions are fraudulent, the Koran was written to reclaim the authentic narratives. The following are examples of Koranic versions: In the third Sura of the Koran, it is said that there was an association between Abraham and Mecca. God commanded Abraham to make a pilgrimage there, where later his footprint was discovered within the sacred enclosure of the Kaaba. And the land God promised to Abraham was, in fact, not Canaan but Arabia. Further, the son of promise was not Isaac but Ishmael. And that is just the beginning of the altered sacred story.

Considering the disregard for truth in the historical method written into their sacred writings, it would not be safe to look to Arab Muslim historians for reliable information. Even their museums are not immune to deletion and fabrication. Bernard Lewis, noted Middle East historian, reports that "the historical museum in Amman [Jordan] tells through objects and inscriptions the history of all the ancient peoples of the region—with one exception: the kings and prophets of ancient Israel are entirely missing…Textbooks used in public schools under the Palestinian Authority…begin with the retroactively Arabized Canaanites and jumps from them to the Arab conquest in the seventh century C. E., entirely omitting the Old Testament, its people and history."[19]

So, we find in the Palestinian school system educators who are intent on recasting history into a fake, self-serving Muslim version in order to cause Jews to virtually disappear from the ancient Middle East. This fabrication is purposive. Its goal is to remove all Jewish rights in Palestine and counter the Zionist claim to any parcel of that land. The history of Israel is labelled a corrupted version, purposely distorted by the Jews in order to gain a claim on the Holy Land. This approach is of one mind with holocaust denial: in that case, we hear reports of statements from Muslim leaders, contending that either the Holocaust never happened or it happened on a much smaller scale than most assert, effectively deeming it insignificant.

This version of history correlates with the Islamic religion. Just as the faith involves complete submission to Allah, so Koranic study offers no supporting evidence of its truth and no textual analysis. Questioning its validity is criminal, for it is written in the heavenly original. Such arbitrary methodology carries over into Islamic historical writings.

This distortion of history is nothing new. To deny the existence of the Jewish people from time immemorial is a public use of slander to gain the upper hand in the war against Israel, and this tactic is as old as the ancients. The Psalmists often complained about it.

They say, "By our tongues we shall prevail;
With words as our ally, who can master us?" (Psalms 12:4)

Hide me from the secret plots of the wicked,
From the scheming of evildoers,
Who whet their tongues like swords,
Who aim bitter words like arrows. (Psalms 64:2–3)

Muslim historians use speech as weaponry. In order to deny Israel's modern connection to the land, the histories of the Jewish people, both secular and sacred, must be discredited. The Tanakh must be besmirched because in its books, Jerusalem is the focal point of Jewish identity, activity, and longing; it's mentioned nearly seven hundred times. But in the Koran there is no mention of Jerusalem. How does one counter this fact? By holding the biblical accounts untrustworthy. Such is the purpose for the brazen and shameless rewriting of Jewish history. As self-designated victims of the Jewish presence in the land, Muslims claim the *right* to falsify the record.

Benny Morris acknowledges the frustration with Muslim historians here when he says that "unfortunately most Arab historians still labor under the yoke of severe political-ideological restrictions that are characteristic of non-democratic societies." [20]

The Strength of the Connection

These rewriters of history contend that the Jewish people are not the same people as the Jews of ancient times; that this nation does not have continuity; that modern Jewry, by and large, is not made up of the descendants of Hebrews of ancient Palestine. They present an interesting case, but there is a preponderance of evidence that contradicts these illusory arguments.

First, there is the Jewish people's common national homeland. From the destruction of ancient Israel by the Roman army to the rebirth of Israel in the modern era, there has been a continual Jewish community in the land. Contrary to common notions, not all Jews went into exile. While the Romans made an effort to wipe out all Jews in Palestine and did decimate the Jewish population, there were many survivors. Many scattered to towns in Galilee, where centers of Judaic study were founded, producing the Jerusalem Talmud. When persecution grew strong, they moved to other towns. By the time of the Crusades, there were enough Jews in Haifa to defend the city. Records dating back to 1099 show that there were Jewish communities throughout the country, fifty of which are known to the Israelis, writes Samuel Katz, former member of the Israeli Knesset and advisor to Prime Minister Begin. [21]

Secondly, consider how fanatical the rabbis were in ancient and medieval times about keeping their lineage pure. Following the dispersion of the Jews in the second century, the rabbis kept a ban on marriage to Gentiles. They also refrained from proselytizing, fearing that too many converts would weaken their community. [22] As noted above, they monitored their communities to keep them solely Jewish.

Thirdly, this most noteworthy piece of Jewish history is grounded in both story and law. From earliest times, exhortations were delivered to Israel to "remember" and to be "mindful." The study of history in Israel was made a solemn obligation.[23]Even when the history was uncomplimentary to the nation, as is often the case in the Tenakh, it still had to be told and studied. Further, the Talmud, which is comprised of oral law that was later written, dates from 445 BC until AD 1600—a span of two thousand years! During that time interpretations of the Torah were handed down, along with additions and further interpretations, to make up the Talmud. The whole compendium was layer upon layer of law, each layer building on the original Torah and all previous interpretations and additions. All contributors were Jewish rabbis, whose names were affixed to their passages. Therefore, the construction of the Talmud itself is a reflection of this connection of ancient Jewry and Judaism to modern Jewry and Judaism.

Charles Krauthammer, noted physician and commentator, states,

Israel is the very embodiment of Jewish continuity. It is the only nation on earth that inhabits the same land, bears the same name, speaks the same language, and worships the same God that it did 3,000 years ago. You dig the soil and you find pottery from Davidic times, coins from Bar Kokhba, and 2,000-year-old scrolls written in a script remarkably like the one that today advertises ice cream at the corner candy store.[24]

So despite the best efforts of Israel's detractors to undermine her history, her history is being validated by the great renewal of her national life upon the very land of her origin.

The connection between ancient and modern Jewry is real and verifiable. I am also of the conviction that there is *a connection between the ancient and modern enmity* existing between Israelis and their neighbors. The neighbors of Israel, both then and now, have made no secret of their desire to see Israel wiped off the map. They have thus done more than just picking quarrels over boundaries and other issues common to neighboring nations. The Torah stories explain that before the ancient Israelites ever approached the Promised Land, nations in the region fought them militarily, sought to have a curse put on them, and prohibited any Israelite feet from stepping on their roadways. Just so, in modern times, the Arab nations have reckoned on driving the Zionists into the sea, sending them back to Europe, or annihilating them with an atomic bomb. This anti-Israelite hatred is part and parcel of the undeniable connection between the ancient and modern experiences of Israel and her people.

INTERNATIONAL RECOGNITION OF THE CONNECTION

In modern times, the State of Israel has had friends, and while they have been few and of the fair-weather variety, they have been beneficial—friends who have acknowledged the historic connection between ancient and modern Jewry. From the standpoint of international law, the first modern international legal mandate pertaining to the return of the Jewish people to Palestine recognized their ancient roots. In the Preamble to the League of Nations Mandate for Palestine in 1922, there is this history-making clause: "Whereas recognition has thereby been given to the *historical connection* of the Jewish people with Palestine and to the grounds for reconstituting their national home in that country."[25] (emphasis mine)

This acknowledgment of the historical connection was accompanied by permission to return. The United States, though not a member of the League of Nations, accepted it de facto. The Ottoman Empire, which controlled Palestine for four hundred years, had prohibited any organized groups of Jews to immigrate there. Their opposition rested on Muslim religion and antinationalist, anti-freedom impulses. Many Christians' growing belief that the Jewish people would be gathered once again in Palestine was viewed as fanciful by some Christian scholars and their adherents. These folks were skeptical as to the claim that Old Testament prophecy contained specific portrayals of future redemptive events. But the events of World War I opened up that very prospect of the return of the Jews to their sacred land.

Before the war, Britain and the Ottomans were allies, so Britain was not going to force the issue of Jewish immigration. However, after the Ottomans foolishly switched their allegiance from the Allied Powers to the German-Austro-Hungary group and found themselves on the losing side of the war, control of the Middle East was transferred to France and Great Britain. *Britain was the only major European power whose leaders had any serious thought of assisting the Jewish people's return to their homeland.* Lord Balfour and Prime Minister Lloyd George could see some advantages to Britain gaining control in the Middle East, but there was more to their interest in Palestine than just strategic advantage. As Walter Laqueur put it in *A History of Zionism*,

> He [Balfour] and Lloyd George wanted to give the Jews their rightful place in the world. It was not right, they felt, that a great nation should be deprived of a home. Balfour believed, as Lloyd George did, that the Jews had been wronged by Christendom for almost two thousand years and that they had a claim to reparation.[26]

The majority of Lloyd George's cabinet was made up of Protestant Evangelicals, schooled in Old Testament scripture. And it was to Britain that the mandate from the League of Nations was granted. Thus, the way was open to the reestablishment of the Jewish national home under the sponsorship of the British. Later, most Americans and the administrations of Presidents Woodrow Wilson and Warren Harding gave their support to the British proposal.

Best-selling author-historian Paul Johnson called the reestablishment of a modern Jewish homeland a miracle, in that many vying interests had to merge to bring it to fruition.[27] One of the greatest of all Zionist philosophers, Ahad Ha'am, though himself an agnostic, made this statement in 1897: "'To gather our scattered ones from the four corners of the earth' (in the words of the Prayer Book) is impossible. Only religion, with its belief in a miraculous redemption, can promise such a consummation."[28]

The small Jewish nation has always needed and received divine intervention to lead her through the vicissitudes of her long life. Even in her anguish, one can trace the hand of Providence. The Torah and prophets can aid in the understanding of her history—yes, even her modern calamitous history. Like no other nation on earth, the Jewish people have been severely tried, and like no other, they have retained a special, divine calling.

The gradual decline of Western civilization and the rebirth of Israel have been occurring simultaneously—two historical phenomena that have become increasingly evident to the world. America and Western Europe are losing their influence. (Any casual search on the world wide web will show how much thought is being given to the weakening of the Pax Americana and decline of Western civilization). The attention of the world is increasingly on the Middle East. In Luke's Gospel, we read this prediction of Yeshua: "[The people of Judea] will fall by the edge of the sword [the Roman army under Titus in AD 70] and be taken away as captives among all nations; and Jerusalem will be trampled on by the Gentiles, *until the times of the Gentiles [the Gentile empires] are fulfilled.*" (Luke 21:24; (emphasis mine). Following the second war between Rome and the Judeans, no Jews were permitted to enter Jerusalem, and the city was renamed Aelia Capitolina. From then until the mid-twentieth century, Gentile empires controlled the city.

Now, in the twenty-first century, America and the West are weakening under the weight of overweening governments on which increasing demands are made. This is partially due to moral decline and the breakup of the traditional family. Governments in the West are now prime caregivers at high cost. Furthermore. challenges to Western leadership in the world are being issued by Russia, China and Iran. The times of the traditionally-strong Gentile nations seem to be nearly over. Meanwhile the tiny nation of Israel, surrounded by enemies, is displaying her technological genius and idealistic intensity.

Chosen Israel has a unique identity. Chosen Israel is in the genes, on the map, and increasingly at the center of geopolitical phenomena. What is lacking is effective spiritual leadership and a resolution to the crisis of her people's faith. Those issues will be taken up in the latter part of this book.

1. Joseph Cardinal Ratzinger, *Salt of the Earth* (San Francisco: Ignatius Press, 1997), 251.
2. Samuel Katz, *Battleground: Fact and Fantasy in Palestine* (New York: Taylor Productions, Ltd., 2002), 10.
3. *NIV Archeological Study Bible* (Grand Rapids: Zondervan, 2005), 360.
4. Mitchell Bard, *The Complete Idiot's Guide to Middle East Conflict* (Indianapolis: Alpha Books, 1999), 224.
5. "The Final Solution," Mitchell Bard, Jewish Virtual Library, 2017, www.jewishvirtuallibrary.org/jsource/Holocaust/finalsolution.html.
6. Herbert Adler, *Service of the Synagogue: New Year and the Day Of Atonement* (New York: Hebrew Publishing), 21
7. Hazony, David; Hazony, Yoram; Oren, Michael B., Editors, *New Essays on Zionism*. Eyal Chowers, "The Zionist Revolution in Time." (Jerusalem and New York: Shalem Press, 2006), 136.
8. Walter Laqueur, *A History of Zionism* (New York: Schocken Books, 2003), 8–9.
9. Milton Himmelfarb, "A Symposium: What Do American Jews Believe?" *Commentary*, August 1996.
10. Ibid.
11. Ibid.
12. Asher Arian et al., and the Guttman Center for Surveys, *A Portrait of Israeli Jews* (Jerusalem: Israel Democracy Institute Publishing, 2012, https://en.idi.org.il/media/5439/guttmanavichaireport2012_engfinal.pdf, 51).
13. Shlomo Sand, *The Invention of the Jewish People* (New York: Verso, 2009).

14. Hillel Halkin, "Indecent Proposal," *The New Republic*, January 9, 2010.

     Halkin is an author, translator, literary critic, and novelist, the son of Abraham Halkin, professor of Jewish literature history and culture at the Jewish Theological Seminary of America in New York.
15. Diana Muir Appelbaum and Paul S. Appelbaum, "Genetics and the Jewish Identity," *Jerusalem Post*, March 6, 2008, 14.
16. Khaled Abu Toameh, "PA Judge: Jews Have No History in Jerusalem," *Jerusalem Post*, August 27, 2009.
17. Samuel Katz, *Battleground: Fact and Fantasy in Palestine* (New York: Taylor Productions, 1985), 130–133ff.
18. "Dennis Ross on Fox News Sunday," Fox News, April 21, 2002.
19. Ron Rosenbaum, *Those Who Forget the Past* (New York: Random House, 2004), 556–57.
20. Benny Morris, *Righteous Victims: A History of the Middle East Conflict, 1881–1999* (New York: Alfred A. Knopf, 1999), xiv.

     Note also: Hillel Halkin, "Out of Andalusia," *Commentary*, September 2003, 41–42.

     "Islam and the Qur'an did deny Jewish reality, right from its very beginning—that is, from the time of Abraham, whose best-loved son, according to Islamic tradition, was not Isaac but Ishmael, and whose life story had been deliberately falsified by the Book of Genesis to conceal the fact that he was the first Muslim. Nor was it Abraham alone. Adam, Noah, Jacob, Joseph, Moses, David, Solomon: the story of every major figure in the Bible is told differently by the Qur'an, which openly charges the Bible with repeatedly lying...To thinking Jews, this made Islam not a less but a more preposterous faith than Christianity. If Christianity was an affront to rational monotheism, Islam was an insult to human intelligence itself, since who could take seriously a religion that, having come into existence 2,000 years after its parent faith, accused the parent of counterfeiting a past of which it now claimed to possess the true version? This was indeed a religion of stolen contraband."

21. Samuel Katz, *Battleground*: *Fact and Fantasy in Palestine* (New York: Taylor Productions, 2002), 88–96.

22. Max I. Dimont, *Jews, God, and History* (New York: Penguin/Mentor, 1994), 128–129.

23. Nahum M. Sarna, *Exploring Exodus* (New York: Schocken Books, 1986), 125.

24. Charles Krauthammer, "At Last, Zion: Israel and the fate of the Jews," *The Weekly Standard*, May 11, 1998, 27.

25. Walter Laqueur and Barry Rubin, *The Israel-Arab Reader* (New York: Penguin Books, 1995), 30.

26. Walter Laqueur, *A History of Zionism* (New York: Schocken Books, 1972), 203.

27. Paul Johnson, "The Miracle." *Commentary*, May 1998.

    Johnson wrote in 1998 that "in the last half-century, over 100 completely new independent states have come into existence. Israel is the only one whose creation can fairly be called a miracle."

28. Arthur Hertzberg, *The Zionist Idea* (Philadelphia: The Jewish Publication Society, 1997), 250.

CHAPTER 2

Israel, Gift to the World

Not to us, O Lord, not to us, but to your name give glory,

For the sake of your steadfast love and your faithfulness.

Why should the nations say,

"Where is their God?"

Our God is in the heavens;

He does whatever he pleases.

Their idols are silver and gold,

The work of human hands…

The Lord is mindful of us; he will bless us;

He will bless the house of Israel;

He will bless the house of Aaron;

He will bless those who fear the Lord,

Both small and great.

—Psalms 115:1–4, 12–13

We cannot understand the Jews if we regard them as one national minority among others. They are a minority and share the fate of all minorities: to become an object of fear and hatred and distracting propaganda if the majority or if the leaders need a sacrifice. That is an outrage, but it does not strike at the depth of the Jewish question. And we cannot understand the Jews if we regard them as one religious group beside others. They are this also, and this has

brought them suffering like many other religious sects that have
become the victims of ecclesiastical lust for power and religious
fanaticism. This is an injustice, but it does not strike at the depth
of the Jewish question. The depth of the Jewish question is that the
Jews are the people of history, the people of the prophetic, future-
judging spirit. This means that we ourselves sin against the meaning
of our own history if we bear guilt against the Jewish people.

—PAUL TILLICH, FROM *AGAINST THE THIRD REICH*, MARCH 31, 1942[1]

WHEN THE LORD CALLED ABRAHAM to be the founder of a new nation,
He was preparing a gift—a light to guide the nations out of hopelessness.
At the time the world was enveloped by the darkness of polytheism. People
compared available gods and chose the ones they preferred. During the early
third millennium in Abraham's land of Mesopotamia, there were some four
thousand deities, all necessitating care and obedience, including the task of
feeding them! But that was not all. The people also took great pains to make
their gods holy, for the gods would carouse and then suffer the ill effects
of drunkenness. Their theologians occupied themselves with establishing the
genealogical connections of these gods and ranking them in order of prominence. The people feared both gods and demons, having no assurance that the
gods would do them any good. Since these deities were so undependable, the
people would guard their homes with protective figurines. It was out of this
pagan and uncertain environment that Abraham was called by the Lord to
go to a land where he and his descendants would be blessed and be a blessing
to the world.

William Foxwell Albright gives us a grim picture of the Canaanites,
whose land Israel conquered. He describes Canaanites serving gods that were
among the crudest, most debased, and most ferocious in the ancient world.
The two dominant figures in their pantheon of gods were Astart and Anath,
goddesses of fertility and war. Anath "massacre[d] mankind, young and old,

from the sea-coast to the rising of the sun." Human sacrifice and sacred pros-
titution of both sexes was common and lasted longer in Canaan than in other
areas. Neither of these forces could be regarded as faithful or compassionate.
Corresponding to the character of their gods, the Canaanite culture was an
extremely decadent one, as Albright has written.[2] Furthermore, the gods, limited in power and themselves chosen and created by mortals, were subject to
superior forces that could be manipulated only through magic. That being the
case, humans had to cope with two powers—first, the gods, and second, the
forces in the primordial realm of existence from which the gods originated.[3]

By contrast, the God of Abraham was the one who did the choosing, ini-
tiating a covenant with this future patriarch. Abraham did not choose God;
God chose Abraham. God Himself outlined the terms of the covenant. He
promised to be a faithful God and to bless both Abraham and his descendants, making the covenant permanent. The covenant would bring forth a
people who would be challenged to reflect the holiness of God, thus enhancing the health of a society instead of corrupting it as pagan culture did.

> Now the Lord said to Abram, *"Go from your country and your kin-
> dred and your father's house to the land that I will show you. I will
> make of you a great nation, and I will bless you, and make your name
> great, so that you will be a blessing. I will bless those who bless you,
> and the one who curses you I will curse; and in you all the families of
> the earth shall be blessed." (Bereshit/Genesis 12:1–3)

After much time had elapsed, a son was born to Abraham and his wife, Sarah,
in their old age, thus proving God's faithfulness.

This set the foundation on which a nation unlike any other that preceded
it would flourish. The nation's people became worshippers of the one true
God, who jealously ordered them to destroy all idols and worship Him only.
His first commandment was "You shall have no other gods besides me." (In

Judaism, however, this is considered the second commandment, the first one being "I am the Lord your God, who brought you out of the land of Egypt." Yes, this initial declaration is considered a commandment even though it lacks an imperative word.) It was a commandment forcefully and repeatedly issued with the threat of punishment—even to the fourth generation after those who rebelled—but also with the promise of steadfast love to the thousandth generation of those who feared Him. Thus biblical monotheism was fully instituted at Mount Sinai, wrapped in fire and smoke and accompanied by thunder, lightning, and a trumpet blast. This seminal event made the new nation unique and has put its imprint on the psyches of Jewish people to this day, as seen in the very center of Jewish liturgy—the recitation of the celebrated *Shema* from the book of Deuteronomy:

> Hear, O Israel: the Lord our God, the Lord is One. You shall love the Lord your God with all your heart, with all your soul, and with all your might. Let these matters that I command you today be upon your heart. Teach them thoroughly to your children. (Devarim/ Deuteronomy 6:4–9)[4]

The surrounding nations were threatened because they could see, by noting its successes, that the Hebrew nation was specially favored and her religion exclusive. Therefore, these Hebrews were continually met with unprovoked hostility.

The Hebrews, now the Congregation of Israel, made their journey from Egypt to Canaan without any assistance from the surrounding nations. In fact, Moses gave his solemn promise to those nations that his people would not disturb anything along their way, would refrain from going through fields or vineyards, and would not drink from wells belonging to others. Not a thing would be taken, nor would it need to be, for the Israelites had learned to be self-sufficient. (There were two reasons for this: they took many riches from Egypt when they left, and God faithfully provided for their needs.)

The Edomites were descendants of Esau, one of Abraham's grandsons, and they announced, "You shall not pass through, or we will come out with the sword against you…and Edom came out against them with a large force, heavily armed." (BeMidbar/Numbers 20:14–21) Moab was another nation that had roadways the Israelites wanted to traverse. The Moabites were descendants of Lot, nephew of Abraham. Their nation originated by means of incestuous relations between Lot and his daughters following the destruction of the corrupt cities of Sodom and Gomorrah. Instead of offering the Children of Israel safe passage on their way to the Promised Land, the Moabite king attempted to put a curse on them. (BeMidbar/Numbers 22:1–24; 25; Sefer Shoftim/Judges 11:14–22)

So in an age when hospitality was the custom of the Middle East, there was absolutely none offered to the Hebrews by their cousins in the Hebrews' trek through the barren wilderness. No assistance. No welcome. Thus the precedent was set for what today's historians call "rejectionism"—other Semitic peoples' rejection of the State of Israel.

Could there not have been cooperation between the children of Israel and their relatives? They had enough common enemies—Egypt, Syria, Babylon, and the Philistines, to name just a few—to prompt them to unite in common efforts. Cooperation with Israel could have benefited their agriculture and commercial activity. It was not to be. Instead, there was enmity and strife from the outset.

THE WORLD WATCHES
The nations of the Eastern Mediterranean watched as this nation of slaves moved up from Egypt to Canaan (Palestine). Spies from the camp of Israel were sent to Jericho before that city was invaded and were directed to the house of Rahab, a harlot. She had a report to give them about the news of the journey of the Hebrews thus far:

I know that the Lord has given you the land, and that dread of you has fallen on us, and that all the inhabitants of the land melt in fear before you. For we have heard how the Lord dried up the water of the Red Sea before you when you came out of Egypt, and what you did to the two kings of the Amorites…whom you utterly destroyed. As soon as we heard it, our hearts melted…The Lord your God is indeed God in heaven above and on earth below. (Joshua 2:9–11)

These events did not happen in secret. The Eastern Mediterranean and the world beyond were watching because Palestine was at the crossroads of civilization, where the great trade routes converged. Therefore, news traveled fairly rapidly, and the light of heaven began to shine in that pagan world. Believing in divine Providence, one can assuredly say that the nation was well situated at the center of the ancient world in order to fulfill the call to be a "priestly kingdom and holy nation" (Shemot/Exodus 19:6). As the Old Testament scholar Christopher Wright points out, her witness "could be either positive… when the nations are impressed with the wisdom of Israel's law (cf. Devarim/ Deuteronomy 28:10); or negative, as when the nations are shocked by the severity of Israel's punishment when they abandon the ways of their God (Devarim/ Deuteronomy 28:37; 29:22–28). Either way, faithful or unfaithful, the People of God are an open book to the world from which we ask questions and draw conclusions."[5] It is surely true that in modern times, contemporary events still bear this out—that the world *watches* Israel: this tiny nation is scrutinized from the halls of the United Nations to television screens around the world.

The United Nations Human Rights Council meets as a tribunal for the shaming of nations that, according to its judgment, violate international law. Israel has been cited more than any other nation. Indeed, according to my research, the Council, in any given year, passes more resolutions for condemning Israel than for all other nations combined. She is the only country that is the object of annual scrutiny, as indicated by a permanent place on the Council's agenda, designated "Agenda 7." Furthermore, at no time in her history has she ever been permitted to have a representative on the forty-seven-member Council. The United Nations does not treat this nation fairly, but it consistently puts her in the limelight. This tiny nation was and is now a major phenomenon among the nations.

THE LAW AND THE PROPHETS

It was at Mount Sinai where Israel received the law that she was first conse-crated as the "holy nation." Under that law, the people were and are repeat-edly directed by the Lord to "be holy because I, the Lord your God, am holy" (Vayikra/Leviticus 20:7). Throughout Jewish history, the more faithful gen-erations delighted in the law. It provided purpose to their existence.

Israel was promised the land of Canaan, where paganism had produced a perverted and inhumane culture. The place had become self-destructive. The fertility gods demanded the sacrifice of babies and called for religious prosti-tution in the temples. By contrast, Israel's moral law was designed to keep the community healthy and cohesive. In the Book of Devarim/Deuteronomy, we read of Moses exhorting the Israelites to keep the law "so that you may live," a phrase often reiterated. The religious and ceremonial law put them into a right covenantal relationship with their God and freed them to live in good conscience.

Israel's religion was not primarily of her doing. It was initiated by the cov-enant-making God in His redemptive acts—releasing Israel from Egyptian bondage and caring for His people in their trek through the wilderness and throughout their subsequent history. Today many voices rise from progres-sive Judaism, boasting that monotheistic religion evolved from their Hebrew ancestors, a rational religion surpassing the primitive forms of polytheism. But Israel's history shows that any boasting here is unjustified because their ancestors persisted in reverting to paganism. The true knowledge of God was renewed by divine interventions of judgment and mercy. The power of Israel's religion was in the calling and mighty acts of the Lord. This point is crucial:

Israel's history shows that *the living and true God has a voice.* The idolatry from which they were freed is "fundamentally an escape from the living voice."[6] Idols have no ears for hearing or mouths for speaking. Israel's religion was more than a manner of acting; it was a relationship, and its winsomeness was in the steadfast love of the Lord.

In the context of His love and care, the law enters to give life! "So that you may live," says the Lord. The commandments, though negative on the surface, would be positive in establishing and preserving their freedom. Wright explains, "Liberation is no advantage in itself unless consolidated into social structures that maintain its objectives for the whole community. The Decalogue [Ten Commandments] is the foundation block of such consolidation."[7]

Israel's newfound freedom from Egypt's tyranny was enhanced by law, which provided the people with a structured framework that brought them wisdom.

Hear Moses in his exhortations to Israel as they are about to enter the land:

See, just as the Lord my God has charged me, I now teach you statutes and ordinances for you to observe in the land that you are about to enter and occupy. You must observe them diligently, for this will show your wisdom and discernment to the peoples, who, when they hear all these statutes, will say, "Surely this great nation is a wise and discerning people!" For what other great nation has a god so near to it as the Lord our God is whenever we call to him? And what other great nation has statutes and ordinances as just as this entire law that I am setting before you today? (Devarim/Deuteronomy 4:5–8)

The Torah itself was a great gift, not only to Israel but to the world. Through the law, protection was offered to the weak in society, foreigners, women, and children. Max Dimont in *Jews, God, and History* says, "The Torah was a giant stride ahead of anything existing at that time…The Mosaic code… was the first truly judicial, written code, and eclipsed previously known laws with its all-encompassing humanism, its passion for justice…In reading these laws formulated some three thousand years ago, one is amazed at their humanitarianism."[8]

As with any society, among the Jews there have been those who disregarded the law and those who looked with disdain upon those who valued it. But in Israel's history, there have been many in every generation who have cherished the Law of Moses, considering it the great gift that it is.

> I have rejoiced in the path of your instruction
> As one rejoices over wealth of every kind…
> My heart pines continually
> With longing for your decrees…
> Your instruction is my continual delight;
> I turn to it for counsel. (Psalms 119:14, 20, 24)

Later in their history, we will see that the Jews set the Torah on a pedestal much too high, expecting too much from it. Through intense study, elaboration, interpretation, and application of the Torah, they expected to heal the alienation between themselves and God. But the law in itself could not accomplish this. Eventually, some observers, both Jew and Gentile, judged that their spiritual existence became a dead tradition as they engaged in exegetical nitpicking and sophistry. Indeed, that same assessment was made of first-century Judaism by Christ and the apostles. (See chapter 10 for an elaboration of this point.)

While the Jews put too much stock in the law, the world should be grateful for the great care they have given to it and its transmission. The vocations of rabbis and scribes were necessary and admirable. They guarded the scriptures against corruption. They ensured the preservation of the law for the use of generations of lawmakers and people of faith in every part of the civilized world. Even the Christian who believes in the great doctrine of justification by faith will—if he or she is wise—be thankful for the law, for in it we are shown how to please God.

Shutterstock/ChameleonsEye
"Torah students in Jerusalem (January 2006) in a program that combines advanced Talmudic studies with military service in the Israeli army."

GOOD GOVERNMENT

How should mortals in Gentile nations be governed, and where should *we* get our models for good governance? People in the West have been taught that the Greek polis and Roman republic were historical models for our modern democracies. Now, however, some eyes are being opened to the major influence that Tenakh-based law has had on civilized nations. Israel, with its confederacy of twelve tribes and its rule of law, was considered by political thinkers as the model of a republic. This was especially true following the Protestant Reformation.

I list here five scholars, some historians, who concur in their judgment that the Tanakh undergirded the political philosophies of well-known seventeenth-century legal and constitutional scholars. Among British thinkers who recognized this connection was John Milton, one of the greatest of all Puritan poets, who pointed to Israel's prophets in *Paradise Regained*:

> As men [the Hebrew prophets] divinely taught, and better teaching
> The solid rules of Civil Government
> In their majestic unaffected stile
> Than all the oratory of Greece and Rome.
> In them is plainest taught, and easiest learnt
> What makes a Nation happy and keeps it so,
> What ruins kingdoms, and lays cities flat.[9]

Fania Oz-Salzberger, a senior lecturer in law and history at Haifa University in Israel, studies the works of political philosophers of seventeenth-century Europe. In her research she has found that the idea of a republic governed by the rule of law was greatly influenced by the Torah and the prophets. She writes,

> In recent years, for the first time, modern scholarship has begun to acknowledge the distinctive character of the Hebrew and Jewish sources of early modern political thought in Western Europe, presented in recent research as political Hebraism. This term, recently put into currency, relates to the European fascination with what John Locke called 'the People whose Law, Constitution, and History is chiefly contained in the Scripture.' Scripture, prominently the Hebrew Bible—which, for several advanced Hebraists, is buttressed by the Talmud, Josephus, and Maimonides—tells the true story of an ancient polity once created by God's chosen people.[10]

Some of the best European jurists of the seventeenth century studied the Tenakh in the Hebrew language and travelled from England to Geneva and

Amsterdam. There, for a time, they met with Jewish rabbis who had come from Spain to discuss the polity (form of government) of the Israelite nation.[11]

Eric Nelson, associate professor of government at Harvard University, in his recent book *The Hebrew Republic: Jewish Sources and the Transformation of European Political Thought*, has taken up this thread, making a corrective observation on European-American political thought:

> Renaissance humanism, structured as it was by the pagan inheritance of Greek and Roman antiquity, generated an approach to politics that was remarkably *secular* in character. The political science of the humanists did not rely on appeals to Revelation…It was, rather, in the seventeenth century, in the full fervor of the Reformation, that political *theology* reentered the mainstream of European intellectual life. The Protestant summons to return to the Biblical text brought with it incessant appeals to *God's constitutional preference as embodied in Scripture*.[12] (emphasis mine)

In fact, Nelson observes that there are but very few references to scripture in sixteenth-century political literature. In contrast, seventeenth-century writings are heavily influenced by Reformation biblical thought. He says, "There is hardly a page of the seventeenth century texts I just mentioned that does not contain several Biblical citations."[13] The writings referred to include those of John Selden, John Milton, Thomas Hobbes, and John Locke, all familiar names to students of British and American history and political science. So the subtitle of Nelson's book is telling: *Jewish Sources and the Transformation of European Political Thought*. It was that thinking—from the Hebrew Bible and also, to a smaller extent, from the Talmud—that was, to a great extent, formative for the republican form of government with limited government, separation of powers, representative legislatures, and religious tolerance. This form became the foundation for the political philosophies of Great Britain and the United States, which in turn led to the democratization of many other nations.

William Lecky, noted nineteenth-century Irish historian, is reported to have stated, "Hebraic mortar cemented the foundations of American democracy." Later, Winston Churchill affirmed this contribution of the Tenakh to the developed world:

> We owe to the Jews in the Christian revelation a system of ethics which, even if it were entirely separated from the supernatural, would be incomparably the most precious possession of mankind, worth in fact the fruits of all other wisdom and learning put together. On that system and by that faith there has been built out of the wreck of the Roman Empire the whole of our existing civilization."[14]

Thus, the scriptures written by the ancient Hebrew servants of God are filled with a wealth of material for political thought. As with God's creation, every part is good and full of wonder; altogether it is exceedingly good. The splendid literary variety of narrative, law, and prophecy in the Tenakh has proven to be foundational for education in nationhood and the bounds of political authority.

A HISTORICAL ACCOUNT

It is important to note that the intent of the authors of the Tenakh was to report actual history. It is not just *sacred history*, as some would call it. That term suggests a collection of stories and wisdom in the form of folklore that has layer upon layer of additions from an original oral-based tradition and therefore is not necessarily factual. It is obvious, however, that the writers of the stories set forth in the Tenakh believed they were reporters of history that had literal meaning; they were recording what God actually said and accomplished.

Most of these biblical stories have place names familiar to archeologists who dig for clues in the land that is the setting of these stories. The Tanakh also contains an abundance of lists of people, lineages, and historical markers. The biblical narratives are increasingly supported by external sources, be they Egyptian hieroglyphs, Babylonian cuneiform, or West Semitic inscriptions—or even tools and household utensils, tombs, temple walls, and all manner of objects unearthed by archeologists.

Moreover, in Israel's calendar of commemorative feasts, there is none that celebrates mythological events such as victories over the dragon of chaos or other monsters characteristic of pagan feasts in ancient literature. That type of story takes one *out* of the realm of actual history. What was reported and is currently celebrated annually in Israel was a deliverance from slavery that occurred in real time in the actual country of Egypt. The story was told orally from one generation to another and then was written down. This long and eventful history following the Exodus down through the Babylonian exile bears the marks of historical reality.[15]

OLD TESTAMENT STORIES

The message of these biblical stories has great significance for people of Judeo-Christian heritage. The meaning of many individual lives derived, to a great extent, from them. The Old Testament provides narratives to live by and heroes to consider as models of character. The stories excite imaginations and give examples of a meaningful existence. They point out how God has shown Himself to imperfect individuals, revealing His mercy and guidance through the stages of a lifetime. The heroes and models of the present generation have very little to offer in comparison. But Abraham, Moses, Joseph, David, Job, and Jeremiah—these figures and others who were accosted by the divine presence and whose lives were disrupted, rescued, enlightened, blessed, and otherwise profoundly affected by the sovereign acts and commands of the Lord God, and who learned obedience and faith—these people demonstrate faith and provide standards upon which to build lives and community. The result of people's failure to know them well and teach the details of their lives to their children has contributed to society's cultural decay. These heroes are needed as prototypes of worthy existence. They are presented to the world in scripture by members of the Chosen People, to whom gratitude is due.

For example, the Exodus of the Children of Israel from Egypt has repeatedly been a source of courage for peoples struggling under the heavy hand of authoritarian rule. The age-old struggle for justice makes this story relevant encouragement for subjugated peoples. Medieval Jews chafing under heavy-handed Christian and Muslim rule; Cromwellian Puritans fighting against an oppressive English monarchy; the black American slaves under the tyranny of institutional slavery; South Africans under the cruelty of Apartheid—these people all took courage from the freeing of the Hebrew slaves under Moses and used it as a paradigm of liberation. The life of Joseph, who was rejected by his brothers but later became a type of savior to them, is an example of a Tenakh hero who resisted temptation and remained faithful to God and his duty. His story is a favorite in Sunday-school classes and is portrayed in contemporary culture in the Broadway musical titled *Joseph and the Amazing Technicolor Dreamcoat*. How can we *not* give credit and thanks for this rich mine of life-changing and character-building literature?

GOD AS LORD

The Hebrew authors spoke of a sovereign deity who was high above all other gods and authority figures and whose moral order was far superior to any other. The awareness of this high God awakened in the Chosen People a sense of their legitimate calling. This sense of calling was both a blessing to other peoples and a source of enmity. To those who saw and accepted the light of God's revelation, paths were opened up to lives of blessedness. For others who envied the success of Chosen Israel and rejected the light, it created deep-seated hostility. Two modern Jewish men, coauthors of a book on anti-Semitism, have put their finger on the chief reason for this hatred:

> In the ancient world, every nation but the Jews worshiped its own gods and acknowledged the legitimacy of others' gods. The Jews declared that the gods of the non-Jews were nonsense: "They have mouths but cannot speak, eyes but cannot see, ears but cannot hear." (Psalms 115:5–6) There is but one God and He had revealed himself

through the Jews. One need not be a theologian or historian to understand why these doctrines bred massive anti-Jewish resentment.[16]

Nevertheless, in spite of anti-Hebrew resentment, the Chosen People and the gifts bestowed upon them by the sovereign God have been a blessing, not a curse. When there is humility and openness to receiving wisdom and love through divinely revealed truth, that blessing is experienced. So isn't it easy to see that without Chosen Israel, history would be radically different? Without the gifts that have come through them, people would continue to search in the wrong places for intimations of the divine.

"In you shall all the families of the earth be blessed," declared God to Abraham in his first approach to this patriarch. Imagine the world situation if this were universally acknowledged. The prophets saw such a time. Isaiah had a vision of this universal blessing through Abraham's offspring:

> In the days to come the mountain of the Lord's house
> Shall be established as the highest of the mountains,
> And shall be raised above the hills;
> All the nations shall stream to it.
> Many peoples shall come and say,
> "Come, let us go up to the mountain of the Lord,
> To the house of the God of Jacob,
> That he may teach us his ways
> And that we may walk in his paths."
> For out of Zion shall go forth instruction,
> And the word of the Lord from Jerusalem. (Isaiah 2:2–3)

The peoples of the world are drawn to Zion, the mountain of the Lord. In streaming ever upward, they go against the usual gravitational pull downward. Today, when Jews of the world immigrate to Israel, they are said to be making *aliyah*—in Hebrew, this means "to go up." The prophecy is that many peoples of the world will eventually make aliyah!

Yet we are still not to the center of the blessings that God promised Abraham, the blessings that came to the world through the Jewish people. We are not there until we look at the Messiah as the featured promise for redemption. The patriarchs, tabernacle, King David, and the prophets all pointed forward to the coming of *Machiach* (Hebrew for "Messiah").

THE MESSIAH

Mashiach did not come unexpectedly, and He did not come unknown. The Jewish prophets and their followers looked forward to His advent, and faithful Jews of the time received Him with joy. The Jewish environment was the manger, so to speak, in which Yeshua/Jesus was laid. Mary and Joseph, Simeon, and Anna were the representatives of the Jewish "church" who recognized Yeshua as the Mashiach/Messiah and received Him for who He was and what He was to be. The old man, Simeon, who met Joseph and Mary and the baby Jesus at the Temple, was a righteous and devout Jew who looked forward "to the consolation of Israel." Simeon took Jesus in his arms and praised God, saying,

> Master (Lord), now you are dismissing your servant in peace,
> According to your word;
> For my eyes have seen your salvation,
> Which you have prepared in the presence of all peoples,
> A light for revelation to the Gentiles
> *And for glory to your people Israel.* (emphasis mine) (Luke 2:25–32)

He did not come in a vacuum but came as the fulfillment of Hebrew prophecy, and when He came, He lay in the arms of faithful Jews. These were the ones who cared for Jesus, heard Him gladly, and witnessed His coming. John the Baptist, the apostles, Mary, Martha, and Lazarus, the seventy sent out to preach, and many others were Jewish hosts who received Mashiach—and to whom, in turn, He ministered. They were the receiving group. It was neither the Greek philosophers nor the Zoroastrians nor the Roman rulers (though there were some who adopted Jewish law and the prophets) who were the cradle of Jesus. No, Jesus Christ came to His own. Yet many of His own did not receive Him. But those who had eyes to see and ears to hear received Him gladly and made His coming continuous with the community of the older covenant. In Jesus's life and ministry, they saw the God of Israel present in power and compassionate service, and as Matthew reports, "they praised the God of Israel." (Matthew 15:31)

Therefore, shall humankind not give thanks for that community of faithful Jews who received Him and bore witness to the light? Shall we not give thanks for the preparation that was made through God's election of this people? Can we not see that the Jewish People, as the Chosen, are witnesses to God's revelation? Should the world not see them as such and, in spite of the unfaithfulness of some of them, respect them and give them their place in this world?

CHRISTIAN SECTS REJECTING THE OLD TESTAMENT

In the history of the Christian church, there have been attempts to destroy the foundational influence of Judaism. For instance, in the second century and beyond, some of the main heresies that infected the church expressed the notion that the religion of the Old Testament was invalid. In fact, they portrayed it as bound up with the forces of darkness, attempting to nullify its influence. They contended that only through the light of Christ was there a revelation of the God of love and mercy. But the church fathers recognized their indebtedness to the Tenakh and the witness of the Hebrew community, refusing to eliminate them, for Jesus and the apostles were heavily dependent on the original covenant. Jesus quotes heavily from the Tenakh in order to resist temptation, undergird His teaching, and show how His life, death, and resurrection were fulfillments of that covenant. So despite efforts to the contrary, the Christian church has viewed the books of the Tenakh as divinely revealed and has always remained grateful and reliant upon them.

ISRAEL'S WITNESS

The twentieth-century Swiss theologian Karl Barth has often been called the greatest theologian since the Protestant Reformation. He believed that theology in the nineteenth and early twentieth centuries had unfortunately developed into the word of man, while he forcefully emphasized the doctrine that divine revelation is a matter of grace—that we cannot know God except as God reveals Himself. In his reflections on "The Election of the Community," Barth includes Israel as a people who have received a divine calling. It matters not that they have frequently been disobedient to the call, Barth asserts; they were chosen to be servants of God, and they remain so.

> God does not wait for Israel's faith before claiming it for this service. For this service is determined and effected with Israel's election quite irrespective of the attitude that Israel takes up towards it...Israel *is* a hearer of the promise. As such, it must and will always bear witness to Jesus Christ, to His election, to its own election, but also to that of the Church...It cannot resign from God's community nor do anything to prevent the sound of its voice reaching not only the ears of all the world but its own ears also in the believing witness of the Church. It can resist the gracious favor of God, but it cannot turn it into disfavour."[17]

No, Israel cannot resign from its own vocation, and because it cannot, those who witness this chosen nation and live with the Jewish people dare not despise them. Humankind is under the obligation to receive and honor them out of respect for the ancient and present vocation of this people. Can the Christian church do this while also recognizing that much of Israel lives in stubborn resistance? Can the church bless those who resist her message and, at the same time, continue proclaiming that message unashamedly in the midst of those who keep that message at arm's length? She is called to do precisely that. Can the church insist to the powers of the world that the Jews be given the protection, care, and land that is needed to preserve them? Sadly, the history of the church displays gross failure in this important commission.

It is essential that the church see her position vis-à-vis Israel in the light of the Apostle Paul's teaching concerning the position of Gentile believers in relation to the Jewish community:

> If some of the branches have been lopped off, and you, a wild olive, have been grafted in among them, and have come to share the same root and sap as the olive, do not make yourself superior to the branches. If you do, remember that you do not sustain the root: the root sustains you…Judged by their response to the gospel, they [the Jews] are God's enemies for your sake; but judged by his choice, they are dear to him for the sake of the patriarchs. (Romans 11: 17–18, 28)

We dare not show superiority or even indifference but rather humility, respect, gratitude, and caring for the welfare of this elect people.

This elect people are the ones who suffer the hostility of a world that, in many times and places, has resented the message of divine revelation. This resentment is carried over to its bearers—Israel and the church. The world often resents the idea of the uniqueness of this revelation—that is, that there is one God who chose a people for His purposes; there is one sacred scripture and one Suffering Servant, Savior, and Redeemer who emerged from this elect people. That is a message often met with stubborn resistance, and the Jewish people (in respect to the Old Covenant) as well as the Christian church feel the heat of that resistance. Because the world wants to create its own gods and formulate its own values. It does not object to additions to its pantheon of gods, but it does mind being told that the worship of these gods is asinine. This was the offence as long ago as Israel's interaction with their cousins, when they were on the way to Canaan. "Your gods are impotent and corrupting" was the message that these peoples received from the very life and observances of the people of the living God. Thus, Israel has incurred hatred and endured suffering from her very outset. She has received this treatment even from segments of the Christian church, which, because it became associated with worldly power, itself became oppressive. "We ourselves sin against the meaning of our history if we bear guilt against the Jewish people," said Paul Tillich in March 1942 as he spoke to the German people, most of whom had been baptized in the churches of Germany.

THE MODERN BLESSINGS OF ISRAEL'S GENIUS

The promise of God to Abraham was not only that He would bless His offspring but also that His offspring would be a blessing to the nations: "In you all the families of the earth shall be blessed" (Genesis 12:3). The blessings proceeding from and through the Jewish people are not limited to the spiritual realm but extend quite naturally into the material. The Jewish people, in their studiousness and industriousness, have contributed to the welfare of humankind disproportionate to their numbers. We have only to look at groupings of people who have risen to the top in their fields of science, art, medicine, and peace in modern life to see how they excel: Jewish achievers account for 20 percent of the Nobel Prizes awarded since 1901. Quite a record for a people who constitute merely 2 percent of the world's population![18]

In the field of modern technology, Israelis are making giant strides, which is largely due to the necessity of defending their nation and very existence. Challenged by terrorist attacks and surrounded by enemies, their technology has given them the edge, with innovations that fascinate the technology industry and global investors everywhere. In a *Wall Street Journal* article published July 5, 2011, author George Gilder is quoted as saying that Israel is "steadily increasing its global supremacy, behind only the United States, in an array of leading-edge technologies. It is the global master of microchip design, network algorithms and medical instruments...Israel is incontestably the world leader in water recycling and desalinization...Israel is also making major advances in longer-range missile defense, robotic warfare, and unmanned aerial vehicles… Israelis supply Intel with many of its advanced microprocessors."

Israel has become a world leader in scientific creativity, innovative engineering, advanced medicine, and leading-edge technology, showing that it is hastening toward the future. Intel, Microsoft, Google, and Facebook are among more than three hundred multinationals that have opened up research and development facilities in Israel. Universal data-compression algorithms, in which Israel scholars specialize, play a foundational role in today's World Wide Web. In his book *The Israel Test*, Gilder speaks of the "Israeli prowess in algorithms," which gives them the ability to take an enormous amount of raw information and interpret it in real time, which is why there are certain technical problems that have only been solved by Israelis.[19] While such technological challenges are beyond the understanding of most, these astounding capabilities are benefiting the entire planet.

Israel's economy has burgeoned since the failed policies of socialism were discarded along with high taxes, suffocating regulations, and government ownership of industry. Natural resources, which were once hard to come by, have now been discovered and give Israel parity with other oil-producing nations of the Middle East. These discoveries propose the real potential of making Israel an exporter of oil and natural gas. So as this little nation is becoming less dependent, other nations are queuing up to contract with Israeli energy companies.

Obviously, much more could be said here about the modern achievements of the Jewish people and the nation of Israel. However, this is not the main thrust of this book; looming high in importance above these physical and temporal benefits is the revelation of the living God that has come to the world through the Hebrews—the understanding, salvation and eternal hope is the essence of the sacred history, law, prophets, wisdom, Gospel, and apostolic writings. All of these point to the Machiach/Christ, or Yeshua/Jesus. In

1838 Lord Ashley of Great Britain expressed his delight when his arguments in favor of a British consul being appointed to the city of Jerusalem prevailed:

> What a wonderful event it is! The ancient city of the people of God is about to resume a place among the nations, and England is the first of the Gentile Kingdoms that "ceases to trod her down.". . .I shall always remember that God put it into my heart to conceive the plan for His honor, gave me influence to prevail with Palmerston and provided a man for the situation.

A few months later he admonished the British people:

> We must learn to behold this nation with the eyes of reverence and affection; we must honor in them the remnant of a people which produced poets like Isaiah and Joel; kings like David and Josiah; and ministers like Joseph, Daniel and Nehemiah; but above all, as that chosen race of men, of whom the Savior of the world came according to the flesh.[20]

RECEIVING THE GIFT TODAY

Through the Jewish people, the world has been endowed with blessings. Yet it does not even enter the minds of most citizens of the world—Christians included—that they should have profound gratitude for this gift from the Jews. It is difficult for the proud peoples of the world to acknowledge their indebtedness to other nations, let alone such a small one. On their land and at other times in the Diaspora, scattered among the world's peoples, the Jewish people have been a singularly impressive sign of God's action in the world. Through them have come assorted blessings to the world's peoples, even though they are sometimes characterized as a stiff-necked people and have been subject to the awful judgment of God in their history. The world should readily see and acknowledge them as a gift for the reasons identified here. Instead, this

Chosen People has been met more often with disdain than with kindness. For this, does not the world bear its own guilt?

1. Paul Tillich, *Against the Third Reich* (Louisville: Westminster John Knox Press, 1998), 14.
2. William Foxwell Albright, *From the Stone Age to Christianity* (Garden City: Doubleday, 1957), 230–236.
3. Nahum M. Sarna, *Exploring Exodus* (New York: Schocken Books, 1986), 58.
4. *The Complete Art Scroll Siddur.* (Mesorah Publication, Ltd., 1990).
5. Christopher Wright, *The New International Biblical Commentary: Deuteronomy* (Peabody: Hendrickson Publishers, 1996), 47.
6. Ibid., 71.
7. Ibid., 65, 71.
8. Max Dimont, *Jews, God, and History* (New York: The Penguin Group, 1962), 44–46.
9. David Gelerntner, "Telling the Story of America's Jews," *Commentary*, November 2004, 43–48.
10. Gordon Schochet, Fania Oz-Salzberger, and Meirav Jones, *Political Hebraism: Judaic Sources in Early Modern Political Thought* (Jerusalem and New York: Shalem Press, 2008), 231.
11. See also Oz-Salzberger, "The Jewish Roots of Western Freedom," *Azureonline* (Shalem Press), Summer 2002.
12. Eric Nelson, *The Hebrew Republic* (Cambridge: Harvard University Press, 2010), 2.
13. Ibid., 2n.
14. "Zionism versus Bolshevism: A Struggle for the Soul of the Jewish People," *Illustrated Sunday Herald*, February 8, 1920, 5.
15. K. A. Kitchen, *The Reliability of the Old Testament* (Grand Rapids: William B. Eerdmans Publishing Company, 2001), 449–500.

16. Dennis Prager and Joseph Telushkin, *Why the Jews? The Reason for Antisemitism* (New York: Simon and Schuster), 2003), 13–14.

17. Karl Barth, Karl, *Church Dogmatics*, II, 2, (Edinburgh: T & T Clark, 1957), 235, 237.

18. Sarna and Krasner, *The History of the Jewish People*, vol. 1 (Springfield: Behrman House, 2006), vii.

19. George Gilder, *The Israel Test* (Richard Vigilante Books, 2009), 155–156.

20. Gertrude Himmelfarb, *The People of the Book* (New York: Encounter Books, 2011), 121.

CHAPTER 3

Israel's Election

Praise the Lord!
Praise the name of the Lord;
Give praise, O servants of the Lord,
You that stand in the house of the Lord,
In the courts of the house of our God.
Praise the Lord, for the Lord is good;
Sing to his name, for he is gracious.
For the Lord has chosen Jacob for himself,
Israel as his own possession.

—Psalm 135:1–4

ONE BEING CHOSEN OUT OF many is a natural phenomenon of life. In auditions, sports play-offs, nominations, elections, promotions, and awards, a selection process chooses one or a few and eliminates the others. This process is widely accepted. But when people speak of God selecting and elevating a few out of the many, some people recoil. The thought of removing power from all collective people and setting up a select group is offensive, especially to those who were brought up in liberal democracies.

However, the repugnance toward divine election will be changed if the world comes to appreciate the God of the Bible as one who is wise,

Israel's Election

condescending, and loving—more wise than we are, more capable of judging and perfect in His ways. Besides that, He is the effectual One, and his word and will are done.

God, in His condescension, acted in human history so those who look with open eyes are able to recognize the work of a superior power. He shows His power and glory to human mortals with impressive phenomena. As we look around us, what do we perceive that stands out? The physical universe shows something of the handiwork of a creator. Beyond that, have there been, in the working out of human history, many developments and events so unusual as to indicate that there must be a divine power at work, guiding, providing, and preserving—something we call Providence.

GOD ACTS AND SPEAKS

The Bible presents the proposition that God is and that He acts, chooses and speaks in ways knowable to us. Yet God's ways stand out from other activity and voices. If they did not startle people, we mortals would not see and acknowledge that the actions and words were of God. So, as we intend to point out, the stories in the Bible relate God's revelatory actions that evoke astonishment. In this way, He and His purposes become known to humankind.

Israel, born into a world thoroughly immersed in idol worship, had to learn to listen for Yahweh's voice. The idol worshippers, rather than listening to their gods, manipulated them. Yahweh is the God who cannot be seen but whose voice was distinct. It might be strange to unbelieving modern individuals, but the experience of Israel at Sinai was powerfully memorable and has become forever etched in the Jewish psyche. Moses later reminded them of it, saying,

The Lord said to me..."Assemble the people for me, and I will let them hear my words, so that they will learn to fear me."...Then the Lord spoke to you out of the fire. You heard the sound of words but saw no form; there was only a voice. (Deuteronomy 4:10, 12)

So says Old Testament scholar Christopher Wright, "As the speaking God, Yahweh reveals, addresses, promises, challenges, confronts, demands. Any attempt to turn Yahweh into a voiceless statue effectively gags God."[1]

In that ancient history of Israel, the word that came to them was often unbidden. It came as they were engaged in worldly pursuits or regular forms of worship. They were startled and often left weak. They were chosen to receive some word from God, who soon became known as Lord. He was the initiator of the relationship.

It was so when He first made Himself known to Moses. Moses observed the bush that was aflame but not consumed and asked this deity for His name so that Moses could tell the people who had chosen Him to be their leader. God said to Moses, "I AM WHO I AM." He said further, 'Thus you shall say to the Israelites, 'I AM has sent me to you'" (or "I WILL BE WHAT I WILL BE has sent me to you") (Shemot/Exodus 3:14). This was an introduction that would confound humans and assert God's freedom. This name indicated that He was not conditioned or determined by any other. In His freedom, He was coming to act on behalf of a people whom He had formed and for whom He would be present.

A TREASURED POSSESSION

From the perspective of the Bible, it is God who is the Lord, who in His freedom chooses a people to bear His name and with whom to establish a covenant. He then acts in such a way as to astonish those who observe His acts on behalf of His people. This people is the vine that He plants and tends. As we have noted previously, the Jewish people are "holy unto the Lord"—that is, set apart from other peoples. They noticeably stand out in their differences from the other nations and peoples. Even though a comparatively small group, they have remained preserved in spite of historical forces and foreign powers that threatened and still threaten their existence. Their preservation is an anomaly. In the darkness of the world's ignorance and corruption, Israel's life and law is revelatory—that is, a showpiece of God's action in the world.

In Israel's history and movements, there is the personal presence of God the Lord, creating freedom and calling them to obedience. Into her national life, the divine revelation came through words and through His very presence. In their journey to the land, His presence was with them in the form of a cloud as He led them in the wilderness. Later, His presence in their worship was symbolized by a cloud that rested upon the tabernacle. "And fire was in the cloud by night, before the eyes of all the house of Israel at each stage of their journey." (Shemot/Exodus 40:38). Just as personal are the linguistic formulas used in the Old Testament: "I am He," and "I am the Lord." This is not a distant god, unmoved by the people's course of action? This language conveys a personal relationship and urgency of communication far different from that of any abstract deity or of a vague power like "the force."

I am the Lord, I have called you in righteousness
I have taken you by the hand and kept you. (Isaiah 42:6)

I am He; I am the first,
And I am the last. (Isaiah 48:12)

The words above were spoken to His people, who were taken into Babylonian exile to pay for their sins. The prophet shows Him as the Lord who yearns for His People to return to Him. Clothed with passion in this yearning, He likens Himself to a woman in her agonizing period of travail: "Now I will cry out like a woman in labor, I will gasp and pant" (Isaiah 42:14). And He is the father who has lost His wayward children and pleads with them to return: "Return, O faithless children, I will heal your faithlessness" (Jeremiah 3:22).

The Lord, though free and unconditioned by any other force or person, is not a god who manipulates Israel like a puppet. Though clothed in holiness and majesty, He is One who chose Israel as a precious covenant partner. "You are a people holy to the Lord your God; the Lord your God has chosen you out of all the peoples on earth to be his people, his treasured possession" (Sefer Devarim/Deuteronomy 7:6).

But you, Israel, my servant,
Jacob, whom I have chosen,
The offspring of Abraham, my friend;
You whom I took from the ends of the earth,
And called from its farthest corners,
Saying to you, "You are my servant,
I have chosen you and not cast you off;" (Isaiah 41:8–9)

WHY THIS CHOICE?

Karl Barth, in his section called "The Election of the Community," speaks of Israel and the church, both of which reflect the intervention of God to, in mercy, draw humankind to Himself.

> The Israelite form of God's community reveals what God elects for Himself when in His eternal election of grace He elects fellowship with man. It is not an obedient but an obdurate people that He chooses. He does not choose a people which has something to give Him but one which has everything to receive from Him. He chooses for Himself suffering under the obduracy of this people, and suffering under the curse and shame and death which this inevitably brings in its train. He burdens Himself with rebels and enemies and at the same time with their merited fall. This is the twofold burden that God chooses for Himself when He elects to make His fellowship with man radically true by becoming man Himself in the person of the Son of David, Jesus; when He elects the people of Israel for the purpose of assuming its flesh and blood.[2]

As Barth indicates, Israel was not chosen as a result of Israel's moral, spiritual, or intellectual superiority. The chosen nation was small and stubborn ("stiff-necked" in the KJV and NRSV Bibles). God elected to deal with a nation of people who questioned His abilities, at times abandoned the covenant with Him, complained before they prayed for help, and often preferred to give homage to other gods. Consider the original children of Israel—the sons of Jacob—conniving, rebellious, and murderous. What good could possibly emerge from such a family? As Barth says, "He [God] burdens Himself with rebels."

THE PROPHETS

Throughout the nation's history, the prophets of the Lord were very critical of the community. Not beholden to anyone but the Lord, they did not exalt their kings as demigods as the Egyptians, Assyrians, and Babylonians did. God was the Lord. The Lord ruled in righteousness, and prophets maintained allegiance, in every circumstance, to Him. They were overwhelmed with His holiness and majesty, and they warned against incurring God's wrath.

The prophet Jeremiah conveyed God's message to unfaithful Israel:

The word of the Lord is to them an object of scorn;
They take no pleasure in it.
But I am full of the wrath of the Lord;
I am weary of holding it in...
They acted shamefully, they committed abomination;
Yet they were not ashamed,
They did not know how to blush...
Hear, O earth; I am going to bring disaster on this people,
The fruit of their schemes,
Because they have not given heed to my words. (Jeremiah 6:10–11,
15, 19)

Though He brought disaster on them, He has never forsaken them, for they are His covenant people. If He had, they would have gone the way of the Canaanite nations that disappeared. His wrath was a covenant response. His raising up of the prophets was a sign of His continuing grace and an expression of his care for Israel. The prophets' calling was a great burden, and most of them were rejected by the people.

The prophets challenged all the powers: kings, priests, elders, false prophets, and the entire nation. But that was not all they were about: they reminded the people of their election; they put steel into the quaking hearts of Israelite kings, and they strengthened the faith of the people when national survival was in question. The message was "Our God is the Lord, who made heaven and earth and called us into being."

Do not fear, for I am with you,
Do not be afraid, for I am your God;
I will strengthen you, I will help you,
I will uphold you with my victorious right hand. (Isaiah 41:10)

Israel's Mind-set

Throughout Israel's history, this election and covenant have been received with ambivalence. In some periods Israel kept the covenant. But in others there were few who welcomed the word of the Lord, most preferring to select the gods of this world, become their own protectors, and adopt their own laws. Being chosen was a burden to them, so they shook it off and took the alternative—assimilation into the prevailing culture, which has always been a temptation, from the time of the conquest of Canaan to Jewish life in modern Europe and America.

In addition, there were always other utopian visions to espouse. In ancient times many Jews turned to Greek philosophy. In modern times some have looked to Marxism as a substitute for the Messianic Age of peace. Karl Marx, himself a Jew, judged his people and their religion harshly, saying that "money is the jealous god of Israel before whom no other god may stand." He argued that there was no vitality left in Judaism and that its days were numbered. He predicted that Judaism would "vanish like an insipid haze in the vital air of society...We recognize in Judaism the presence of a universal and contemporary anti-social element whose historical evolution...has arrived at its present peak, a peak at which it will inevitably disintegrate." Other Jewish philosophers following Marx echoed the same line and contended that it was time to discard the notion of chosenness.[3] Even since the birth of the modern State of Israel, many modern liberal Jews, with their vision of universalism and world government, have advocated assimilation, which would end the Jews as a cohesive people.

The book *The Jewish State: The Struggle for Israel's Soul*, by the Israeli philosopher Yoram Hazony, is subtitled *The Jewish State Doesn't Live Here Anymore*. In it he describes the mood of discomfort many Israeli young people, intellectuals, and government officials feel when speaking of "Jewish values" or the "interests of the Jewish people." Published in 1999, this work notes that many leaders in Israeli politics and culture have lost any sense of Jewish purpose. For example, in the education ministry, Hazony relays, it was announced that "the Jewish people would be included in the new curriculum, 'but certainly not as a subject of primary importance.'...On the Supreme Court, the Chief Justice had devised a new constitutional doctrine whereby the 'Jewish' character of the state had to be interpreted 'at the highest level of abstraction' so that it became identical with the universal dictates of what is acceptable in any generic democracy; prominent officials and public figures had begun to talk of changing the Israeli national anthem (to remove the words 'Jewish soul')." As Hazony began the task of founding the Herzl Institute in Jerusalem, he observed that by the 1990s, "The post-Jewish condition had become a matter of national policy—to the point that one could easily imagine the Jewish state, for which such a fantastic price had been paid in sweat and blood, actually being dismantled in favor of a non-Jewish state: a state for which the ideals and memories, traditions and interests of the Jews would be—simply irrelevant."[4]

How shocking to those who love the Israeli nation! Yet it is encouraging that Professor Hazony is now serving on the Israel Council for Higher Educations's commission reviewing the General Studies and Liberal Arts programs in all of Israel's universities and colleges.

Readers might wonder if this attitude toward Jewishness is still to be found among certain segments of Israeli society. The answer is in the affirmative, and one must point out that the attitude has *always* been present but in the general public there is ambivalence. As Ofir Haivry, a colleague of Hazony, writes in *New Essays on Zionism*, the general consciousness in Israel reveals a basic Jewish outlook and identity, especially at times of festivals and in the use of Jewish symbols. However, norms of conduct and rules of the rabbis meet widespread rejection. Adding to that, there exists an astounding ignorance of and dismissive attitude toward Jewish history. People's efforts to survive and make gains in their lifestyles take precedence.[5]

There is a variation on this theme of Jewish identity found in the Jews not in Israel but in the Diaspora, especially that of American and European Jewry. In a survey of American Jews by Pew Research that was released in October of 2013—a survey called "explosive" by Jonathan S. Tobin in *Commentary* magazine—94 percent of respondents said they were proud of being Jewish. There is no problem there. However, as Tobin says, "The stunning finding of Pew's *A Portrait of Jewish Americans*—the most comprehensive portrait of the community in 20 years and, in the richness of its detail, perhaps of all time—is the degree to which American Jews are not choosing to live as Jews in any real sense...The study's analysis of what being Jewish means to its respondents reveals just how much irreligion has taken center stage in American Jewish life." Several generations of Jews in the United States "have allowed themselves and their children to become functionally illiterate about Judaism, its belief system, its history, and the obligations of Jewish peoplehood." The consequence of this secular lifestyle and manner of thinking is that the community of Jews in the United States will continue its rapid shrinkage. For if there is nothing particularly desirable or special about being Jewish, then assimilation in America's inclusive society—as well as intermarriage with Gentiles, which carries no stigma—will mean the end of Jewish life.[6]

Loyal Jews

Still, both in Israel and the Diaspora, there are other modern Jews who have embraced the identity and vocation of their people with vision and courage.

We must mention some shining examples. The world has heard them. We know them. They are the greats among modern Jews. Below, attention will be given to three.

Theodore Herzl comes into view first. He was not the first of the Zionist thinkers. There were many before him—philosophers and rabbis who in the nineteenth century lectured and wrote on the merits of returning to the land. But Herzl was different in that he was a man of the world with the resources to effect change. He was awarded a doctoral degree of law from the University of Vienna and became an accomplished journalist; he traveled widely, maintaining contacts throughout Europe. As he observed his Jewish compatriots, he burned with compassion for those who suffered the ignominy of every type of persecution in a Europe fairly saturated with anti-Semitism. In a pamphlet he created in 1896, he wrote, "Hatred grows apace. The rich do not feel it much. But our poor! Let us ask our poor, who have been more severely proletarized [reduced to a lower level] since the last resurgence of anti-Semitism than ever before."[7] The solution to Jew-hatred, he knew, was not for the Jews to assimilate with Gentile society. That would not solve the problem of Jew-hatred. It had been tried. He felt too that anti-Semitism was an international problem needing an international solution.

In the First Zionist Congress (1897), which Herzl himself organized, he declared, "One of the first results of our movement, even to be perceived in its larger outlines, will be the transformation of the Jewish question into a question of Zion…The Congress will concern itself with the spiritual means to be employed for reviving and fostering *the national consciousness* of the Jews."[8] (emphasis mine) The "Jewish question" was the phrase used in Europe to discuss the pressing issue of the standing and acceptance of Jews. Herzl's great contribution was fulfilling his own goal of changing that issue to this one: Zion, or his people's return to the Jewish fold, both religiously and geographically. Though he had lived a secular life, he knew that the renewal of his people and the return to the land would need to be prompted by the power of their religious tradition.

The problem of the Jewish identity is a binding theme of this book. Herzl embraced it at his own expense, both financially and physically. He used every means of persuasion available to him, talking to audiences and high officials of many nations. After bringing the world Zionist Movement to fruition, he died at age forty-four from overwork.

Proceeding to the 1930s, the thirteen-year-old Anne Frank, confined to an attic with her family to evade the searching Gestapo police in Holland, asked if there was meaning in Jewishness. In her hiding, she was not content merely to bemoan her isolation and its inconveniences for a young lady; she also considered "the Jewish question."

Shutterstock/Olga Popova
"A German Stamp with Picture of Annelies Marie Ann Frank (1929–1945), circa 1979"

"Who has inflicted this upon us?" Frank asked. "Who has made us Jews different from all other people? Who has allowed us to suffer so terribly up till now? It is God that has made us as we are, but it will be God, too, who will raise us up again. If we bear all this suffering and if there are still Jews left, when it is over, then Jews, instead of being doomed, will be held up as an example. Who knows, it might even be our religion from which the world and all peoples learn good, and for that reason and that reason only do we have to suffer now."[9] In her youth she confidently—and with hope in God—affirmed her identity with her suffering people, obviously believing in the divine election and vocation of her people. In a place and time of great peril, she courageously wrote what could be used against her.

Further on in the twentieth century, Natan Sharansky gained recognition as a notable voice of Jewish identity. Born in the Ukraine and at first a loyal citizen of the Soviet Union, he was willing to adapt to the totalitarian regime. But his life changed when he was awakened through the study of Judaism and Zionism, and he was freed from Communist thought-slavery. He then became a dissident and was charged with treason by the Kremlin. For nine years he was a political prisoner in Soviet prisons and a Siberian labor camp (gulag). Though put through mental and physical torture, he never caved, always encouraged by the knowledge of his wife's and friends' attempts to free him. But that was not all. He found hope and meaning in a book of Psalms that he obtained by going on a hunger strike. His release came in 1986; he was the first political prisoner freed by Mikhail Gorbachev under the urging of President Ronald Reagan.

Sharansky's crime was his attempt to gain an exit visa to Israel in 1973. He realized that to live authentically, he must embrace his identity as a Jew. After he immigrated to Israel, he served in four successive governments, including in the positions of minister and deputy prime minister. In his book *Defending Identity*, he points out that many thinkers in the educated classes are proponents of the idea that nationalism is out of date and that Israel fosters a selfish identity. They say we now live "in a world that has moved beyond identity into a utopia of 'individual rights, open frontiers, and international law.'" Even if "'for many years, Israel had a special meaning for the Jewish people,' that time has passed, and indeed puts other Jews in danger."[10] In the *Jerusalem Post*, he is quoted as saying, "Europe is abandoning its identities, with the multicultural idea that there will be no such thing as nation-states or religion. In post-identity Europe, there is less and less space for Jews for whom it is important to have both identity and freedom."[11] But he argues that it is all-important for the State of Israel to insist that the world recognize its right to exist as a *Jewish* democratic state. It is important because "identity is what gives meaning to our lives, what connects us with the past and with the future."[12]

These highly honored Jewish individuals saw that there was a purpose for their race. In each of them, there was a conviction—or at least a positive intuition—that his or her people have been chosen by God and set apart for a select service to humanity. Some Jews, like Sharansky, see this as a commitment to freedom and democracy; there are others, like the very Orthodox, who are convinced that the rebirth of Israel is a sign that the Day of Redemption and the coming of their Messiah is near and that they must live faithfully in readiness for these events.

THE GENTILE PERSPECTIVE

The question now is, how shall the Gentile peoples view this race? Will they deny any question of the Jews being divinely elected? Will the idea bring only scorn? And in world politics, will Gentile nations, like the ancient cousins of the new nation of Israel—the Ammonites, Moabites, and Edomites—prefer that the Jews live in obscurity?

Those who reject the Jews are rejecting God's interests and actions in history. They do not look with appreciation at this startling phenomenon; they ignore it. Some have developed a disdain for this Chosen People and, when considering them at all, consider only the aspects of their darker side. But they cannot change this divine initiative, which is an initiative of grace, and they cannot totally ignore it. For it is there for all to see, exposed and cemented in the history of the human race.

Gentiles who appreciate divine revelation and the covenants God makes with humankind will surely not be disposed to despise His chosen ones.

Rather, these understanding Gentiles receive the Jewish people as a sign of divine providence. They are fascinated with God's means of revelation. They love the stories of the call issued to Abraham, Moses, and the prophets. They relate to Jacob's struggle with the messenger of God. They love the songs and prayers of Israel's worship leaders recorded in the Book of Psalms. And they are fascinated, therefore, with the community of Israel and watch its history with great interest. They do not resent its election. On the contrary, they count it a privilege to be called "the Israel of God," St. Paul's designation for Christian believers—that "in Christ Jesus the blessing of Abraham [has] come to the Gentiles" (Galatians 6:16; 3:14).

These Christian believers with a scriptural perspective look upon Israel's history since the fall of Jerusalem in AD 70 with pity and sorrow. They look upon her modern history of suffering and persecution with grief and penitence. And they even look upon her recalcitrance with compassion. They would honor the Jews if they would receive it. They would embrace them in the name of Yeshua, their Messiah and ours, if this people could or would accept Him. And they ask, "What is objectionable about election—God's choice of a people to bring hope to the human race? Why should God not appoint a certain people to receive the revelation of His love so it can be seen and heard throughout the whole earth?" The existence and calling of these Israelites, this small community of God's elect, show that He is faithful even when humankind is unfaithful. Even in unbelief, people are witnesses to the God who overrules human unbelief and shows His love in spite of it and even through it. And so in honoring the Jewish people, we honor the faithful God of Abraham, Isaac, and Jacob. In honoring them, we remind them of their calling.

HAVE THEY EARNED ELECTION?

Do the Jews deserve this election? Have they shown faithfulness, consistency, and steadfastness in their devotion to God? No, they have not. But interest in them stems from a desire for closeness to them because of the covenant they made with God, because He their God is faithful even when they are unfaithful. His mighty works are done in and through them even in their unfaithfulness, for that is how God works. Even through periods of rebellion, He retains them as His People. Through them He shows His patience and mercy. "He does not retain his anger forever, because he delights in showing clemency" (Micah 7:18). Regard for the Jewish people is right because God regards them as His servants. Interest in Jewish history arises because God acted decisively in and through that history. "He has not dealt thus with any other nation" (Psalms 147:20).

ISRAEL, THE CRADLE OF THE MESSIAH

In Israel, God elected the covenant community and chose them to be the cradle (Luther's metaphor) to hold and put on display the chosen man, the Messiah, Jesus Christ. The chosen community and the Chosen Man both proceeded (humanly speaking) from the same history. The Chosen Man entered the world, having been prophesied, then identified with His people, calling them forth to be a worshipping and observing community. The elected Man, as Karl Barth says, emerged from Israel, the elected people. They provided His environment.

> As the environment of the elect man, Jesus of Nazareth, the elected community of God is the place where God's honour dwells, i.e., where this Jesus as the Christ (Messiah) and Lord, and therefore in Him God's covenant purpose, His intervention for lost man, the execution of His judgment and mercy, is effective and visible among men. It [the elected community] is elected to serve the presentation (the self-presentation) of Jesus Christ and the act of God which took place in Him—as a testimony and summons to the whole world...He [God] chooses out of the treasures of His own nature righteousness and holiness, peace and joy, life and blessedness. He chooses for man His own self as Brother but also as Leader, as Servant but also as Master, as

Physician but also as King. He therefore chooses for man the reflection of His own glory. He does this by electing flesh and blood from Judah-Israel to be His tabernacle and the Church of Jews and Gentiles to be His sanctuary, to declare to the world His gracious turning.[13]

The elect Man and the elect people—both were given to the world to show the righteousness and grace of God, who is the Lord of creation and history. "O the depth of the riches and wisdom and knowledge of God! How unsearchable are his judgments and how inscrutable his ways!" (Romans11:33)

§

In the Jewish service, the *Amida* is the central prayer of the liturgy. In it there are nineteen blessings, which are to be said while one stands and faces Jerusalem. They express gratitude for gifts that the Lord God bestows upon His people. The Amida is a prayer of the Chosen People and conveys a yearning for the Chosen Redeemer. Here is a brief excerpt from the Orthodox Siddur:

> Blessed are You, LORD our God and God of our fathers,
> God of Abraham, God of Isaac and God of Jacob,
> The great, mighty and awesome God, God Most High
> Who bestows acts of lovingkindness and creates all,
> Who remembers the lovingkindness of the fathers
> And will bring a Redeemer to their children's children
> For the sake of His name, in love...
>
> To Jerusalem, Your city,
> May You return in compassion,
> And may You dwell in it as You promised.
> May You rebuild it rapidly in our days
> As an everlasting structure,
> And install within it soon the throne of David.
> Blessed are You, LORD, who builds Jerusalem.

May the offshoot of Your servant David soon flower,
And may his pride be raised high by Your salvation,
For we wait for Your salvation all day.
Blessed are You, LORD, who makes the glory of salvation flourish.[14]

1. Christopher Wright, *The New International Biblical Commentary: Deuteronomy* (Peabody: Henrickson Publishers, Inc., 1996), 71.
2. Karl Barth, *Church Dogmatics*, vol. 2, pt. 2, (Edinburgh: T & T Clark, 1957), 206–207.
3. David Hazony, Yoram Hazony, and Michael B. Oren, *New Essays on Zionism* (Jerusalem and New York: Shalem Press, 2006), 135–136.
4. Yoram Hazony, *The Jewish State: The Struggle for Israel's Soul* (New York: Basic Books, 2001), xix-xx.
5. Hazony, Hazony, and Oren, *New Essays on Zionism*, 86–88.
6. Jonathan S. Tobin, "How America's Embrace Is Imperiling American Jewry," *Commentary*, November 2013, 11–16.
7. Arthur Hertzberg, *The Zionist Idea* (Philadelphia: The Jewish Publication Society, 1997), 224.
8. Ibid., 227.
9. Anne Frank, *The Diary of a Young Girl* (New York: Bantam Books, 1993), 207.
10. Nathan Sharansky, *Defending Identity* (New York: Public Affairs, 2008), 183.
11. Sam Sokol, "The End of European History," *The Jerusalem Post*, August 15, 2014, 1.
12. Nathan Sharansky, *Defending*, 185–187.
13. Karl Barth, *Church*, 205, 211.
14. Rabbi Lord Jonathan Sacks, *The Koren Siddur* (Jerusalem: Koren Publishers, 2015).

CHAPTER 4

The Land

When Abram was ninety-nine years old, the Lord appeared to Abram,
and said to him, "I am God Almighty; walk before me, and be
blameless. And I will make my covenant between me and you, and
will make you exceedingly numerous…And I will give to you, and
your offspring after you, the land where you are now an alien, all the
land of Canaan, for a perpetual holding; and I will be their God."

—Bereshit/Genesis 17:1–2, 8

Intimate attachment to the land, waiting for the renewal of Jewish life
in the land of Israel, is part of our integrity, an existential fact. Unique,
sui generis, it lives in our hopes, it abides in our hearts…To abandon
the land would make a mockery of all our longings, prayers, and
commitments. To abandon the land would be to repudiate the Bible.

—Abraham Joshua Heschel[1]

The sliver of land granted to Abraham and the promised nation has the
Mediterranean Sea on the west side and the Arabian Desert on the other side.
Its geology and agronomy require rain for agricultural production, for the
land has no great rivers running through it. Its people depend on weather pat-
terns for good harvests. It is not like Egypt, where people can rely on irrigation

from the Nile waters. Therefore, historically, Israel's people could either be blessed by an abundance of rain or be tested by the withholding of it. It is a good land, flowing with milk and honey, but prayers were seasonally offered there to ensure sufficient rainfall.

The Book of Beginnings (Bereshit/Genesis chapters 12, 15, and 17) and also Deuteronomy/Devarim state that the land was promised. It was a sacred holding. The transaction was sealed not by a third-party notary or agent but by a covenant between the Lord and Abraham. Throughout the whole lives of the people of Israel, there has been an attachment to this same land—a historical curiosity. What other people have remained attached to the same land for such duration? What other peoples have experienced such national traumas in exiting their native country, and such triumphs in returning to it?

The gift of this land was contested from the very beginning of Israel's habitation there. People said, "It is ours, not yours." Moreover, when Israel was dispersed, some contended that the land was no longer a sacred holding of the Jewish people. Those people said, "You have been absent for generations; it is no longer yours." But even though the world has not always noticed, there has *always* been a remnant population of Jews on the land throughout the last two and a half millennia, and there have always been descendants of Abraham who, accepting the land as a sacred trust, yearned for its restored occupation.

Observant Jews have always claimed the land as a gift. Secular Jews see it differently. To them, the story of the Exodus is religious mythology evolved from an unreliable oral tradition. But the longing for the land has remained, throughout the ages, in the collective soul of the Jewish people and especially the lower-class oppressed Jews for whom assimilation in other cultures was not an option. They said, "It is the only land we have, and our God is the giver."

•

Walter Brueggemann, professor of the Old Testament at Columbia Theological Seminary, in his book *The Land*, says,

The land for which Israel yearns and which it remembers is never unclaimed space but is always *a place with Yahweh*, a place well filled with memories of life with him and promise from him and vows to him. It is land that provides the central assurance to Israel of its historicality, that it will be and always must be concerned with actual rootage in a place which is a repository for commitment and therefore identity.[2]

Gifted land it is, but it was not simply dumped into Israel's lap. The Israelites had to trudge through the desert from Egypt, where they were oppressed but at the same time securely rooted. In their fear of the unknown, they hankered for Egypt after leaving. In their cowardice, they detested the wilderness trek. In their doubt, they wondered how Yahweh could deliver. At the border of this land of Israel, they grew increasingly nervous and threatened revolt and return to Egypt. Later, in conquering the land, the Israelites often made errors and showed a lack of resolve. Yet in spite of it all, the land eventually became theirs because of the Lord's faithfulness.

> When the Lord your God has brought you into the land that he swore to your ancestors, to Abraham, to Isaac, and to Jacob, to give you—a land with fine, large cities that you did not build, houses filled with all sorts of goods that you did not fill, hewn cisterns that you did not hew, vineyard and olive groves that you did not plant—and when you have eaten your fill, take care that you do not forget the Lord, who brought you out of the land of Egypt, out of the house of slavery. (Devarim/Deuteronomy 6:10–12)

Israel was a recipient who, although not passive, was also undeserving. She received a "good land"—one where there were already cities, houses, cisterns, vineyards, and groves. The good life was there waiting for her People to claim it. Satisfaction was guaranteed. "You will lack nothing...You shall eat your fill" (Devarim/Deuteronomy 8:9–10).

Among the festivals and sacred years that the Hebrews were to observe in this land was the Year of Jubilee, the fiftieth year. In that year purchased land would revert to the previous owner. In a modern economic system, this would be revolutionary. To Israel it was a year of liberty and return. Liberty was proclaimed throughout the land. Debtors were released; prisoners and slaves were set free. During the Year of Jubilee, all people were released from labor to live off the produce of the untended land. It was a reminder of their release from bondage in Egypt. It discouraged the accumulation of huge holdings of property. This was a concrete demonstration of God's ownership and humankind's stewardship. "The land shall not be sold in perpetuity, for the land is mine; with me you are but aliens and tenants" (Vayikra/Leviticus 25:23). Sadly, we have no indication that this Year of Jubilee was faithfully observed.

By no other people was this land ever seriously viewed as a gift from a deity. It was conquered by the Romans, who subdued the recalcitrant Jews. It was later subdued by the Muslim caliphs (vice-regents of Allah) as part of their empire. Jerusalem did not become a major Islamic center, and the Islamic peoples did not pray facing Jerusalem as the Jews did. Arabs turned toward Mecca with their backs toward Jerusalem. The city of Jerusalem is not once mentioned by name in the Qur'an, whereas in the Hebrew scriptures it occurs 778 times. It has never been the capital of any other people since it was conquered by King David. Under the Jordanian occupation between 1948 and 1967, it never had the status of a capital. In the interval between the destruction of the Jewish state in AD 70 by the Romans and the birth of the State of Israel in 1948, "Palestine never became a national homeland for any other people, has never been regarded as a geopolitical entity and has never been an independent state. It was conquered and re-conquered no less than fourteen times in thirteen centuries. Each conquest absorbed it as occupied territory to be ruled from without."[3] No other people have historically claimed it as the land of their heritage. Dr. Abraham Joshua Heschel, twentieth-century Jewish spiritual leader and biblical theologian, states,

The land of Israel was not merely a place where, historically speaking, the Jews had once dwelt. It was the homeland with which an indestructible bond of national, physical, religious, and spiritual character had been preserved...For these many ages, in many lands, whether in Spain or in India, in Egypt or in Poland, no day, no evening passes without praying for Zion and Jerusalem. We pray for her recovery, we pray for her redemption, for her prosperity and for her peace... Attachment to the land of Israel so dominates our liturgy that the prayers for dew and for rain accord with the seasons of the Holy Land rather than with the climates of the lands in which the worshipers recite the prayers.[4]

LIVING IN EXILE

What people have more to tell us about the meaning of exile than the Jews? The length of it, the yearning to return, the ghetto-inflicted isolation, the ostracism, the expulsions, the periodic threat of pogroms, and every form of persecution, including massacres—these have been part and parcel of the Jewish experience of exile. Their prolonged dispersion has given them the opportunity to watch the ebb and flow of multiple civilizations. And in that exile, they have always been wary, concerned about whether persecution might force them to flee, for they have always known that a disturbance in their adopted land could mean trouble for them. They would be singled out as the scapegoat. In his novel *The Fixer,* Bernard Malamud writes of the Jewish people in exile being deeply and profoundly involved in human history. Yakov (Hebrew for Jacob) was a prisoner in Russia with no prospect of being released—a prisoner because of false accusations and the authorities' anti-Semitism. His story is representative of the Jews who have been enmeshed in nations and cultures throughout the ages and always subject to harassment.

We're all in history, that's sure, but some are more than others, Jews more than some. If it snows, not everybody is out getting wet. He

[Yakov] had been doused. He had, to his painful surprise, stepped into history more deeply than others—it had worked out so.[5]

The meaning of the people's exile was well understood by a significant number of traditional Jewish rabbis in the following way: God was angry with them and forcibly removed them from the land just as He had cautioned in the Torah:

> If you disobey me, and continue hostile to me, I will continue hostile to you in fury; I in turn will punish you myself sevenfold for your sins…I will lay your cities waste, will make your sanctuaries desolate…I will devastate the land, so that your enemies who come to settle in it shall be appalled at it. And you I will scatter among the nations. (Vayikra/ Leviticus 26:27–32)

Agony and grief attended the exiled people. Yahweh departed from His sanctuary, and so, therefore, did His people. And those who love the Chosen People participate in their sadness, empathizing with them and praying for their complete restoration in God's time.

One might ask, why didn't the Jews return to the Holy Land before this last century? While a few did return periodically, many were prohibited from travel. Restriction of movement was just one of the many impositions on the Jews. Others who were poor could not afford relocation. Some rabbis declared that efforts to return to the land were unlawful, as they believed that only God Himself should initiate such a return. That, they said, would happen only with the appearance of the Messiah.

Nonetheless, Jewish history since the Roman destruction of Jerusalem is full of stories of attempted and realized immigration to their land. When Jews did go, they often consigned themselves to lives of extreme poverty. Under Muslim rule, beginning in the seventh century, Jews were to be protected as a "people of the book." However, like the Christians, they were forced to pay confiscatory taxes, including a poll tax and a land tax, which, combined, were a crushing financial burden. Still, they went. Despite the slaughter of Jews during the Crusader occupation of the land, the prominent rabbi Yehuda Halevi (1075–1141) issued an invitation to his people to immigrate. Then, following the defeat and expulsion of the Crusaders, there began a trickle of brave Jews who ventured back to the land. For example, hundreds of rabbis from Europe and North Africa settled in Jerusalem in the early thirteenth century. Others followed, and from then on, there were periods of immigration and expansion of the Jewish presence in Jerusalem, Safed, Hebron, and Tiberias.[6] In 1936, Chaim Weizmann, then president of the Zionist organization, appeared before the Peel Commission gathered in Jerusalem and said, "If the Commission would take the trouble to study the post-Roman period of the Jews and the life of the Jews in Palestine, they would find that during the nineteen centuries which have passed since the destruction of Palestine as a Jewish political entity, *there was not a single century in which the Jews did not attempt to come back.*"

The empires and nations that swept through the land since the time of Jesus were many, and the atrocities and brutal rape of the land is legendary. The Romans, Byzantine Christians, various Muslim imperial dynasties, Turks, Crusaders, Kharezmians and Mongols, the Ottoman Turks—these conquerors had no lasting devotion to the land. The Muslim Mamluks even ordered that the Palestinian coastal plain be a desert. Obviously none of these imperial powers showed any interest in the survival and well-being of the Jewish people who were there through it all, eking out a bare subsistence. Abraham Heschel looks back in history and declares,

> Throughout the ages we said No to all the conquerors of Palestine. We said No before God and man emphatically, daily. We objected to their occupations, we rejected their claims, we deepened our attachment, knowing that the occupation by the conquerors was a passing adventure, while our attachment to the land was an eternal link. The

Jewish people has never ceased to assert its right, its title, to the land of Israel…How did the Jews contest and call into question the occupation of the land by the mighty empires of East and West? How did they assert their own title to the land? Our protest was not heard in the public squares of the large cities. It was uttered in our homes, in our sanctuaries, in our books, in our prayers. Indeed, our very existence as a people was a proclamation of our link to the land, of our certainty of return.[6]

The Ottoman Empire conquered Palestine in 1516 at the beginning of the modern era. During its reign, Palestine was not named; its territory contained portions for three different eyalets (or provinces). It went undifferentiated until the British Mandate of 1920. It went unclaimed by any national group until the rebirth of Israel. It had no official name of its own. And until that time, it lay in a pitiful condition. Mark Twain visited Palestine in 1867 and was surprised by its bleakness and desolation. He reported his grim impressions in *The Innocents Abroad*:

Of all the lands there are for dismal scenery, I think Palestine must be the prince. The hills are barren, they are dull of color, they are unpicturesque in shape. The valleys are unsightly deserts fringed with a feeble vegetation that has an expression about it of being sorrowful and despondent…It is a hopeless, dreary, heart-broken land… Palestine sits in sackcloth and ashes. Over it broods the spell of a curse that has withered its fields and fettered its energies…Nazareth is forlorn…renowned Jerusalem itself, the stateliest name in history, has lost all its ancient grandeur, and is become a pauper village. The noted Sea of Galilee…borders are a silent wilderness…Palestine is desolate and unlovely.[7]

Thirty years after Twain made his observation, the Zionist movement was born. The population of the land was only approximately five hundred thousand. The land was ripe and ready for tilling, dressing, and development.

Before the destruction of the Second Commonwealth in AD 70 (in the Second Temple Period, 530 BC to AD 70), this land that was traveled by Jesus and the apostles had in it busy cities, productive agriculture, impressive estates, and caravans of merchants traveling the trade routes of the Middle East. It was civilized, developed, and well populated, even though there were areas of poverty. But in the early sixteenth century until the end of World War I, the land was under the control of a progressively corrupt, cruel, and inefficient Turkish administration. It was largely forsaken until the Jews began returning in the late nineteenth century. It constituted no administrative entity but was part of the Ottoman province of Syria, with Damascus as the capital. "The British Consul in Palestine reported in 1857 that 'the country is in a considerable degree empty of inhabitants and therefore *its great need is that of a body of population.*'"[8] The population was decreasing, and villages were being devastated by the Bedouins. The legendary beauty of the Plain of Sharon was gone. The irrigation and canal systems were gone. These descriptions are confirmed by archeology as well as by population statistics.

James Parkes, a British historian, Palestinian researcher, and Church of England clergyman, writes about the condition of the land in the nineteenth century:

> Leading up to the Zionist movement, there was almost constant warfare between tribes and villages which exceeded anything that was known in the most turbulent centuries of early feudal Europe...The Turkish governors were not averse to a continuation of this state of affairs, since they had no desire to see the power of any of the local landowning families consolidated on the permanent basis which peace and security would have ensured...In the wars between villages it was far too common a practice to cut down fruit trees and olives and to destroy crops, and this in the end caused as much loss of life through hunger as was caused by the actual casualties of fighting. Bedouins freely destroyed the crops of villages which they raided, and killed or carried off their livestock. They filled wells with stones and

broke down reservoirs and cisterns. They often caused such insecurity in whole districts that wide fertile areas were for years left completely uncultivated, while streams and rivers because dammed, malaria became endemic and the unlucky peasants fled elsewhere or starved in the towns...In spite of the immense fertility of the soil, it is probable that in the first half of the nineteenth century the population sank to the lowest level it had ever known in historic times.[9]

It was during this period—mid- to late nineteenth century—that conditions for millions of Jews in Russia and Eastern Europe became desperate. The most acute situation was in Russia, where the unusually large population of five million Jews was being persecuted. There had been some temporary relief under Czars Alexander I and II, who abolished serfdom and lightened some restrictive laws. But after the murder of Alexander II, conditions worsened. *Pogrom* was the term given to organized massacres and destruction of whole residential areas; pogroms became commonplace. Fanatical mobs frequently massacred entire villages. The government and its administrators did little to help, while law-enforcement agencies, at times, aided the terrorists.

A few Jewish leaders began to pose the question of emigrating from Russia. This would not be easy. There were strict laws limiting movement, specifically for the Jews. Most lived within the ghetto, or *pale*, as it was termed. They could not live close to the national border. They were held hostage within their designated areas. Complicating matters, some wealthy Jewish financiers were opposed to mass emigration, feeling that it would furnish the anti-Semites with more cause to accuse the Jews of disloyalty to the Russian Motherland. They held out with the hope that emancipation was imminent. Still, out of a sense of desperation, there were Jews who began talking and writing to their people about rising up from this terrible state of affairs and helping themselves. Masses of Russian Jews braved the journey and immigrated to Western Europe and the United States, while others began to discuss the feasibility of going to the Holy Land. In 1881–1882 associations of young Russians began to spring up in a number of cities, promoting immediate immigration to Palestine.

Was this convergence of events and conditions a providential sign? The land of Israel was lying desolate, without true resident ownership, at the very time when it was desperately needed by the Jewish people, most of whom had a passionate longing for it and all of whom had a historic attachment to it.

This state of affairs was reminiscent of the Iron Age around the fourteenth and thirteenth centuries BC. Canaan was the name of the land when it was populated by Canaanites, and this civilization had grown so corrupt that it was ripe for takeover. Conditions familiar to declining civilizations had set in: decadence, political fragmentation, and economic weakness. Egyptologist Kenneth A. Kitchen writes, "That Canaanite religion appealed to the bestial and material in human nature is clearly evidenced by the Ugaritic texts and in Egyptian texts of Semitic origin or inspiration."[10] This confirms the Genesis account in which God, in His promise to Abraham, said that his descendants would be aliens and slaves in another land (Egypt) until the iniquity of the Amorites was "full" and they could not be a viable society any longer. Then, in that "fullness of time," they would be led to conquer and occupy the land. When the previous ownership was corrupt, then God permitted the conquest. Only then.

Likewise, the return of the Jews to Palestine began at a time when the land was at its most desolate and the society most corrupt. Thus, there is a correspondence between the condition of Palestine under ancient Canaanite rule and Palestine during modern Ottoman rule: it was in a pitiful condition both times. Palestine in the late nineteenth century was a nonstate, poorly and corruptly administered, populated by a people who had no national identity—politically fragmented and loyal only to tribe and family—agriculturally unproductive, and owned for the most part by a few wealthy nonresident Arabs. These owners extorted profits so severely that the residents were repeatedly forced to move from place to place to seek work. The population of peasants not only had to pay the landowners but also were so highly taxed that it seemed as if they had to pay for the very air they breathed. In both eras (the time of the ancient conquest and the late nineteenth century), the land was crying for new residents and new stewardship.

In summary, observant Jews firmly believe that the land originally became theirs because of an ancient, divine promise and gift. The Hebrews existed in that land in the Eastern Mediterranean for over a millennium, though exile to and assimilation in other lands was the destiny of some. Secondly, the Jews never abandoned the land, and they never surrendered it, even to the Romans; they merely succumbed. In the period between the fall of Jerusalem in AD 70 and the birth of the State of Israel in 1948, there was a continuous presence of a Jewish community in Jerusalem and some outlying towns and cities. During the Ottoman Empire, numerous Jewish communities flourished there. Thirdly, in that same time period of almost nineteen hundred years, the Jews in the Diaspora made many efforts—most of them aborted—to return to the land. "Though it was only at the coming of the Messiah that the rabbis expected a mass movement, it was held at all times to be a meritorious action to settle and live in the land of Israel."[11] Fourth, those in the Diaspora who valued their faith and observed its laws yearned to return to the land and prayed at their feast times (both then and now), "Next year in Jerusalem." Fifth, in that same time period, as mentioned above, the land never became an independent state for any other people. Indeed, from the long-reigning Ottoman Empire until the British gained the land as a result of World War I, it was considered not as a separate geographical entity but rather as the province of southern Syria. Finally, ever since the Hebrew conquest of the land in the early Iron Age, there has been an uninterrupted presence of Jewish people there—from five to seven million people during the time of Jesus, to a few thousand at the beginning of the nineteenth century.

THE BIRTH OF ZIONISM

In Europe, the latter part of the nineteenth century was a pivotal period in the Jewish experience. Anti-Semitism was a problem that wouldn't go away. There were brief periods of toleration; then the vilification and hostility erupted anew. A few individual Jewish voices were heard telling their people to emerge from their cocoons and prepare for change—to move from their settlements, ghettos, and the Russian pale and go where they could once again be one nation and take responsibility for their own protection and survival. Theodore Herzl, the founder of the World Zionist Organization, was one of those voices.

Herzl was not sure where the Jews should immigrate, but he believed they had to find a homeland. Having traveled throughout Europe as a journalist, he understood that anti-Semitism was not going away, even with Europe's advances in culture and technology. He saw, too, that assimilation was not viable for the masses of poor and ghettoized Jews. His people were treated as aliens, even though they were loyal citizens. "In vain are we loyal patriots...in vain do we make the same sacrifices of life and property as our fellow citizens; in vain do we strive to enhance the fame of our native land in the arts and sciences, or her wealth by trade and commerce." He then predicted: "In the world as it is now and will probably remain, for an indefinite period, might takes precedence over right...I think we shall not be left in peace."[12]

So in the latter part of the nineteenth century, when Europe was talking about the world moving toward a permanent peace, there was no peace for the Jews. They were unable to fight their oppressors, and the option of moving to a homeland was set before them. At one point Britain suggested Uganda as a resettlement destination for the Jews. Herzl, in his eagerness to get his oppressed people out of their ghetto existence, actually advocated on behalf of the plan at one of the Zionist congresses. He believed that the Turks of the Ottoman Empire would never permit settlement in Palestine. It was, therefore, futile to hope for it. In the Sixth Zionist Congress of 1903, where the Uganda proposal was discussed, the delegates were sent into shock at the suggestion of a homeland other than Palestine. It almost divided the movement. So in his closing speech, Herzl admitted that only Palestine was the land for his people, and he closed the congress with an uplifted right hand, crying out the words of the Psalmist: "If I forget thee, O Jerusalem, may my right hand wither!"[13]

THE BRITISH INITIATIVE

What would break the impasse? How could the Jews return to their homeland in any significant numbers when the ruling Muslim Turks would not permit it? The answer lay in an overture by a different colonial power moving down into the Middle East to defeat and evict the Turks. In reality, while Europe was talking peace at the turn of the century, its nations were gearing up for war. Britain saw that the reform movement in the Ottoman Empire (headed by the Turks) was not working and anticipated its impending collapse.

World War I did indeed result in the defeat of Turkey and the dismantling of the Ottoman Empire. As part of the postwar settlement, Britain gained control of Palestine and what is now Jordan. This "territory" had, as pointed out earlier, been a part of the province of Syria. It now became a territory mandated to Great Britain; Britain's goal was to develop the land into a self-governing nation. The geographical position of Palestine was advantageous for Britain because control of the territory on the Eastern Mediterranean would enhance its trade routes as well as its military position.

As an added incentive for England, Palestine was a sacred place that provoked great interest. Britain was a nation where, at that time, biblical literacy was high and the place names of Palestine were familiar. The English Bible had been a major force in British life since the sixteenth century, beginning with the Tyndale Bible, then the Geneva Bible, and finally the King James Version. At this critical juncture in the birth of Zionism, the British prime minister, Lloyd George, happened to be a man steeped in Torah literature who had much sympathy for the plight of the Jews. It wasn't bad politics at the time to propose that Palestine once again be the homeland of the Jewish people. "Unlike his colleagues he was keenly aware that there were centuries-old tendencies in British Nonconformist and Evangelical thought toward taking the lead in restoring the Jews to Zion. Indeed they formed the background of his own Nonconformist faith."[14]

France and Great Britain negotiated the new boundaries and administration of the Middle East in what became known as the Sykes-Picot Agreement. Lloyd George "told the cabinet that it would be an outrage to let the Christian Holy Places in Palestine fall into the hands of 'Agnostic Atheistic France.'"[15] In fact, the French disliked the idea of the Holy Land being controlled by the Jews and the Protestant British. As for Russia, when British diplomat Sir Mark Sykes, spoke with his Czarist hosts in Petrograd during the war, they "persuaded him that Zionist Jews were a great and potentially hostile power within Russia."[16] Despite the Russians' open hostility toward the Jews, the totalitarian regime would not let them go.

Thus, Britain remained the only European power with both concern for the Jewish cause and the power to open up the way for a return to the land. It was Britain alone that had a few men at the top of the government with personal interests in Palestine. In the middle of the war, these men were promoted to the top seats of government just in time to frame this crucial new Middle East agreement. Lloyd George succeeded Lord Asquith, and Sir Arthur James Balfour became foreign secretary. Both were pro-Zionists, inclined to respond to the Jewish longing for restoration. Lord Balfour authored the Balfour Declaration in November 1917, the document that recognized the right of the Jewish people to reclaim their national homeland in the Middle East. Lord Balfour acknowledged that "Christian religion and civilization owes to Judaism an immeasurable debt."[17]

The League of Nations' understanding was that it was not *creating* the rights of the Jewish people to inhabit their national home; it was *recognizing a preexisting right*. The connection of the Jewish people to their historic land was acknowledged by those world leaders at that time. The British Mandate, confirmed by the League of Nations on July 24, 1922, states, "Recognition has thereby been given to the historical connexion of the Jewish people with

Palestine and to the grounds for reconstituting their national home in that country." It was, without a doubt, providential that Britain was given the Palestinian Mandate by the League of Nations.

The perennial prayer of the Jewish people for the recovery of the land was in a political first stage of finally being answered. Those familiar with Hebrew scripture can hardly be faulted for recalling a text such as this:

> But the Lord will have compassion on Jacob and will again choose Israel,
> And will set them in their own land;
> And aliens will join them and attach themselves to the house of Jacob.
> And the nations will take them and bring them to their place. (Isaiah 14:1–2a)

1. Abraham Joshua Heschel, *Israel: An Echo Of Eternity* (New York: Ferrar, Strauss, and Giroux, 1969), 44.
2. Walter Bruggemann, *The Land* (Philadelphia: Fortress Press, 1977), 5.
3. Abraham Joshua Heschel, *Israel*, 56.
4. Ibid., 57, 64.
5. Bernard Malamud, *The Fixer* (New York: Farrar, Straus and Giroux, 1966),
6. Abraham Joshua Heschel, *Israel*, 54–55.
7. Mark Twain, *The Innocents Abroad* (Hartford: The American Publishing Company, Dover Edition, 2003), 606–608.
8. Joan Peters, *From Time Immemorial: The Origins of the Arab-Jewish Conflict over Palestine* (Chicago: JKAP Publications, 2002), 159.
9. James Parkes, *Whose Land: A History of the Peoples of Palestine* (New York: Taplinger Publishing Company, 1949, 1970), 214–215, 220.
10. J. D. Douglas, ed., *The New Bible Dictionary*, 3rd ed. (Downers Grove: Inter-Varsity Press, 1997), 161–164.

11. James Parkes, *Whose Land*, 143ff.
12. Walter Laqueur, *A History of Zionism* (New York: Schocken Books, 2003), 86.
13. Ibid., 129.
14. David Fromkin, *A Peace to End All Peace: The Fall of the Ottoman Empire and the Creation of the Modern Middle East* (New York: Henry Holt and Company, 1989), 268.
15. Ibid., 270
16. Ibid., 197
17. Barbara Tuchman, *The Proud Tower* (New York: The Macmillan Company, 1966), 366.

CHAPTER 5

Rejoicing in the Land

When the Lord restored the fortunes of Zion,
We were like those who dream.
Then our mouth was filled with laughter,
And our tongue with shouts of joy;
Then it was said among the nations,
"The Lord has done great things for them."
The Lord has done great things for us,
And we rejoiced.

—Psalms 126:1–3

May Zion rejoice
As her children are restored to her in joy.
Praised be Thou, O Lord,
Who causes Zion to rejoice at her children's return…
Praised be Thou, O Lord our God,
King of the universe,
Who created joy and gladness,
Bride and groom,
Mirth, song, delight and rejoicing,
Love, brotherhood, peace and fellowship.
O Lord our God,
May there soon be heard

In the cities of Judah
And in the streets of Jerusalem,
The voice of joy and gladness,
The voice of bride and groom,
The jubilant voice of those
Joined in marriage under their bridal canopy,
The voice of young people
Feasting and singing.

—BENEDICTION FROM THE JEWISH WEDDING RITUAL[1]

FOR MANY JEWS, THE LAND excites the imagination. Those who embrace their heritage love it and are drawn to absorb its history and culture. They feel compelled to enter, settle, and rejoice in the land. They tend and caress it; they fight hard for it; they are willing to learn the language; they endure suffering, hardship, and the world's disdain for them and the land, and they subject their children to the dangers inherent in defense of the land. The closer they are to the land, the closer they feel to their tradition, ancestors, and, often, the Torah. Some eventually, by way of this passion, find themselves drawn closer to the God of their ancestors.

Before the advent of the Zionist Movement, there were small groups of Jews settling bravely in the beloved land despite her barrenness, pestilence, and squalor. In the year 1810, under conditions of hardship, a group of disciples of the great Talmudic scholar the Vilna Gaon settled in the land and reported,

Truly how marvelous it is to live in the good country. Truly how wonderful it is to love our country…Even in her ruin, there is none to compare with her, even in her desolation, she is unequaled, in her silence there is none like her. Good are her ashes and her stones.[2]

DAVID BEN-GURION

The first prime minister of the new State of Israel was born into a Jewish family in Czarist Poland. As recounted in *Ben-Gurion, Prophet of Fire*, by the time Ben-Gurion was eight, he had at home been immersed in the expectation of the redemption of the Promised Land. He was chosen to attend a special school for gifted children, where he studied the Torah, the Talmud, and Hebrew grammar. Not only was he remarkably gifted; he was also highly opinionated, concluding at this early age that the Torah was precious, while the Talmud, so full of minute interpretation of laws, was unimportant. So between the pages of his copy of the Talmud, he secretly kept Zionist literature, which he avidly read while other class members listened to the teacher lecture on the fine points of the law. As a teenager, Ben-Gurion and two other boys formed a young Zionist organization and met in homes. Against the wishes of the local rabbis, they promoted Zionism, learned Hebrew, studied the Bible, and read poems composed by David. (The rabbis in David's town, as well as many others, believed that Hebrew should be spoken only in prayer and that the Jews would return to their land only in connection with the advent of the Messiah.)

David left for Palestine in the summer of 1906. His spirits were high, for he was soon to be in *Eretz Israel* (land of Israel).[3] He had to forge a group passport and then, once on board the ship, suffer the worst kind of indignities forced upon his group by the entire crew, who treated them as Jewish scum. The landing at Jaffa was not pleasant, as David and his friends were confronted with extreme poverty. Ragged idlers, mosques with moldy domes, rows of shanties, filthy bazaars, and cursing Arabs seeking *bakshish* (tips) all greeted his group. Emaciated Jews on the waterfront greeted them as well, telling them they were fools and admonishing them to return to Poland on the next ship! But David was not to be disheartened in the least. This was *Eretz Israel*, the land of promise! His heart beat wildly. He was euphoric. He was sure that, with the industrious work of the young Zionists, the living standards would be raised and the land would become productive and bloom. They were in an environment of decay and backwardness, but that would change.

David refused, against the wishes of young hosts, to remain long in Jaffa but hurried the group along to the settlement of Petah Tikvah in Judea. On the way, the young people sang, danced, and joked as they traveled through orange groves, swamps, and wilderness. Upon their arrival at Petah Tikvah, "the gate of hope" did not look the part. It was in a swampy area full of animal carcasses, ridden with disease, and close to Arab residents. Yet there were also fields of corn and groves of olive and orange trees, blossoming acacia, and the pleasant sound of distant sea waves.

All was strange and bewildering, as though I were errant in a legendary kingdom. Could it be? Joy turned to exaltation. My soul was in
tumult, one emotion drowned my very being: "Lo, I am in *Eretz
Yisrael!*" and Eretz Yisrael was here, wherever I turned or trod…All
night long I sat and communed with my new heaven."[4]

The Ethiopian Jews

We turn from the towering giant of Israel's emerging statehood to 20th-cen-
tury illiterate villagers in the African nation of Ethiopia. Many live in grass
and mud huts. Surprisingly, a portion of them are Jews. Other Ethiopians call
them *Falashas* ("strangers"), but the Jews call themselves *Bet Israel*—"House of
Israel." Certain observers say they are descendants of Solomon, who had many
foreign wives. Others suspect they are descendants of Moses, who married a
Cushite (African). The Ethiopian Jews themselves have a founding narrative,
which is that King Solomon and the Queen of Sheba produced a son, Menelik
I, who was founder of an Ethiopian Solomonic dynasty. They recognize firm
evidence indicating that Judaism was firmly established in Ethiopia at least
by the fourth century AD. Their version of Judaism is purely Torah-oriented;
nothing from the Talmud is known to them, indicating their utter isolation
from the world and other Jews. They have no information about the Talmud

or Judaism as it existed without the sacrificial system. But what has been fore-most in their minds over many centuries has been the city of Jerusalem—the city of David. They testified that Ethiopia was not their homeland, and given their adherence to the Torah, this was understandable. They knew not the way to Jerusalem, yet they held in their hearts a deep longing for and had visions in their sleep of that glorious city—the city which their tradition had held up as the center of worship and celebration of life with the one Lord God. And, as far as they knew, in their heart-of-Africa isolation, they were possibly the last living Jews.

These "Falashas" or "Beta Israel" had experienced nothing of modern life and had no resources to travel any distance. They didn't know how they might travel to Jerusalem. They had never seen airplanes on the ground. However, in the early 1980's, the Israelis were told of these black Ethiopian brothers and sisters. A groundswell of interest in them formed, and in due course, certain officials in the Israeli government and defense forces resolved that the Ethiopians would have the opportunity to immigrate to Israel. But at that time, the Ethiopian government was close to being overturned by rebel forces, and the ruling regime was making group emigration nearly impossible. However, after World Jewish organizations heard of this and pressed for rescuing these reticent but desperate people, plans were devised with assistance from the American government. The most dramatic of these was "Operation Solomon" in which non-stop flights of Israeli aircraft were chosen to make the flight to Tel Aviv.

The planning for "Operation Solomon" was held secret, and in 1991 the people of Beta Israel made the dangerous and arduous trip to Addis Ababa on foot or hidden in trucks to avoid discovery by rebel forces. There, in and around the city, they found clandestine positions until time for the flights out of the country.

Thirty-five Israeli aircraft were utilized for this 1600-mile journey. Some of these had the seats removed to create more seating space. The Ethiopians were forbidden to take luggage of any kind since every bit of space was utilized to seat people. One El Al plane had on board 1,122 passengers which could only have been done given the light weight of these people. Babies were born inflight, and many people turned sick and were taken to hospitals upon arrival. Nevertheless, on disembarking barefoot from the planes, many of these small black Africans were ecstatic, cheering and kissing the ground, while the pilots and Israeli soldiers who were aboard were weeping with joy and relief over the successful mission.[5-6]

The Israelis too were ecstatic over this record-breaking airlift. Gifts of cribs, clothing and accessories came showering down to meet the needs of these immigrants who owned only the clothes on their backs.

Imagine the adjustments these immigrants had to make to adapt to an advanced modern-day culture. Many articles and books have been written to describe the post-traumatic stress disorders of these Ethiopians and the trauma treatments that social workers and psychiatrists gave to them. Their ancient dream of living in Jerusalem was now fulfilled, and they experienced joy mixed with nightmares of their dangerous foot journey to reach the airport. Starvation, murders, rapes, robbery, and illness were endured on the group's journey. As might be expected, their adjustment to modern life and assimilation into Israeli culture was fraught with many difficulties. Never before had they used bathrooms or seen modern appliances. Unemployment, poverty, and even discrimination were experienced by those who, over the course of the years, were successful in making the journey. Nevertheless, they were now at home, with no danger of being slain for observing Jewish laws and practices.[6-7-8]

The Russian Jews

In Russia, under the totalitarian rule of the Communist Party, all religious expression was suppressed. An extraordinary effort was made to extirpate Judaism by shutting down all synagogues, closing Hebrew schools, and forbidding Jewish worship. Opposition to Zionism was openly expressed in the state-controlled mass media. It was outlawed in the Soviet code and attacked as a tool of international capitalism. A large number of published anti-Semitic books portrayed

Judaism as a religion with, ironically, Nazi characteristics. Exile to Siberia was the lot of many Jews who were declared or even suspected of Zionist activity. Consequently, the second generation of Jews living under Soviet indoctrination had little knowledge of their Judaism. Observers in Western countries predicted that the third generation living under this religious suppression would—in addition to having little knowledge of Judaism and Zionism—possess little religious curiosity and be thoroughly assimilated into the Soviet system and culture.

Then came the Six-Day War. Israel decisively countered and prevailed over the aggression of its Arab neighbors, thereby becoming "occupiers of the West Bank" (or Judea and Samaria, to use the Israeli-preferred biblical nomenclature). Then the sons and daughters of the second generation living under Russian Communist domination—the young people who had been brought up by the "lost generation"—began to feel a sense of solidarity with their fellow Jews. A yearning for the land was born in their souls and, with it, a feeling of alienation from Soviet Russia and its values. A collective conversion took place, bringing inquisitiveness about Hebrew thought and history.

Applications for immigration to Israel began in a slow stream, though the Russian government was purposely slow to act, thinking the new stirring would soon lose its fascination. Leaders of the movement were imprisoned, generating protests both in the Soviet Union and abroad. Visitors to Russia from Western countries traveled there to visit the dissidents. This third generation of Russian Jews defied the authorities and demanded their right to leave the country, a right that was in the Soviet Constitution but had not been honored. They were determined enough to declare that they would go on foot, if necessary, to reach the land for which they yearned. By the late 1980s, the Soviet-Jewish protest movement had gained worldwide attention, and the Russian authorities began to relent.

The courage these young citizens of the Soviet state showed energized their parents, and a wave of immigration began. When the liberalizing policy of *perestroika* (meaning "restructuring") was put into gear by Mikhail

Gorbachev, the wave became a tsunami. In the 1990s, 772,239 Jews emigrated from the USSR to enter the land of their dreams and dwell with their own people. The longing for the return to Zion was so intense that nothing could stop it. The time was ripe. Russia as an imperial power had weakened and yielded to pressure at the very time when Israel was positioned to receive her own. It was yet another amazing exodus and joyous return.[9]

It is hard to imagine two groups of Jews more fundamentally different than the Russian Jews and the Ethiopian "Bet Israel." The latter group were isolated from the entire world but had kept the religious traditions of the Torah, observing them meticulously. The Russian Jews, many of whom were educated and cultured within the Russian environment, were utterly ignorant of their religion--isolated in this spiritual aspect from the world Jewish community. But different though they themselves were and different as their expectations of the land were, these two groups chose to immigrate to the same land, and their choice led to this land where the cultural differences are huge. Millions of Jewish people from the ends of the earth have taken the same step: with differing traditions, looks, occupations and political and social structures they are forming a fantastic new state. The amazing process of amalgamation will continue, promising to make a most wonderfully diverse community of Israel the Chosen.

The land is the venue for the ingathering—from east, west, north, and south; from Asia, Europe, Africa, and the Americas—from more than one hundred countries speaking more than eighty languages. The Diaspora is returning home. The exile is over, and the welcome mat is out for the sons and daughters of Jacob. The land is a melting pot, but unlike that of America, this one has one predominant nationality—yet the diversity within that nationality is startling: Sabras (see Glossary), Ashkenazi, Sephardim, Ethiopian, Mizrahi (from the Middle East), to name a few. The return to the land has brought with it the return of the use of the biblical language of Hebrew and, with it, a revival of interest in Hebrew scripture and tradition—the Torah and the Talmud. There are Gentiles making aliyah (see Glossary) too. Africans and Asians are streaming into Israel because of the economic opportunities and personal liberties the country affords, consequently swelling the Christian population. The children of these worker-immigrants are being granted the rights of citizenship.

The people rejoice! In spite of threats from without and within and perpetual dissatisfaction with government corruption, the people of Israel, at this stage, are a happy people.

Caroline Glick, editor of the *Jerusalem Post*, wrote in April 2013 that in a recent survey carried out by the Organization for Economic Co-operation (OECD), Israelis are ranked among the happiest people in the world. Israelis work harder, complain more, and yet, she says, "are among the happiest people in the OECD." And she goes on to elaborate on one aspect of that happiness. "Today, with an average of three children per family, Israelis are the fecund outliers of the industrial world. And as David Goldman at PJ Media has demonstrated, there is a direct correlation between children and human happiness. This is why fruitful Israelis have the lowest suicide rate in the industrial world. When you have children, you have a future. And when you have a future, you work hard to secure it, and have a generally optimistic outlook."[11]

More recently, the "World Happiness Report" which is published annually by the United Nations Sustainable Development Solutions Network and the Earth Institute at Columbia University shows that in 2016 Israel ranked 11th among the nations for citizen happiness. The United States is at 13th, France is 32nd, Egypt 120th.[12] That's surprising considering the turmoil in the Middle East--that Israel's neighbors rank close to the bottom and that Israel is one of the most hated nations of the world. But Israel is a nation still growing, still receiving her own people year after year, making phenomenal progress in technology, while underneath all these modern phenomena is the deep-seated conviction in many of her citizens that she is built on a Biblical foundation.

ABRAHAM JOSHUA HESCHEL

Heschel (1907–1972) was professor of ethics and mysticism at the Jewish Theological Seminary of America. He is widely known in Christian as well as Jewish circles for his profound insights. He wrote of his personal impressions as he strolled with friends through Jerusalem after the Six-Day War of 1967. Nothing but the work of God, he declared, could have brought about this great moment in Jewish history. All of Jerusalem was finally opened, and there was great rejoicing in the streets:

> This is the work of Providence and who is to say that there is nothing new under the sun?...Those of us who were in the land following the end of hostilities walked in amazement, in silent gratitude, overwhelmed and spellbound. In our eyes it was as if the prophets of ancient Israel had risen from their graves and walked through the streets of Jerusalem. How to welcome them? What should we say to them?
>
> We were carried away by an awakening of the soul, overwhelmed by a vision of the profound seriousness of Jewish history. Suddenly, we sensed the link between the Jews of this generation and the people of the time of the prophets. Despite the distance of time and the difference of cultures, we are that very same living people, parts of the body of Israel of all generations.
>
> In the days that have just passed even the unlettered among us saw that which Ezekiel could not see. Every one of us had a moment in which he said, "This is my God and I will praise him, my father's God and I will exalt Him." (Exodus/Shemot 15:2).[13]

1. Joshua Abraham Heschel, *Israel: An Echo of Eternity* (New York: Farrar, Straus, and Giroux, 1969), 62–63.

2. Samuel Katz, *Battleground: Fact and Fantasy in Palestine* (New York: Taylor Productions, Ltd., 2002), 101.

3. Dan Kurzman, *The Prophet of Fire* (New York: Simon and Schuster, 1983), 74–99.

4. Ibid., 80.

5. Donna Rosenthal, *The Israelis* (New York: Free Press, 2003), 149–151

6. "Operation Solomon," *Wikipedia*, https://en.wikipedia.org/wiki/Operation_Solomon

7. Judy Siegel-Itzkovich, "Trauma from a Brave Exodus," *The Jerusalem Post*, February 13–19, 2015, 14–15.

8. Mitchell G. Bard, *From Tragedy to Triumph: The Politics Behind the Rescue of Ethiopian Jewry* (Westport, Connecticut: Praeger, 2002), 199.

9. Samuel Katz, *Battleground*, 82–84.

10. David Margolis, "The Fabulist," *The Jerusalem Report*, April 18, 2005, 40, 41.

11. Caroline Glick, *carolineglick.com*, April 19, 2013.

Continuing Glick's report: "Then there is our newfound energy wealth. Israel became energy independent on March 30, when the Tamar offshore gas field began pumping natural gas to Israel. In two to three years, when the Leviathan gas field comes online, Israel will become one of the most important producers of natural gas in the world. Moreover, in 2017, Israel will likely begin extracting commercial quantities of oil from its massive oil shale deposits in the Shfela Basin near Beit Shemesh. Geologists assess that the field alone contains some 250 billion barrels of oil, giving Israel oil parity with Saudi Arabia. Chinese, Russian and Australian firms are lining up to sign contracts with Israeli energy companies. International analysts assess that Israel's emergence as an energy power will have a stabilizing impact on the global economy and international security. Israel can end Asia's oil and gas hunger. It can reduce European dependence on Russia. It will remove OPEC's ability to dictate world oil prices through supply manipulation."

12. "Israel World's 11th Happiest Country," *BreakingIsraelNews,* March 18, 2016, https://www.breakingisraelnews.com/63830/israel-worlds-11th-happiest-country-jerusalem/#GgDKKclQyYlcWOpV.97.
13. Joshua Abraham Heschel, *Israel,* 209–210.

CHAPTER 6

The Rejection

§

O God, do not keep silence;
Do not hold your peace or be still, O God!
Even now your enemies are in tumult;
Those who hate you have raised their heads.
They lay crafty plans against your people;
They consult together against those you protect.
They say, "Come, let us wipe them out as a nation;
Let the name of Israel be remembered no more."
They conspire with one accord,
Against you they make a covenant—
The tents of Edom and the Ishmaelites,
Moab and the Hagrites,
Gebal and Ammon and Amalek,
Philistia with the inhabitants of Tyre;
Assyria also has joined them;
They are the strong arm of the children of Lot…
Make their nobles like Oreb and Zeeb,
All their princes like Zebah and Zalmunna,
Who said, "Let us take the pastures of God
For our own possession."

—Psalms 83:1–8, 11–12

Israel particularly sticks in the craw of Islamists...because even
though it exercises sovereignty over only one-five-hundredth
of the territory of modern *Dar al-Islam* (House of Islam), it's
geographically smack in the middle, frustrating a Greater Islam...
When Arabs castigate Israel as "a cancer in the body of the Arab
nation" or "a dagger in the heart of the Arab"—rhetorical overkill
to Westerners—they're making perfect sense within Islamic
ideology, which calls for "Islamic hegemony over the world."

—Carlin Romano, reviewing "Peace: The
Arabian Caricature" by Arieh Stav [1]

The liberation of that land [Palestine] is an individual duty binding on
all Muslims everywhere. This is the base on which all Muslims have
to regard the problem; this has to be understood by all Muslims.

—The Hamas Charter

[Israel] has no cure but to be annihilated.

—A tweet from Iran's Supreme leader,
Ayatollah Ali Khamenei [2]

THE STATE OF ISRAEL IS noticeably absent from the official Arabic maps of
Lebanon, Saudi Arabia, Syria, and the Palestinian Authority. In a map of
the Middle East published in America for use in English-speaking schools
in the Middle East, the state of Israel has been omitted. A spokesperson for
the publisher is reported to have said that "supplying maps including Israel
would be 'unacceptable' to customers in the Gulf countries and the map was
a response to 'local preferences.'"[3] So, the very existence of neighbor Israel is

denied. Official maps are just one sign among many that show the abhorrence in the Middle East of this tiny nation.

Hatred toward Israel and the Jews is stirred up in government-run schools beginning in the first grade, with schoolbooks poisoned with anti-Semitic and anti-Israel propaganda. Examples: "Palestinian children are taught in school that Jews are descended from apes and pigs and that the most noble thing they can do is to kill Jews."[4] David Horowitz of the "Center for the Study of Popular Culture" writes that "elementary school children in Palestinian Arab schools are even taught to chant "Death to the heathen Jews" in their classrooms as they are learning to read."[5]

The malignant spirit of anti-Semitism fills the airwaves, newspapers, and all forms of communication. Hitler's *Mein Kampf* is a best seller in Egypt. The myth entitled *Protocols of the Elders of Zion*, a classic piece of racist literature, was discredited long ago as being a Czarist forgery, but it too has been widely circulated in the Arab world. This slanderous book accuses the Jews of poisoning wells, spreading the plague, and using the blood of Christian children for baking matzos for the Feast of the Passover.[6]

Nonie Darwish in her autobiography, *Now They Call Me Infidel*, recounts her memories of this nauseous spirit pervading the culture where she grew up in Gaza and Egypt. Of her life in Gaza, she writes: "The hatred of Israel and our obligation to pursue jihad was somehow worked into every subject we discussed in school....Peace was never discussed as an option, and we were made to feel that peace with Israel would bring only shame to our Arab pride....Jews were portrayed as devils, pigs, and an evil, occupying foreign force." And she writes of living in Egypt during the rule of Gamal Abdel Nasser: "Despite the extreme hardships and poverty our society was suffering, the Egyptian media had only one agenda, and that was jihad—to destroy Israel...I remember cartoons depicting the blood-thirsty Jews who wanted to kill Arabs for fun."[7]

Can anyone explain the reason for this toxic racism? Can we find the answer to this question: Why did Hashem, the God of Israel, place His people where they would experience such antagonism? Both ancient and modern Jewish thinkers have raised this question. Moses Maimonides, twelfth-century Jewish philosopher, voiced this as he contemplated the Muslim neighbors of Israel: "God has cast us into the midst of this people, the nation of Ishmael, who persecute us severely, and who devise ways to harm us and to debase us... None has matched [them] in debasing and humiliating us."[8]

ANCIENT REJECTIONISM

This same type of antagonism was shown by Semitic peoples when the Hebrew people first approached the land. Looking at some incidents in the early history of Israel will broaden understanding of the scope of anti-Semitism.

In a different—or perhaps better—world, there may have been cooperation between the Israelites and the other children of Abraham. In fact, there is evidence of some having occurred. The text of the Book of Bereshit/Genesis gives us the origin of other peoples of Palestine and Arabia. For example, following the death of Sarah, Abraham wedded Keturah in his old age and produced six sons. He thus fathered additional nations, which settled east of the Jordan River and southeast in the Arabian Peninsula. As Leon R. Kass points out in his work *The Beginning of Wisdom: Reading Genesis*, these half-brothers of Isaac "are not purely vessels of enmity for Isaac and his line...Many of them crop up in later stories, both for good and for ill. Perhaps most important are the Midianites, who figure prominently in the future life of Israel. It would be Midianites who rescue Joseph from the pit...It will be a priest of Midian, Reuel, who takes in the fugitive Moses, escaped from Egypt, and gives him his daughter, Zipporah, as a wife...It will be the same Midianite, now called Jethro, who tells Moses to establish a law for his emancipated nation of slaves."[9]

Thus individuals might conceive of a history of cooperation between the Children of Israel and their cousins. They had sufficient common enemies to prompt them to work together against these adversaries—Egypt, Syria, and the Philistines, to name just a few. Such cooperation also could have greatly benefited their agriculture and commercial activity. Why could they not have peacefully coexisted? What did the Israelites do to provoke the aggression that surfaced immediately upon Israel's sojourn from Egypt to Canaan?

The enmity stemmed from a resentment of Israel's ethical monotheism and the successes that came with it. The One God, Hashem, had chosen Israel and acted on her behalf. This One God had given her a unique law. The fraternal enmity was a reaction to this singular God, to Israel's chosenness, and to her law. Israel was scorned. We learn from the Torah that it was an arrogant, contemptuous rejection. Those nations rejected the monotheism of Israel, preferring instead the little gods they possessed and manipulated. They hated the superior ethic of the Torah, which the One God had given, and they hated Israel for adhering to it.

The Book of Bereshit/Genesis sets forth the original enmity between Ishmael, Abraham's firstborn son to Hagar (Sarah's maidservant), and Isaac, the "son of promise" born to Sarah, Abraham's formerly barren, elderly wife. Many Muslim Arabs today consider themselves descendants of Ishmael, for Islam in its sacred literature points to Ishmael as the "son of promise" out of whom would come the Chosen People. This convoluting of the ancient biblical story is a way for Islam to bring credibility to its origin. To Muslims, the Torah is in error, and the correction of the error came with Mohammed. Their objective is to recover the ascendancy of Ishmael over Isaac—that is, of Ishmael's descendants over the Jewish people. Charles Malik, Arab Christian of the mid-twentieth century, Harvard college professor, and Lebanese states-man, saw this Arab identification with Ishmael as a key to understanding the modern Middle East crisis:

> The Old Testament theological challenge has to deal with the great
> mystery of Ishmael and Isaac. Whoever broods with a pure and lov-
> ing heart upon this mystery and contemplates in its light the present

spiritual situation between Jews and Arabs in the Near East must experience a profound emotion of wonder...To dismiss the present conflict between the children of Isaac and the children of Ishmael, who are all children of Abraham, as just another ordinary politico-economic struggle, is to have no sense whatever for the awful and holy and ultimate in history. When history shall finally reveal its secret (of which we here and now already catch a real glimpse), the present confrontation between Isaac and Ishmael may turn out to be...one of the major keys unlocking that secret.[10]

People of the Western world may wonder if such ancient events can possibly have a bearing on today's enmities. One could argue that they do. Both Judaism and Islam claim legitimacy on the basis of their ancient stories. Both hold them implanted in their collective subconscious and conscious minds. Their stories are religious and foundational. The things they claim were divinely given—land and military success, for example—are very precious. By these gifts their fate is largely determined. They honor the ancestors who originally received them. Therefore, their identity is built on changeless narratives.

For the Muslim, the ancient history of Israel is a false narrative; the Islamic version recognizes only Arabs as the children of Abraham. Abraham's son Ishmael, not Isaac, is the son of promise. But in the Bereshit/Genesis account of Ishmael's birth, the angel of the Lord prophesied that Ishmael "shall be a wild ass of a man, with his hand against everyone, and everyone's hand against him; and he shall live at odds with all his kin" (Bereshit/Genesis 16:12). The question is, do Arab Muslims acknowledge this prophecy and see its fulfillment in their own history?

Not only Ishmael (the half-brother of Isaac) but also Isaac's eldest son, Esau, was to be the father of a nation. The Edomites proceeded from Esau—Abraham and Isaac being common patriarchs of both the Israelites and Edomites. As briefly noted in chapter 1, the Israelites asked permission to pass through Edomite territory on their way from Egypt to Canaan (Palestine), since that route would shorten the distance they had to travel. The biblical narrative records their request, identifying their close relationship.

"This message is from your brother Israel. You know all the hardships we have encountered, how our ancestors went down to Egypt, and we lived there for many years. The Egyptians ill-treated us and our fathers before us, and we cried to the Lord for help. He listened to us, sent an angel, and brought us out of Egypt. Now we are here at Kadesh, a town on your frontier. Grant us, we ask, passage through your country. We shall not trespass on field or vineyard, nor drink from your wells. We shall keep to the king's highway, not turning off to right or left until we have crossed your territory." But the Edomites refused, and marched out to oppose them with a large army in full strength. Since the Edomites would not allow Israel to cross their frontier, Israel turned and went a different way. (BeMidbar/Numbers 20:14b–21)

One might think that their common parentage, combined with a humanitarian impulse, would have moved the Edomites to grant the requested permission. (In the ancient world, hospitality was a custom generally and generously extended.) The appeal to their better instincts failed. The response of the Edomites showed not just indifference but militant hostility. This was an omen of subsequent Edomite and, later, Arab action.

Indeed, later in history, these Edomites gloated when the Babylonians destroyed Jerusalem and took the Israelites into captivity. They travelled to Palestine and celebrated with jubilant demonstrations as all homes were set afire and the Jewish inhabitants were forced out to be led like cattle on the road to Babylon. The prophet Obadiah denounces Edom for this hateful spirit:

The words of the Lord God about Edom…
For the violence done to your brother Jacob.

You will be covered with shame and cut off forever...
Do not gloat over your brother when disaster strikes him,
Or rejoice over Judah on the day of his ruin.
Do not boast when he suffers distress,
Or enter my people's gates on the day of their calamity. (Obadiah 1,
10, 12, 13)

So from the outset, the Israelites were fiercely rejected by the very peoples who should have shown kindness, their hateful action establishing a precedent for the ages.

Later Rejectionism

In the seventh century AD, the Arab Muslims gained ascendancy in the Middle East through military might. They were certain they would never have to tolerate a *nation* of Jews as neighbors. Nevertheless, the Jews were, at this time, a sizeable segment of the population in the Middle East. The Arab and Turkish Muslims could control, humiliate, and on occasion slaughter them with the backing of Islamic law. They had had the upper hand for all these centuries—conquering their world, establishing Islamic culture, gaining adherents, and subjugating "infidels." With the Arab Muslims' heavy-handed rule, how could the Jews come in strength and claim land in their midst? Not until the latter part of the nineteenth century did any of them contemplate such a possibility.

At that time Zionists, some of whom hoped to establish a state, began immigrating to Palestine. However, the immediate purpose of many of them was to escape the persecution they and their people had experienced for centuries in Russia and Eastern Europe. These immigrants arrived, thrilled to be in the land of their forebears, ready to work on the land to prepare it for farming. They had no plan to expel the Palestinian Arabs. Their priority was to purchase land from the Arabs for cultivation. They did not take it by force but bought it from rich Arab landowners, the "effendis," most of whom were aristocrats who lived in Damascus or some other urban area with serfs (*fel-lahin*) working for them. Some of these Zionists bought land from the Greek Orthodox Church. Early land purchases were mostly in the coastal plain between Jaffa and Haifa and in the Jezreel and Jordan Valleys. As previously noted, much of this area was swampy, heavily-infested with mosquitos, and sparsely inhabited.

The arrival of these Jews, by small increments at first, was appalling to their Arab Muslim neighbors. What temerity these Jews have, they thought, to move from Europe and settle in the land. Further, it was galling to observe their success in establishing prosperous farms and medical facilities.

Thus, in the early years of Zionism (late nineteenth and early twentieth centuries), Palestinian Arabs were infuriated that Jews, who were supposed to be *dhimmi* (see Glossary), would be living next to them. The Arab Muslims had been accustomed to seeing Jews cower. In Islamic countries, both Jewish and Christian *dhimmis* were considered people of the book (the Bible) and, on this basis, were to be given protection. Beyond that, they were afforded almost no rights. Muslim law ordained that dhimmis should be much more heavily taxed than Muslims, thus producing monetary gain for the state. The law required dhimmis to lower their eyes and make way for Muslims on the road, and keep silent unless spoken to. In most Arab Muslim countries, dhimmis had no legal or social rights—no right to defend themselves in public or in court. In countless ways, the Christians and Jews had to practice self-debasement and move about warily to avoid the slightest offense. Consequently, it was vexing, both to the Palestinian Arabs and the Ottoman-Turk authorities, to see Jewish immigrants entering the land, settling there, and becoming prosperous. The notion of the low and vile Jews settling in their land was viewed as unnatural and contrary to their law.[11]

Yet it was not only the Muslims who objected to Jewish immigration. Walter Laqueur, in his volume *A History of Zionism*, writes that Christian churches in Palestine were among the most vocal in their protests against

Jewish settlement. Christians were prominent in the educated class and, therefore, more influential. Newspapers in Syria and Palestine were managed by Christians. Regarding rejection of the Jewish immigrants, Eliyahu Sapir wrote in 1899 that "the main blame was with the Catholic Church, and in particular the Jesuits."[12]

RESISTANCE TO ALIYAH

As previously noted, the Hebrew word *aliyah* means "to go up" or "to ascend." A Jewish aliyah is immigration to Israel. This word is used for the waves of immigrants to Israel in the modern age, beginning with the first aliyah of 1880 to 1900. It was spearheaded by young Jews from a high-school and university group in Kharkov, Russia, and founded in 1881. Its name, Bilu, is an acronym for "*Bet Yaakov lechu ve nelcha*" ("O house of Jacob, come ye, and let us go") (Isaiah 11:5). Out of a group of three hundred, only sixteen survived the hardships of travel and arrived in the Holy Land. Even this small community of Jews seemed to pose a threat to the Turkish Ottoman Empire that ruled "lower Syria," as Palestine was then identified. Even before the Jewish group had left Odessa, Russia, by boat, the Turkish consul general there announced a prohibition of anyone to settle in Palestine. This was but the beginning of proclamations to bar any Jews from immigrating to Palestine. They were not welcome and not to be allowed in. Abdulhamid II said in June 1891, after being informed of renewed Zionist pressure on the gates of Palestine, "Why should we accept those whom the cultured Europeans turned back and expelled from their own countries?"[13]

Occasionally, the Ottoman authorities incited the local Arab population to bring violence against the settlers. All this was before Zionism was organized—before Theodore Herzl proclaimed his vision of a new homeland for the harassed Jewish people of Europe and before the First Zionist Congress of 1897. Thus, from the very hint of the beginning of return to their ancient homeland, the Jews were despised and rejected by the authorities who controlled the land of their forefathers—the same land where there had been a continuous Jewish presence since the conquests under Joshua some fourteen hundred years before Christ. Nevertheless, under pressure from the Great Powers, bribery, and the inefficient bureaucracy of the Ottomans, the immigration of the Jews began.

It is perhaps understandable that immigrants were rejected and harassed in a land and culture where the underclass and savage stalked the land. The Bedouins and the debased *fellah* (peasants) who worked the effendis' lands were not the kind of open-minded and open-hearted people who would graciously welcome newcomers. "The novelist Brenner recalled that soon after landing at Haifa, he was rushed by a group of Arab youth shouting 'Yehud, Yehud' (Jew, Jew). His initial instinct was to hit them...By 1913 Brenner was writing of the hatred that existed between Jew and Arabs—and 'so it must be and will continue to be.'"[14] Unfortunately for the Jews, the attitude of this lower segment of Palestinian and Arab society was not exceptional save in the tactical approach of their rejection. With every new aliyah, there were new and more vehement ways the world of Middle Eastern peoples conveyed, "You are not welcome in the land of your origin."

The second aliyah continued from the turn of the century through 1914. It was inspired by hundreds of pogroms in Russia. Thousands of Jews were killed or injured, property was destroyed, and synagogues were burned. Intimidation and persecution were widespread and severe. Zionism itself was not the primary factor that brought the second wave of immigrants to the land; it was simply the need to escape from anti-Semitic terrorism. Many Jews fled to Western Europe and the United States, while others, influenced by the Zionist appeal, settled in Palestine.

Many of the early Zionist leaders argued for the development of good relations with the resident Arabs. For those who had the time and energy in the midst of their efforts to survive and build neighborhoods, this was the prevailing sentiment. Some thought the tension between Jews and Arabs—since it stemmed from mutual ignorance of each other's language and culture—could be overcome with enough time and effort. After World War I, no Zionist Congress was held without passing recommendations or declarations on the necessity of establishing good relations with Arab nationalists and the Arab population generally. Previously, at the seventh Zionist Congress in 1905, Yitzhak Epstein, a teacher and agriculturist, encouraged his fellow Jews to promote peaceful relations with the Arabs. Land purchases should be made only if there would be mutual benefit. The Arabs should be helped to find their own identity and build hospitals and schools. Everyone present agreed that the Arabs had already profited from the presence of the Jews. The Zionist newcomers wanted it that way, but it was exceedingly difficult to establish a sense of brotherhood when there was such enmity toward the Jews. Epstein admitted that it was a difficult task to buy the friendship of the Arabs. "Why then try so hard? History was full of examples showing that the more the Jews tried to ingratiate themselves with other peoples, the more they had been hated."[15]

In 1917 the Arabs reacted furiously to the Balfour Declaration, whereby Britain recognized the right of the Jews to establish a homeland in Palestine. British intelligence officers reported widespread opposition among Palestinian Arabs. As early as 1918, they began to organize against its implementation. Arab attacks on Jewish settlements became increasingly frequent. In 1920 rioting in Jerusalem broke out, and placards were put up, reading, "Death to the Jews" and "Down with Zionism." Six Jews were killed, two hundred wounded, and hundreds more rendered homeless. In 1921 the rioting ensued; forty-seven Jews were killed, and 117 were wounded. Palestine was supposed to have been a shelter from pogroms. Now, in their new homeland, the immigrants experienced what they had sought to leave behind them in Russia. At this point the British suppressed the violence and beefed up their forces. But the Arabs had shown the intensity of their antagonism, and it would continue in various forms.

Arab leaders caught wind of discussions among Jewish leaders about whether or not there might have to be a transfer of some Arabs to other areas, such as Transjordan. This, of course, enraged the leaders. But such a proposition was never approved. Though some recent historians said that David Ben-Gurion was one who suggested this, most backtracked and acknowledged that he was never a serious proponent of the idea. To the contrary, he declared, "*We do not wish, we do not need to expel Arabs* and take their place...All our aspiration is built on the assumption...that there is enough room in the country for ourselves and the Arabs."[16] And later, "The Arab policy of the Jewish State must be aimed not only at full equality for the Arabs but at their cultural, social, and economic equalization, namely, at raising their standard of living to that of the Jews."[17]

For its part, the British Administration tried strenuously to placate the Arabs by jailing the key Zionist leader, Ze'ev Jabotinsky, and assuring them that the Balfour Declaration would not result in a Zionist administration. In 1929 more violence erupted after a series of Arabs' inflammatory statements contained accusations that the Jews were desecrating the Temple Mount (called by Arabs "al-Haram al-Sharif"), the third holiest site in Islam and the Jews' most holy site. It was at this site where at least the second ancient biblical Temple was situated, if not, both the first (Solomon's) and the second. (Following the Six Day War of 1967 when the Israelis won control of Old Jerusalem, the then prime minister, Levi Eshkol gave control of access to the Mount to the Jerusalem Islamic Wapf. Since then, Arab propagandists have occasionally accused the Jews of wanting to not only take over this area but also destroy Islam's sacred structures. Furthermore, every part of the land was considered by Arabs to be sacred soil, since it once was in Muslim control. There were demonstrations by both groups. The risk for the Jews was highest when thousands of Arabs emerged from worship. Muslim emotions were inflamed by sermons, which resulted in Jewish pedestrians being attacked, as well as in shops being looted and set afire. In some rural areas and villages, Jews were massacred as the violence spread throughout the country. British High Commissioner Sir John Chancellor characterized the attacks as "unspeakable savagery."[18]

It was evident that British forces could not control the unruly mobs, since the British forces were much too small to prevent the destruction. The Jewish Haganah, a clandestine organization for the defense of the Jewish population, upgraded its organization and began to smuggle in arms from abroad. If the Yishuv (the Jewish community of Palestine) was to survive, it would have to bear responsibility for its own defense. The Arabs were intent on ending Jewish immigration and ridding themselves of these nonsubservient Jews.

In April of 1936, the Arab effendis called a general strike and formed a Supreme Arab Committee. Their purpose was to close down shops, factories, and ports until the British put a stop to Jewish immigration and banned land sales to Jews. Violence erupted in the cities and the countryside, with bomb throwing, arson, crop destruction, and clashes with the British. It was not until October that the Arabs held their fire, only after learning that the British High Commissioner was willing to meet nearly all their demands.

The antipathy of Palestinian Islamic Arabs to the Jewish people was so extreme as to block any humanitarian concern. They wanted neither Jewish immigration nor any rights of ownership to be transferred to Jews. Was there any display of concern for their cousins when the Jews of Europe were suffering anti-Semitism of every kind, even pogroms and, ultimately, the Holocaust? No. Instead the record shows how Arab leaders cooperated with the Axis powers leading up to and during World War II in the planned destruction of the Jewish people.

Haj Amin al-Husseini, the grand mufti of Jerusalem, is a prime example of Arab-Nazi collaboration. He operated from headquarters in various countries throughout the Middle East, finally settling in Germany. There he established branch offices in other parts of Germany and Italy to carry out his plan to assist the Nazis in their execution of the "Final Solution." Joan Peters, in her book *From Time Immemorial*, documents the cooperation that the grand mufti, who interpreted Islamic law, gave to the Nazis. He was a "staunch friend of Hitler and coordinator with Germany in the 'Final Solution' to the Jewish problem" and in that capacity was "personally responsible for the concentration camp slaughter of hundreds of thousands of Jews, if not more."[19] In one instance, nine hundred Jewish children who were being aided in an escape plan to Palestine were finally sent to extermination camps as a result of the mufti's intervention with Hungarian authorities.

Here again it seems quite appropriate to consider the ancient enmity of Israel's cousins as a foreshadowing of the attitude of modern Middle East Arabs toward the Jews. Though separated in time by over three thousand years, both ancient and modern Semites have so deeply despised the Jews that no humanitarian impulses surfaced at times of extreme neediness in the Jewish community. What conclusion can be drawn? This inquiry is worthy of informed reflection.

In the post–World War II period, Arab unity was easily garnered for the purpose of blocking Jewish immigration and preventing the founding of a Jewish nation. Such unity took the form of the Arab League, founded in 1945. The first secretary general of the League, Abd al-Rahman Azzam, was assured by Jewish representatives that the Arab world had nothing to fear about Jewish immigration and that there was no thought of Jewish expansion. The Jews made on offer consisting of a guarantee that a Jewish state would not encroach on the boundaries of neighboring states. Active cooperation and development, they assured Azzam, would continue to benefit both Arabs and Jews materially as well as culturally. But Azzam was adamantly opposed to any sliver of land being allocated to the Jewish people. He spoke of the Arab peoples' resentment of the Jewish presence in terms of Arab collective consciousness. He declared the following to his Jewish counterparts:

> For me you may be a fact, but for them you are not a fact at all—you are a temporary phenomenon. Centuries ago the Crusaders established themselves in our midst against our will, and in 200 years we

ejected them...You will achieve nothing with talk of compromise or peace...You speak of the Middle East. For us there is no such concept; for us there is only the concept of the Arab world. Nationalism is the great force that moves us. We do not need economic development. For us there is only one test, the test of strength. If I were a Zionist leader, perhaps I would behave as you do. You have no choice. In any case, the problem is likely to be solved only by force of arms.[20]

Accordingly, Arabs refused the UN proposal to once again partition Palestine and offer the Jews a small portion. Unable to prevail against partition, the surrounding Arab nations went to war, endeavoring to bring about the new nation's destruction. In bellicose language, they told the Arab Palestinians to leave their land until the job of wiping out the new nation was accomplished, which, they said, would take but a short time.

When Israel's War of Independence ended and the partition was put in place over Arab objections, their leaders refused to accept or rehabilitate the Palestinians who had fled the land upon receiving that direction during the war. Arabs rejected not only the Jews but also Arab Palestinians. The Arab world used them as pawns, leaving it to the UN, the United States, and other Western nations to maintain the Palestinian encampments. The historian Paul Johnson explains:

A treaty...[to the Arabs] appeared to them a kind of surrender. That was why they did not want the refugees resettled because it meant the final disposal of a moral asset. As Cairo radio put it: 'The refugees are the cornerstone in the Arab struggle against Israel. The refugees are the armaments of the Arabs and Arab nationalism.' Hence they rejected the 1950 UN plan for resettlement without discussion. Over the subsequent quarter century they refused even to receive repeated Israeli proposals for compensation.[21]

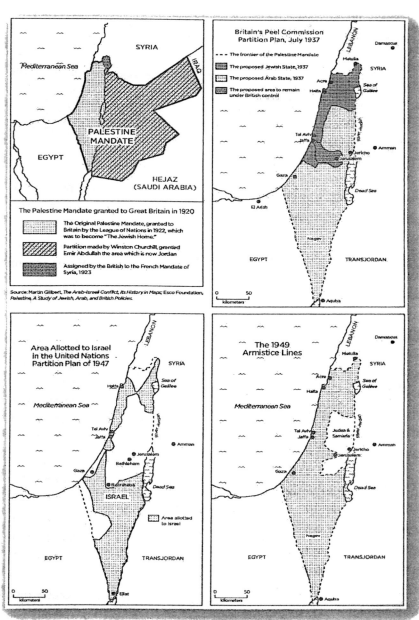

Partitions, Territories, and Borders

ejected them…You will achieve nothing with talk of compromise or peace…You speak of the Middle East. For us there is no such concept; for us there is only the concept of the Arab world. Nationalism is the great force that moves us. We do not need economic development. For us there is only one test, the test of strength. If I were a Zionist leader, perhaps I would behave as you do. You have no choice. In any case, the problem is likely to be solved only by force of arms.[20]

Accordingly, Arabs refused the UN proposal to once again partition Palestine and offer the Jews a small portion. Unable to prevail against partition, the surrounding Arab nations went to war, endeavoring to bring about the new nation's destruction. In bellicose language, they told the Arab Palestinians to leave their land until the job of wiping out the new nation was accomplished, which, they said, would take but a short time.

When Israel's War of Independence ended and the partition was put in place over Arab objections, their leaders refused to accept or rehabilitate the Palestinians who had fled the land upon receiving that direction during the war. Arabs rejected not only the Jews but also Arab Palestinians. The Arab world used them as pawns, leaving it to the UN, the United States, and other Western nations to maintain the Palestinian encampments. The historian Paul Johnson explains:

A treaty…[to the Arabs] appeared to them a kind of surrender. That was why they did not want the refugees resettled because it meant the final disposal of a moral asset. As Cairo radio put it: 'The refugees are the cornerstone in the Arab struggle against Israel. The refugees are the armaments of the Arabs and Arab nationalism.' Hence they rejected the 1950 UN plan for resettlement without discussion. Over the subsequent quarter century they refused even to receive repeated Israeli proposals for compensation.[21]

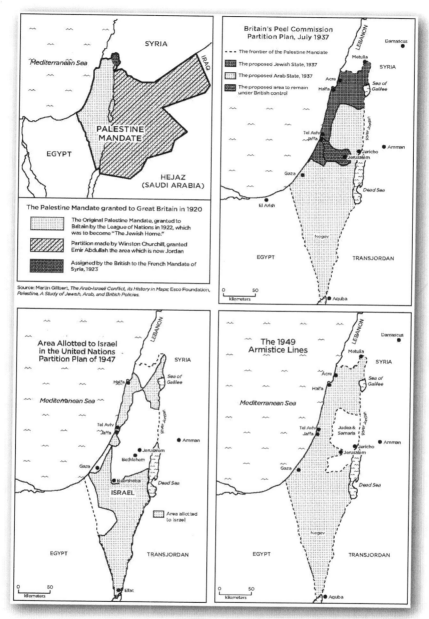

Partitions, Territories, and Borders

The Catastrophe

"The Day of Catastrophe" ("Nabka") is what Arabs called the birth of the Israeli nation. It was indeed a catastrophe for the half million Palestinians who fled. Most of them fled because of two reasons: first, their leaders had already left the scene when reports of fighting first circulated; secondly, many were told by the Arab military that the Jews would soon be slaughtered and that they would be able to return in a very short time.

The war was a catastrophe, but it was begun by the Arab Palestinians after the United Nations authorized a partition plan for Palestine on November 29, 1947. One part of the partitioned land was to be given to the Palestinian Arabs and the other to the Israelis. In an effort to prevent Israeli independence, attacks by both local Palestinians and a pan-Arab irregular army under the leadership of Hajj Amin Husseini began two days following the UN authorization. When the British Mandate expired on May 14, 1948, Israel declared itself a state. On the day following the declaration, armies from Egypt, Iraq, Lebanon, Transjordan, and Syria invaded the fledgling Israeli nation.

Here we must consider the Jewish population residing in Muslim-Arab countries. For them Israeli independence did indeed produce a catastrophe. As the rebirth became a reality, anti-Semitism became fierce. These Jewish communities, which had existed in Arab Middle Eastern and North African countries for many centuries, were devastated. As Israel was gaining her independence, much of the Jewish people in these Arab countries were forcibly thrust from their homes, and in most cases, their investments and property were confiscated. Some of the Arab leaders adopted the Russian and Nazi anti-Semitic policies of instituting pogroms; thousands of Jews were killed and their homes and businesses destroyed. Because these Arab governments did not want the new State of Israel to gain in population, they initially made it nearly impossible for Jews to leave their countries. Yet with persistence and help from the world community, the Jews were finally able to flee, albeit without their possessions. The harassment was especially severe and often fatal for those Jews who were identified as Zionists. It is estimated that between 550,000 and 700,000 Jews left Arab countries under duress between 1948 and 1967.[22]

Following the War of Independence, the Arab League formally instituted a complete economic boycott of Israel. The boycott was directed against all Israeli companies and Israeli-made goods and was broadened to include non-Israeli businesses from any other nation that maintained economic relations with the State of Israel or were thought to support it. The United States Congress passed a law prohibiting this boycott, and through the years it has had a lessening impact. However, as of this writing, some Arab nations—including oil-producing ones—continue to observe the boycott and urge the League to become stricter in its enforcement. Most of these Arab nations still want Israel to have no trade, no recognition, and no friends.

The leaders of the Muslim Arab nations surrounding Israel have never ceased calling for the elimination of the new nation. At the end of Israel's War of Independence, these nations refused to make peace. There were no peace treaties, only armistice agreements that the Arab leaders viewed as elaborate cease-fire agreements, thus making it clear that there remained an ongoing state of hostility. Egyptian president Gamal Abdel Nasser was a virulent instigator of renewed hostilities directed at Israel. Fedayeen raids (small groups of suicide squads) were used to penetrate Israel's borders and terrorize the population; the Suez Canal was closed to Israeli shipping, and the Egyptian arsenal was rebuilt.

Israel's search for peace partners among her neighbors was in vain. Those who had moved to the land with the hope of finding peace and security soon had their eyes opened to the modern form of the enmity that had existed from time immemorial. They soon realized that the truce following the War of Independence was only a Muslim Arab tactic to buy time in order to gain strength, attain superiority, and annihilate her.

MORE WARS AGAINST ISRAEL

Then came subsequent Arab aggression by way of wars against Israel. In 1967, as a prelude to the Six-Day War, Egypt blockaded the Straits of Tiran, blocked the Port of Eilat, which was Israel's gateway to the East, and moved about six divisions of the Egyptian army into the Sinai desert, poised to invade Israel. Egypt's president, Nasser, ordered the United Nations' peace-keeping forces completely out of the Sinai Peninsula. These were unprovoked acts of war. Egypt then entered into military pacts with Syria and Jordan and invaded Israel's air space, another act of war. Nasser made bellicose statements to his nation, predicting that Israel would be driven into the sea. Before the actual fighting broke out, he was using words as well as acts of war to provoke Israel and prove his prowess to the Arab world. "Our basic objective," he proclaimed, "will be the destruction of Israel. The Arab people want to fight." The Arab world was clamoring for war, especially in Syria, where Defense Minister Hafez Assad said, "Our forces are now entirely ready not only to repulse the aggression, but to initiate the act of liberation itself, and to explode the Zionist presence in the Arab homeland...I, as a military man, believe that the time has come to enter into a battle of annihilation."[23] Genocide was their stated aim. By this time it was clear that this was not an Arab-Israeli conflict over territorial rights but, simply and obviously, a renewal of the ancient hatred against the Jewish people.

While Nasser and Assad inflamed the Mideast by throwing down the gauntlet, Israel made every effort to avoid all-out warfare, in spite of the acts of war already perpetrated on her and the military alliances being made against her by the surrounding nations. The Israeli government tried to initiate negotiations through complaints to the United Nations. Israel contacted United States President Lyndon Johnson, reminding him of the US guarantee to Israel in 1957 to act if the Straits of Tiran were ever closed or if the Sinai desert was ever remilitarized. An official plea was sent by the Israeli government to King Hussein of Jordan, asking him to refrain from joining forces to invade Israel. He flatly refused. It is noteworthy that at this time, Jordan was, in fact, illegally occupying what is commonly referred to as the West Bank (officially designated by Israel as being Judea and Samaria, parts of the biblical Northern and Southern Kingdoms, respectively, of ancient Israel).

Israel then, out of self-defense, preemptively struck with their army and air force and, in six days, defeated the combined forces of Egypt, Syria, and Jordan, which received additional help from Kuwait, Algeria, Saudi Arabia, and Iraq. In pursuing their enemies, the Israeli Defense Forces (IDF) captured the Sinai desert, Golan Heights, Gaza Strip, and West Bank. However, Israel fully intended to make territorial concessions and return some of the land. On June 19, 1967, almost immediately following cessation of the war, the Israeli cabinet agreed to offer the Sinai to Egypt and the Golan Heights to Syria in exchange for peace. Other concessions by the victors would no doubt have come later. But in Khartoum that September, the Arab League made this telling declaration: "No peace with Israel, no recognition of Israel, no negotiations with it."[24] The Arab leadership was responding to the Arab "street," as an Egyptian broadcast indicated: "The Arab masses will never let any responsible Arab person remain alive who would dare negotiate with Israel."[25]

In 1973 the Arab nations again went to war against the Jews, this time to regain their pride and the territory lost in 1967. Egyptian President Anwar Sadat had been threatening war for two years, demanding that Israel return the territory gained in the previous war. He needed a war to divert attention from severe domestic problems, but no one expected him to follow through. However, on October 6, 1973—a date that coincided, that year, with Yom Kippur, Israel's holiest day of the year and during the Muslim holy month of Ramadan—Egypt made a surprise attack across the Suez Canal, which was followed by a Syrian advance into the Golan Heights, both armies crossing the cease-fire lines of the Six-Day War. At least nine additional Arab states came to the aid of Egypt and Syria in attacking Israel. The Israeli army suffered initial setbacks, but the advantage soon turned to the IDF. Once it did, there were numerous calls from the United Nations and separate nations for the fighting to end.

During what came to be called the Yom Kippur War, Arab oil-producing countries slapped an embargo on oil exports to the United States, which had shipped massive amounts of military hardware to Israel. This resulted in long lines at the gas pump and skyrocketing gas prices in America. In addition, the war sobered the Israeli people as they calculated the heavy losses incurred and wondered how many wars they would have to fight for their very existence.

Peace Treaty with Egypt

This most recent war was mental preparation for negotiation between Egyptian President Sadat and Israeli Prime Minister Menachem Begin, which resulted in the first ever peace treaty in modern times between their nations, signed on March 26, 1979. Israel made a great sacrifice by giving up its occupation of the Sinai, from which Egyptian military forays could be made into Israeli territory. The relinquishment meant that seven thousand Israeli residents of the Sinai were forced from their homes because Egypt would not allow Jews to reside in its territory. The Egyptians made certain that the Sinai would be 100 percent free of all Jews.

Peace Treaty with Jordan

In 1994 a peace treaty was signed with Jordan, a country heavily populated with Palestinians who loathe Israel. In the October 26, 2014, issue of the Jordanian newspaper *Al-Arab Al-Yam*, the front-page leading article was entitled, "Twenty Years of Odious Peace with Israel." Though Jordan's King Abdullah entered into an agreement for the purchase of Israeli natural gas, he continued to make outrageous charges against Israel, such as claiming that the Israelis kill Arab children *en masse*. The treaty with Israel had and would be benefitting Jordan in many ways, including ensuring mutually beneficial water sharing and a gas deal that could mean energy security for the foreseeable future.[26] But the Jordan street got no news from Israeli television—only from Al-Jazeera—and, as a result, continued to harbor deep-seated enmity against Jews while showing no appreciation for the benefits they received as a result of the treaty.

Military threats from every side continue to unnerve the Israeli people. Since the founding of the State of Israel in 1948, more than sixty thousand rockets have fallen on their land. (This figure was published in February, 2012). Note that this figure is not the number of rockets poised for Israel but only those that have actually been shot into the country. There are hundreds of thousands more on Israel's periphery ready for launching.[27] In addition, there is the increasing nuclear threat not only from Iran but also from other Arab nations that are preparing to join the nuclear-weapons-capable group of nations. Preparations for the eventuality of yet another war have resulted in a booming Israeli protection industry, with the construction of bomb shelters, security rooms in homes, multistoried underground hospital units, and alternative technology systems.

THE PALESTINIANS

In late 2013, as new peace talks were being commenced once again, the Palestinian Authority's president, Mahmoud Abbas, declared that he would not authorize any new agreement if it gave permission for even one Jew to reside in a new state of Palestine. He also declared that he would never crack down on Palestinian terrorism. In their speeches, writings, and long-range planning, Palestinian leaders have repeatedly made it clear that their goal is the complete destruction of the State of Israel. Fatah, the largest political arm of the Palestine Liberation Organization (PLO), has historically stated its objective as being the "liquidation" or "uprooting" of the Zionist entity. (Note: President Abbas has been Chairman of the PLO since 2004). Fatah's great passion is to gain *vengeance*—a term that has been often used in its literature.

Article 9 of the Palestinian National Covenant reads as follows: "Armed struggle is the only way to liberate Palestine. Thus it is the overall strategy, not merely a tactical phase. The Palestinian Arab people assert their absolute determination and firm resolution to continue their armed struggle and to work for an armed popular revolution for the liberation of their country and their return to it…. Article 22 "Zionism is a political movement organically associated with international imperialism and antagonistic to all action for liberation and to progressive movements in the world. It is racist and fanatic in its nature, aggressive, expansionist and colonialist in its aims, and fascist in its methods."[23] Muslim honor has been violated by Jewish control of land in the Middle East, and Western nations are to blame for collaborating with the Zionists.[28] Also, codified in Palestinian Authority law are measures to richly reward the families of martyrs. The statutes pledge to the families of these terrorists an income for life of three times the average salary in the West Bank. It must be remembered that the American government provides foreign aid to the Palestinian Authority, reportedly 4 billion dollars over the last ten years.[29]

Palestinian school systems have written their own curricula, which, at every grade level, are infused with hate-filled anti-Israeli propaganda. Their children quickly learn that the violent destruction of Israel is a vision of their own people. Caroline Glick says that "with the exception of Pakistani students in madrassas, few societies have undergone the mass indoctrination that the Palestinians have undergone over the past 20 years of Palestinian Authority rule. ….They are told that it is an Islamic duty to fight Jews and destroy Israel. This is as true in the regular PA schools as it is in schools run by the United Nations Relief Work Agency."[30] (published 11/7/2014)

A Curious Disparity

In mosques throughout the Middle East, including the West Bank and Gaza, there is a familiar litany spoken in loud chorus by Arab men with fists raised in the air: "Death to the Jews." It doesn't matter that in the twentieth century, twenty-two new Arab states had their legitimacy acknowledged by international law, along with the tiny State of Israel, or that Israel has initiated one peace effort after another since the founding of the State, or that in Israel the Arabs have more rights than they have anywhere else in the Middle East. It doesn't matter that the infant mortality rate for Arab babies is lower in Israel than in all other Middle Eastern countries. The Jews are despised and, therefore, not welcome there. The question remains: Why has there been no acceptance?

History is in the making as the Jewish people return to the land long ago promised to them—a land that has proven to be a thousand times more productive when the Jews reside and work the land there. But it is all resistance and precious little acceptance. No warmth and understanding. No pity for the Jews who escaped the pogroms, massacres, and genocide of Europe's anti-Semitic peoples. Instead, there is antagonism and rejection. There are peace movements in Israel but none in Arab-ruled nations and territories around her. There are human rights enforced by liberal courts in Israel for the Israeli Arabs. There are jobs, Arab universities, and quality health care in the land of Israel for its Arab citizens. But in the surrounding Arab countries (Syria, Egypt, Jordan, Iraq, Lebanon, Iran), there is neither room nor rights for Jews. Only in a few areas are small residual Jewish communities permitted, and these are under conditions of third-class citizenship—they're harassed and severely restricted.

What do the current plans of radical Islam include for itself and the Jewish nation? The answer for many Muslims reveals the following: a global caliphate, uniting the Islamic states into one, a theocracy governed by Sharia law and headed by a politico-religious leader—the Caliph. Along with that, the Islamist goal is to lay waste the infrastructure of American industry and culture, thereby rendering the US system of government incapable of assisting or influencing other nations. Then Israel, and its supporter, would be destroyed.

The growing weakness of the West is giving opportunity to Iran, Russia, and the Middle East nations to exploit, such as by building up sophisticated weapons arsenals, making terror tunnels in the West Bank and Gaza areas, establishing new army and naval bases in that area, and financially supporting Hamas and Hizbollah. The Iran Nuclear Agreement is the first treaty the United States has negotiated with a country whose aim is genocidal. Ayatollah Ali Khameni has declared that Israel's destruction is guaranteed.

The Zionist Jews are hated for establishing their own land, small sliver though it is. Their possession of a land that is considered to be Allah's brings the wrath of Muslims worldwide. Early Jewish immigrants did not anticipate such ancient enmities to still be prevalent with such intensity in the modern era. What those Jews seem not to have grasped is that Muslims consider the religious basis of Judaism—the Tenakh, with its emphasis on Israel's chosenness—a fabrication, a fabrication that remains a severe impediment to a Muslim-dominated world.

The scriptures are quite clear about this: those who are the chosen will be rejected and hated. We must soberly acknowledge this. The chosen are lambs in the midst of wolves. Standing out from the greater part, guided by law and imbued with an ethical mission, they are despised and extremely vulnerable. In all times, in varying circumstances and contexts and in many different forms, this rejection has been fiercely expressed and fearfully realized. The Jewish people are experiencing an amazing phenomenon: they are returning to their historic homeland. And as anti-Semitism increases in Europe and America, that return will continue. But as they continue to gather, they are becoming more vulnerable than ever before to annihilation in their tiny country.

1. Carlin Romano, a review of *Peace: The Arabian Caricature*, by Arieh Stav, Gefen Press, *The Weekly Standard*, October 22, 2001, 37–38.
2. Ruth R. Wisse, "Obama's Racial Blind Spot," *Wall Street Journal*, July 31, 2015, op-ed section.

3. Lamiat Sabin, "Israel not included in Harper Collins map used by children in Middle East," *The Independent*, "2 years ago," as of 2/9/2017, http://www.independent.co.uk/news/world/middle-east/Israel-not-included-in-harpercollins-map-used-by-children-in-middle-east-9951550.html.

4. "Racism in the Islamic World." *Flame*, San Francisco: Facts and Logic About the Middle East, a 501(c)(3) organization.

5. David Horowitz, *Why Israel is the Victim in the Middle East* (Los Angeles: Center for the of Study of Popular Culture, 2002), 15.

6. Kenneth Levin, *The Oslo Syndrome: Delusions of a People Under Siege* (Hanover, NH, 2005), 168.

7. Nonie Darwish, *Now They Call Me Infidel* (New York: Penguin Group, 2006), 9, 41.

8. Benny Morris, *Righteous Victims: A History of the Zionist-Arab Conflict, 1881–1999* (New York: Alfred A. Knopf, 1999), 11.

9. Leon Kass, *The Beginning of Wisdom: Reading Genesis* (New York: Free Press, 2003), 375.

10. Arthur W. Kac, *The Rebirth of the State of Israel* (Chicago: Moody Press, 1958), 340.

11. Benny Morris, *Righteous*, 39.

"The Sublime Porte's claim to the caliphate, or succession to Muhammad, included the role of protector of Islam's holy places. The sultan was often to declare that he 'could never part with Jerusalem.' Moreover, there was something unnatural, not to say downright blasphemous, in the notion of the Jews—a *dhimmi,* inferior race—harboring, and attempting to further, political ambitions, and what's more, Muslim land...The Jews were viewed as actual or potential agents of hostile penetration and expansion, at once backed by and enhancing the hated Capitulations, which gave the European powers extra-territorial rights in the empire and subverted Ottoman authority."

12. Walter Laqueur, *A History of Zionism* (New York: Schocken Books, 1972, 2003), 212.

(Quotes E. Sapir, *Hatred of Israel in Arab Literature* [Hashiloah, 1899], 222 et seq.

13. Benny Morris, *Righteous*, 11.
14. Ibid., 44.
15. Walter Laqueur, *A History*, 216–217.
16. Efraim Karsh, *Fabricating Israeli History* (London: Frank Cass, 1997, 2000), xvii.
17. Ibid., 45
18. Benny Morris, *Righteous*, 112–116
19. Joan Peters, *From Time Immemorial* (Chicago: JKAP Publications, 2002), 363.
20. Efraim Karsh, *Fabricating Israeli History,* (London, Portland: Frank Cass and Co., 2000), 74, 75.

    (Citing Caplan, *Futile Diplomacy*; citing Cohen, *Israel and the Arab World*; citing David Horowitz's account)
21. Paul A. Johnson, *A History of the Jews* (New York: Harper and Row, 1988), 530.
22. Ibid., 529.

    Paul Johnson gives Jewish population figures moving from these countries as follows: "252,642 from Morocco, 13,118 from Algeria, 46,255 from Tunisia, 34,265 from Libya, 37,876 from Egypt, 4,000 from Lebanon, 4,500 from Syria, 3,912 from Aden, 124,647 from Iraq and 46,447 from the Yemen."
23. Mitchell Bard, *An Idiot's Guide to Middle East Conflict* (Indianapolis: Macmillan USA, 1999), 225–226.
24. Howard M. Sachar, *A History of Israel: From the Rise of Zionism to Our Time* (New York: Alfred A. Knopf, 2003), 676.
25. Michael B. Oren, *Six Days of War* (New York: Ballantine Books, 2003), 318.
26. Ariel Ben Solomon, "Reigning Theories," *Jerusalem Post*, October 31, 2014, 14.

27. Giulio Meotti, "Israel Makes Preparation for War," Commentary/ Contentions, February 15, 2012, https://www.commentarymagazine. com/foreign-policy/middle-east/israel/israel-iran-war-preparations/.

28. Y. Harkabi, *The Palestinian Covenant and its Meaning* (London: Vallentine, Mitchell, Co,, Ltd, 1981), 61, 88.

29. David Aufhauser and Sander Gerber, *Daily Alert*, January 30, 2017, http://www.dailyalert.org/archive/2017-01/2017-01-30.html.   Mr. Aufhauser was Chairman of the National Security Council Policy Committee on Terrorist Financing and the general counsel of the Treasury Department after 9/11. Mr. Gerber is a fellow at the Jerusalem Center for Public Affairs. (Wall Street Journal)

30. Caroline Glick, "Terror Decentral," http://carolineglick.com/terror-decentral/, 11/7/14.

CHAPTER 7

The Peace Offers

In my distress I cry to the Lord,
That he may answer me.
"Deliver me, O Lord,
From lying lips,
From a deceitful tongue…"
Too long have I had my dwelling
Among those who hate peace.
I am for peace;
But when I speak,
They are for war.

—PSALMS 120:1-2, 6-7

The problem of what is to become of the Jews in the postwar world ought to engage all of us, not only because a suffering people has a claim upon our compassion but because the very quality of our civilization is involved in the solution. It is, in fact, a scandal that the Jews have had so little effective aid from the rest of us in a situation in which they are only the chief victims.

—REINHOLD NIEBUHR IN *LOVE AND JUSTICE: SELECTIONS FROM THE WRITINGS OF REINHOLD NIEBUHR*[1]

THE MODERN HISTORY OF ATTEMPTS to create a Palestinian state is filled with efforts to find peace. The most ingenuous minds in the field of international relations have focused on the Middle East conflict for a century or more, proposing peace plans dating back to the 1930s. The introductions to these proposals have typically spoken of the time as "a fateful hour." Each proposal has had, as one key part, an offer to the Palestinians of land for a Palestinian state in exchange for peaceful coexistence with the State of Israel.

JEWISH SUCCESS AND ARAB REACTIONS

Following World War I, the Palestine Mandate was awarded to Great Britain, and the Yishuv began development of the area in earnest. In the 1920s the building of Jewish industry in the country proceeded rapidly. By 1930 there were growing Jewish industries in textiles, clothing, metal goods, lumber, chemicals, stone, and cement. Exports were rising sharply, and while the rest of the industrialized world was facing depression, the Yishuv was experiencing rapid economic growth with a high rate of job creation. The Histadrut (the Jewish Labor Federation of Palestine) was founded in 1920 and proceeded to organize unions with members from both rural areas and urban centers.

The Palestinian Arab population became alarmed as they saw the expansion of Jewish population and business. They saw the land purchases (though land of cultivable soil was still only 5 percent to 20 percent Jewish owned). They watched as Jewish farmland became highly productive, with three times the amount of land in citrus production in 1936 as in 1931.[2] Palestine was no longer a depressed area; it was being transformed by high idealism and hard labor. Arab cries of resentment and fear were heard throughout the land.

From 1932 through 1935, Jewish immigration into Palestine reached a new level. The population in the Yishuv stood at 185,000 in 1931. In 1932, Jewish immigration figures were at 12,500, rising to 37,000, 45,000, and 66,000 in 1933, 1934, and 1935, respectively. Consequently, the Jewish population in

Palestine nearly doubled within three years to 375,000.[3] At the same time, there was an insidious spread of anti-Semitism in Central and Eastern Europe, which precipitated the immigration of fearful Jews into Palestine as well as the United States and Great Britain.

The nationalists among the Palestinian Arabs, though few relative to their population, now became more vocal, spreading fear and warning of a Zionist takeover. Further, Arab Muslims in the Middle East were leery of economic progress and the social change accompanying it, fearful that it would undermine Arabic and Islamic values. The grand mufti of Jerusalem, Hajj Amin Al Husseini, and his allies instigated rioting in a three-year effort to discredit the British Mandate for Palestine and bring immigration to a halt.

However, alongside the flood of Jewish immigration was a simultaneous flow of Arab immigration. Joan Peters, in her well-documented book *From Time Immemorial*, points out that Palestine was a receptacle of illegal Arab immigrants and that British officials looked the other way except for the most flagrant cases. To the British and other observers, these illegal entrants became part of the native population—this after the British Mandate from the League of Nations had designated Palestine as the future home of the Jewish people. True, the Mandate's protective clause was that the local population in the country was to be accepted and their rights honored. No one disputed this. But under the Mandate, Palestine was to be a land open to Jewish immigration, for it was the Jewish people whom the world acknowledged as needing a homeland, while the Arabs who surrounded Palestine were living in countries native to them according to culture, language, and history.

Peters states that there is "hard evidence" to indicate that thirty-five thousand Arabs, in 1930, were known to have been deported from the Hawran area of Syria to Palestine. The Palestine Royal Commission received startling testimony that there were immigrants entering Palestine not only from Syria and Trans-Jordan but also from Egypt, the Sudan, and Yemen.[4] Unemployment lists were being swollen by this Arab influx. Furthermore, figures on these reports were inflated in order to bolster the argument that there were insufficient jobs to accommodate more *Jewish* immigrants. A 1930 British White Paper dealing with these issues recommended that Jewish immigration be suspended. As Peters points out, "The Jews, who had been explicitly granted the position in the land 'as of right and not on sufferance' by international mandate, were now being relegated to a permanent minority status."[5] In deference to the Arabs, the British now began to set severe immigration restrictions on the Jews *just at the time when those at the mercy of the Nazis needed a receptive destination.* As history has shown, the British government was, at that time, in a mind-set for appeasement.

In the midst of this inclination to change course in Palestine, letting the Jewish people down in their time of anguish, it was none other than Winston Churchill who challenged the British Parliament with these words:

Can we strengthen ourselves by repudiation [of the mandate]? Never was the need for fidelity and firmness more urgent than now. By committing ourselves to this lamentable act of default we will cast our country, and all that it stands for, one more step downwards in its fortune.[6]

Tragically, Churchill was alone in his sentiments. The British were not interested in backing up what had become an unpopular agreement. They needed the full-fledged allegiance of the Arabs—or so they thought—for oil as well as their military support, should another war break out.

Meanwhile, the Arabs continued to be alarmed at the growth and productivity of the Yishuv. Arab terrorists began destroying Jewish property, ruining crops on Jewish farmland, and murdering Jewish residents. In May of 1936, an extended strike against the British government's immigration policy was called by the grand mufti of Jerusalem, Haj Amin Al Husseini, and this was enforced by his hoodlums. It lasted a full six months, immobilizing the government and transportation systems. Ironically, the effects were felt mostly by the Arab population, which resulted in Jewish workers supplanting the cheaper Arab labor. Despite this detriment to Arab employment, the revolt continued. "Committees for the Defense of Palestine" were organized in surrounding Arab countries, which sent in hundreds of volunteers each month. Three years of bloody riots instigated by the mufti and his allies resulted in hundreds of Jewish casualties and an estimated forty-five hundred Arabs killed, many by the mufti himself, who took revenge on Arab notables not of his party.

THE PEEL COMMISSION

In the midst of this violence in November of 1936, the British sent a Royal Commission of Inquiry to the region for the purpose of determining the causes of the rebellion. The six distinguished commissioners were headed by Lord William Robert Peel, grandson of the nineteenth-century prime minister. The Arabs, represented by the Arab Higher Committee, determined in advance that they would reject any conciliatory efforts and at first snubbed the Commission. Their answer to the problem: stop Jewish immigration entirely. The Peel Commission reported that "though the Arabs have benefited by the development of the country owing to Jewish immigration, this has had no conciliatory effect. On the contrary...with almost mathematical precision the betterment of the economic situation in Palestine meant the deterioration of the political situation."[7] The Commission acquiesced and cut the Jewish quota from forty-five hundred to eighteen hundred. They then made a recommendation: *a second partition of Palestine.* It should be noted that the first partition had sliced off what was known as Trans-Jordan, the land east of the Jordan River. This land had been previously awarded to the Arab prince Emir Abdullah as a concession. And so the territory that had been designated by the League of Nations to be part of the Jewish Homeland was now Palestinian Arab land. This *second* partition was clearly unfavorable to the Jews as well: *less than one-fifth of the remaining mandated territory would be for the Jewish homeland!*

(SEE MAP.) THE PEEL COMMISSION PARTITION PLAN

Churchill protested. He saw no evidence that Jewish immigration had created hardship for the Arabs. "Why is there harsh injustice done if people come in and make a livelihood for more and make the desert into palm groves and orange groves? Why is it injustice because there is more work and wealth for everyone. There is no injustice. The injustice is when those who live in the country leave it to be a desert for thousands of years."[8] Indeed, the Commission had found that Arab complaints about the Jewish acquisition of land were baseless. The report pointed out that a good portion of the land now blossoming with orange groves had been uncultivated sand dunes or swamp when it was purchased by the Jews. Further, it was reported that there was, at the time of the earlier sales, little evidence that the Arab owners possessed the resources or the training needed to develop the land.

The Zionist leaders were astonished at the proposal even before the ratio of land was announced. Chaim Weizmann, then president of the Zionist Organization, protested that it was like cutting the child in two. The Zionist Congress assembled a month after the report and agonized over the issue. To many of the delegates, such a partition was unthinkable, yet the majority favored at least exploring the plan. Having their own state, no matter the size, would give them a place where they could determine the rate of immigration and welcome the harassed and persecuted Jews of the world into their own homeland.

The Arab opposition to the report was complete and unqualified. They stoutly opposed any plan that would give even the smallest parcel to the Jews. They feared future expansion of the Jewish area, even though they had seen how little—how miniscule—the portion the recent proposal suggested be set aside for a Jewish presence. Simply put, the Arabs had no room for the people who were developing the land, who were offering to cooperate with them, and who had already brought a level of prosperity to the country unseen since Roman rule. Palestinian Arabs, with their numbers increasing, had seen their wages and standard of living rise more than the Arabs of any other Middle Eastern country. And yet to them, the land of Palestine was Muslim land—conquered Muslim land. And land, once in Muslim hands, could not be ceded to the control of non-Muslims. Any land not part of *dar al-Islam* (the abode of Islam) is *dar al-harb* (the abode of war).

In July 1937 the Arab Higher Committee took official action to categorically reject the Peel Commission plan of partition. By September the Arabs once again resumed their rebellion and, according to historian Benny Morris, "launched 438 attacks—109 of them against the British police and military, 143 against Jewish settlements, and 109 against 'Arab houses.'"[9] In the midst of this renewed uprising, German officials began to take an interest in Arab resistance, and the Nazi propaganda machine reached into Palestine, facilitated by businessmen, permanent residents, and diplomats. Some Arab businessmen and villagers were unenthusiastic about the rebellion, but the poison of anti-Semitism joined forces with Muslim jihad. In September 1937 a congress of the Committee for the Defense of Palestine at Bloudan, Syria, met with five hundred delegates from neighboring countries. The purpose of the meeting was to spread anti-Zionism. There was a call for the extermination of Palestinian Jewry by a former prime minister of Iraq, Naji as-Suweidi Pasha. To the believers of Muslim tradition, not only was there no room for a Jewish state; there was no room for self-sufficient Jews. And for the Arabs who were indoctrinated with fascism, there was no room for *any* Jews. Palestine should be *Judenfrei* (free of Jews).

THE UNITED NATIONS PARTITION PLAN OF 1947

There also wasn't room for the Jews in Europe. The attempt to exterminate a whole race of people had been carried out there while Britain and the United States focused on their war efforts. Paul Johnson points to the harsh reality that "the British and American governments were in theory sympathetic to the Jews but in practice were terrified that any aggressively pro-Jewish policy would provoke Hitler into a mass expulsion of Jews whom they would then be morally obliged to absorb."[10] The number of survivors on the European continent was small. Walter Laqueur, in *A History of Zionism*, sets forth the figures: "The extent of the Jewish catastrophe became fully known during 1944…Of more than three million Jews in Poland, fewer than a hundred thousand had survived; of 500,000 German Jews—12,000. Czechoslovakia once had a Jewish community of more than 300,000, of whom about 40,000 were still alive. Of 130,000 Dutch Jews some 20,000 still existed, of 90,000 Belgian Jews—25,000; of 75,000 Greek Jews—10,000…It is estimated…that the Jewish population of the Soviet Union was halved…Of the remnant of European Jewry many were refugees from their native lands…The smaller European countries were eager to get rid of the aliens, but where were they to go? Few of them were ready to start life afresh in Germany, or indeed anywhere on a continent which had become the slaughterhouse of their families and their people."[10]

Shutterstock/Dmitrijs Mihejevs
"Classical Historical View of Auschwitz Death Camp"

Immigration remained the hot issue in the 1940s as the situation in Europe continued to be crucial for the very survival of the Jewish population there. The British were allowing eighteen thousand immigrants per year into Palestine—more than was stipulated in their previous declaration. Following World War II, great numbers of displaced persons (DPs) traveled from Eastern Europe to the western zone of Germany to escape pogroms and harassment that had broken out in Poland and the Balkans.[11] But residing in Germany, where the recent genocide had occurred, caused great unease. While they may not have been Zionists before the war, now nearly all European Jews were convinced and avid Zionists, many of whom were determined to move to the homeland. Even the Jewish skeptic, Harold Laski, Chairman of the British Labor Party, said at the conclusion of World War II that "he felt like the prodigal son coming home. He did not believe in the Jewish religion and was still a Marxist; before the war he had been an advocate of assimilation and had thought that to lose their identity was the best service which the Jews could do for mankind. But now he was firmly and utterly convinced of the necessity of the rebirth of the Jewish nation in Palestine." The authors of *A History of Zionism* point out that "before the war Zionism had been a minority movement—sometimes a small minority—in the Jewish community. But in 1945 even its former enemies rallied to the blue and white flag…They were all Zionists now."[12]

The Anglo-American Committee, specially formed for the purpose of finding places for these Jewish victims, concluded that Palestine was the best place for them, as no other country was ready or willing to receive them. The Committee recommended that one hundred thousand visas should be issued as soon as they could be processed, and immigration should proceed swiftly. President Harry Truman then approved and, in addition, recommended the partition of Palestine and Jewish statehood. In this he was at odds with the position of Prime Minister Clement Atlee of Great Britain and his foreign secretary, Ernest Bevin. At the news of Truman's acceptance of the plan, Bevin went into a rage, declaring publicly that "the Americans favored the admission of 100,000 Jews into Palestine because 'they did not want too many of them in New York.'"[13] A strong protest was sent to Washington. The Committee's work thus came to naught, and within weeks, the British cabinet recommended the abandonment of the Palestine Mandate! Meanwhile, as British forces were attempting to contain the frustrations of the Jewish Yishuv, Jewish paramilitary forces were exerting extreme pressure on the Brits, demanding the admittance of European Jews. In February of 1947, because of the inability of British forces in Palestine to stop the violent actions of the Jewish underground in its efforts to admit desperate holocaust survivors, Britain turned to the United Nations for help.

Enter UNSCOP, the United Nations Special Committee on Palestine. The troubling issue of Palestine was handed over to yet another committee. The members of it were drawn from ten different nations, none of which was from the Great Powers. This group reiterated the Arab argument that the Peel Commission had made: the land was unable to absorb more immigrants. Menachem Begin, the future prime minister of Israel, countered that five to seven million people lived in Palestine in ancient times, and the land could support a similar population now. After long months of meetings in several countries, another partition proposal was presented. Many Jews opposed it because of the narrow strip of land it allotted for the Jewish homeland. However, they finally agreed, knowing this was the best they would get. The plan would have given the Palestinian Arabs an area including the western Galilee, the hill country of central Palestine (except for the Jerusalem enclave), and the coastal plain from a line south of Isdud (Ashdod) to the Egyptian border. The remaining territory would be the Jewish homeland, with the exception of the Jerusalem-Bethlehem area, which would be internationalized. Similar to the Peel Commission Report, this plan would give the land a checkerboard appearance with disconnected sectors. The two states, Palestinian and Jewish, would be linked by an economic union. A board of commissioners made up of three Jews, three Arabs, and three representatives of the United Nations would administer economic affairs. The Jewish nation would provide a regular subsidy for the new Arab nation. Jewish immigration would be strictly limited to 6,250 per month in the first two years, followed by a limit of 5,000 per month in succeeding years as long as such constraints were necessary.[14] *No limits to Arab immigration into Palestine were proposed* by the Special Committee.

Mitchell Bard says, "It is interesting to note that no Arab leader demanded the creation of a Palestinian state at any time during the UN debate" in the General Assembly. "The Palestinians had no sense of nationalism, no political attachment to the land."[15] (The Arab High Committee officially boycotted UNSCOP. The few Arabs who did come before the Committee wanted all the illegal Jewish immigrants to be expelled, while they wanted the influx of Arab immigrants to be retained—in other words, the Arabs entering for the economic opportunity which the Jewish presence had made possible. They argued for a unitary Arab state in which Jews would have no political rights. Their intention was that Jews would have to be subservient and required to accept the status of dhimmitude (a legal and social situation in Muslim nations characterized by repressive rules, excessive taxes, and humiliating practices).

The Zionists were disheartened by the proposal, to say the least. However, it did offer them a sovereign state and steady influx of immigrants. In a secret meeting, Jewish Agency officials sought to assure the Arabs that they had no expansionist intent and offered guarantees to that effect. But there was no Arab willingness to negotiate.

The British cabinet immediately decided to pull out of Palestine. The Arab nations quickly proceeded to impose economic reprisals and supply men and weapons to the Palestinian Arabs. They threatened war if the report received a favorable vote in the UN General Assembly. A three-day protest strike was called. Riots throughout the country ensued, resulting in the murders of seven Jews and the injuries of several more.

The United Nations General Assembly did adopt the plan on November 29, 1947. The Arabs stalked out of the hall and again threatened war if the resolution was implemented. It was not an idle threat. Mob violence and strikes began, and the first stage of the Israeli War of Independence, though undeclared, commenced. The chairman of the Arab Higher Committee announced that they would fight for every inch of the land. (Yet ever since, in all the attempts to secure a peace agreement, it has been the Palestinians who have tried to make the legal case of being innocent victims of Israeli aggression and dispossession and therefore entitled to recover their territory and housing.) In May of 1948, on the day following Israel's Declaration of Independence, the armies of five neighboring Arab nations joined the Palestinians in attacking the fledgling state.

The Arabs had been offered an independent Palestinian state in Judea, Samaria, part of Gaza, and part of Galilee. They didn't even consider it. They chose war instead and ended up with a pathetic Palestinian diaspora. They had wanted two things: first, to get all the land back into Muslim hands and, second, to nourish their ages-long enmity. Instead, the Israelis won the war, resulting in Israel obtaining more territory than the UN Partition Plan had ever allotted.

CAMP DAVID ACCORDS OF 1978

In May 1977 the Likud Party in Israel came to power for the first time, with Menachem Begin as prime minister. The nation was still shaken by the beating it took in the Yom Kippur War of 1973 (even though it had eventually prevailed). The economy was weak, and a minor financial scandal (secret bank accounts being kept in the United States, which was against Israeli law) of Labor Prime Minister Yitzhak Rabin and his wife, Leah, had forced Rabin's resignation.

The new prime minister was the first Israeli leader who was not from the political left. As a young man in Poland, Begin had come under the influence of Zeev Jabotinsky, head of the Revisionist Party wing of the Zionist movement. The Revisionists claimed that the entire British Mandate of Palestine, which included Gaza, the West Bank, and the land now consisting of the nation of Jordan (which was split off from Mandatory Palestine in 1922) should constitute the new nation.

Begin shared the Revisionists' vision of an "undivided Land of Israel" and was, therefore, an unlikely negotiating partner for a Middle East peace plan. In 1947–48, he had been a leader of the revolt that used terrorist methods against British forces in Palestine. He was considered demagogic even by many Israelis, ignored by former Prime Minister Ben-Gurion, and scorned in the press. But now, as prime minister, his mind turned toward negotiating a peace agreement with the Arabs, so long as it did not mean any withdrawal from the Judea and Samaria. He began to look for a bargain he could make with President Anwar Sadat of Egypt, and he let it be known that Israel was ready to trade land for peace. The territorial concession that Israel was considering was a part of the Sinai desert that had been successfully taken during the 1967 war. As for Sadat, he made the dramatic and politically unprecedented move of visiting Jerusalem, where he addressed the Knesset (the Israeli Parliament). He had good reason to take this risky step. First, it seemed that Sadat genuinely wanted peace. Second, repeated wars had devastated the Egyptian economy, and he knew he could count on American financial aid if he offered to negotiate. Third, he knew that Israel's military capability made any Arab military action impossible.

In the United States, President Jimmy Carter was anxious to act as peace-maker in the Middle East, believing that he could accomplish where others had failed. His plan was to sit down with all concerned parties in Geneva and negotiate a peace plan. This did not bode well for the Israelis. They feared that with all the Arab parties present, the result would be that no Arab leader would offer concessions that might lead to peace, for fear of looking soft. Discussions involving the three nations and UN representatives began with lower-level talks followed by meetings among Begin, Carter, and Sadat. The focus was two-pronged: Egyptian-Israeli issues and the Palestinian problem.

As the process unfolded, other Arab states in the region, led by Syria and Iraq and supported by the PLO, declared an economic and diplomatic boycott of Egypt. Benny Morris wrote, "As the months passed, Sadat seemed increasingly concerned only with a bilateral Egyptian-Israeli accord. Perhaps he had never cared that much about the Palestinians to begin with; without doubt, PLO opposition to his peace efforts had taken its toll; perhaps Begin's rigidity over the West Bank and Gaza had persuaded him that only a deal on Sinai was possible." As this process took place, "there was a succession of Palestinian terrorist attacks against Egyptian, Israeli and Western targets." Sadat's reaction was fierce. He called the PLO leaders "pygmies and hired killers" and declared that he was excluding the PLO from his lexicon. While he became disheartened with the talks, he desperately wanted the Sinai to be returned to Egypt, and Begin was increasingly inclined to give back all of it in order to keep the West Bank off the negotiating table.[16]

When Carter made the bold move of calling a tripartite summit to be held in the United States at Camp David, Begin and Sadat promptly accepted. The talks lasted for eighteen days and were filled with tension, rage, bluster, threats of termination, and exhaustion. In the end Egypt got back the entire Sinai, insisting that all Jewish settlements in it be disbanded and all Jewish people be banned from it. The area had to be completely free of Jews. The early-warning stations situated on mountains in the Sinai and all military installations had to be vacated. In return, Egypt promised to establish peaceful relations with Israel.

The "Framework for Peace," which evolved out of the talks, concerned Israeli relations with the Palestinians and provided a "mechanism for negotiating a resolution to the problems of the West Bank and Gaza Strip, which would include some measure of self-rule for the Palestinian inhabitants during a protracted interim period." There would be a "peaceful and orderly transfer of authority in the West Bank and Gaza with 'transitional arrangements' for a period of up to five years...The Arab inhabitants should receive 'full autonomy,' while Israel should withdraw its military government and civil administration, which would be replaced by an elected, Arab 'self-governing authority.'...No later than three years after the start of this transitional period negotiations were to begin (between representatives of Israel, Egypt, and Jordan and those elected in the West Bank and Gaza) 'to determine the final status of the West Bank and Gaza' and the relationship between these areas and their neighbors (that is, Egypt, Jordan, and Israel) and to conclude a peace treaty between Israel and Jordan...The negotiations would determine boundaries and security arrangements, and would 'recognize the legitimate rights of the Palestinian people and their just requirements. In this way the Palestinians will participate in the determination of their own future.'"[17] The problem of displaced Palestinians from the 1967 war would be addressed by a committee that would include Israeli representatives and would allow for some form and method of return.

The reaction in the West was enthusiastically positive. In Egypt there was a jubilant reception for Sadat that was only partially staged. The Egyptian people were tired of war and the poverty that accompanied it. There were pockets of dissent, notably from the Communist Party, the Muslim Brotherhood, and the Muslim clergy. However, the Palestinian people themselves were *unanimous in their outright rejection* of the framework. Their assessment of the plan was cynical in every respect, saying that the "autonomy" promised to them was only a cover for continued Israeli control. Camp David was proclaimed an anti-Palestinian conspiracy. A one-day strike was called. An Arab summit meeting was called for the purpose of expelling Egypt from the Arab League if Sadat went through with the framework. Egyptian entities conducting business with Israel were to be boycotted. A new financial fund was set up for continued resistance to Israel.

Yet another offer to the Palestinians that assured them self-governance— an offer made by Egypt, the United States, and Israel—was peremptorily and entirely rejected.

The Oslo Accords

In June 1992, Prime Minister Yitzhak Rabin led the Labor Party to a narrow victory in the Israeli national elections and formed a coalition government.

Immediately, a freeze on Jewish settlements in the West Bank was declared, and the willingness to negotiate a "land for peace" agreement was announced.

Early in his administration, Rabin had forbidden Foreign Minister Shimon Perez from establishing even indirect talks with the PLO, as contact with that organization was prohibited by Israeli law since formation of the PLO in 1964. The prohibition was the result of the PLO's stated intention not to "liberate" the West Bank and Gaza but to *"liberate" Palestine and destroy the Jewish state.* However, in December 1992, highly secretive meetings were, in fact, initiated by Norwegian researcher Terje Rod-Larsen between Israeli professor Yair Hirchfeld and PLO finance and trade minister Abu Alaa (Suleiman Ahmed Qurai). They met first in London and then in Oslo, Norway. By March 1993 Rabin and Perez were first informed of the secret meetings, and both were dubious, yet they permitted the talks to continue, knowing they could always void any adverse results as being unauthorized.

The negotiators agreed that the most to be hoped for at first would be a general agreement, followed later by specifics. That limited goal produced what was termed the "Declaration of Principles." The first key issues were the following: Israeli withdrawal from Gaza, gradual transfer of economic authority to the Palestinians, and international economic assistance to the proposed new governing authority in the Gaza Strip. Later, after more rounds of negotiations, agreements were reached on elections in the territories, Palestinian autonomy in the interim period before final settlement, gradual withdrawal of Israeli forces from the territories, and transfer of powers in the West Bank and Gaza. At this point the Israeli government was fully involved, while Arafat, chairman of the PLO, had been involved from the beginning. By mid-July, there was an indirect exchange of letters between Rabin and Arafat, which resulted in an agreement to discuss mutual recognition between the PLO and Israel.

The matter of mutual recognition was expressed in letters. Morris says, "In his, dated September 9, 1993, Arafat stated that the PLO 'recognize[s] the right of the State of Israel to exist in peace and security...accepts UN Security Council Resolutions 242 and 338,' commits itself to the peace process and 'to a peaceful resolution of the conflict...renounces the use of terrorism and other acts of violence,' would try to prevent all 'PLO elements' from resorting to violence (an implicit affirmation of an end to the Intifada, which the PLO refused to make explicit), affirms that the articles in the Palestinian Covenant that deny Israel's right to exist 'are now inoperative and no longer valid,' and 'undertakes to submit to the Palestinian National Council...the necessary changes in regard to the Palestinian Covenant.' In his brief response, dated September 10th, Rabin stated that 'the Government of Israel has decided to recognize the PLO as the representative of the Palestinian people' and to negotiate peace with it."[18]

It looked like the Jewish people and their cousins were going to work out their problems, accept their commonality, and respect the rights of each to live in the land. Perhaps a partition agreement was viable after all and the two nations of Israel and Palestine could coexist side by side.

Morris again reports, "The two sides agreed to negotiate the establishment of 'a Palestinian Interim Self-Government Authority' in the West Bank and Gaza Strip for 'a transitional period' not exceeding five years. This would then lead to a 'permanent settlement' based on [UN] Resolutions 242 and 338."[19] A council would be elected, which would constitute the Palestinian Authority (PA) in the territories during the transitional period. This was known as "Oslo I"—the Declaration of Principles and the letters of recognition. Seven months later, a more specific agreement, known as the "Cairo Agreement," was reached regarding the military withdrawal of Israeli forces. Security would be administered by Palestinian forces for the Gaza Strip and the Jericho area. During the month of May 1994, this transfer of authority took place. Arafat and thousands of his men from his home in Tunis flooded Gaza, receiving a tumultuous welcome.

However, it did not take long for the excitement to wane. The high expectations of the Palestinian people soon evaporated and were replaced by disillusionment. Immediate results were anticipated—results like quick economic rebound and more freedom to move about. Instead, because of continuing terrorist attacks, Israel used border closings for protection; funds that were promised to the PA were slow in arriving because of pledging countries' fears that obvious PLO corruption would divert the allocations from infrastructure development to support the PLO's financial empire. Such suspicions later proved true. The PLO became an engine of fraud, money laundering, payoffs, and drug dealing. Reports made public a few years later brought this to light: Arafat and his associates had purchased expensive villas in France and several late-model Mercedes Benz vehicles. Their appointments to office transformed them into beneficiaries of the high life. Some rushed to make deals with shady businessmen in order to enrich themselves quickly with monopolies on gas, food supplies, and other commodities. Most had no inclination to work for the good of the people. Some were simply thugs.

The most basic parts of the agreement did not materialize. Arafat and his forces only went through the motions, arresting suspects and then quickly releasing them. There was no restraining the militant Arab groups Hamas and Islamic Jihad. The Israelis quickly became aware that Arafat's forces were not going to enforce laws against perpetrators of acts of terror. As the Oslo talks continued, the shootings, stabbings, and suicide bombings actually increased in number and widened in geographical reach. Arafat had so far reneged on his pledge at Oslo to change the PLO Covenant, which currently called for the elimination of the Zionist state. Still, the talks continued. Rabin and Peres had committed the nation to a negotiated peace. They would not be deterred.

The talks progressed until September 28, 1995, when what was to be known as Oslo II was completed and signed. Termed the "Israeli-Palestinian Interim Agreement on the West Bank and Gaza Strip," it was meant to be an additional step in the reconciliation of the Palestinians and the Israelis, even though the first step had not been effectually implemented. Furthermore, Israeli troops were to be removed from Arab-populated areas in the West Bank. Eventually, Israeli forces would remain only in Jewish settlements and military installations. In the areas with the most Arab towns and villages, the PA would immediately wield full civil authority. Israel would release all Palestinian detainees and prisoners, except those responsible for fatality or serious injury. Israel and the PA would begin negotiating the permanent status of the territories—discussing issues such as Jerusalem, settlements, the Palestinian refugees, relations with neighboring countries, borders, and security arrangements. Elections for the PA were to be free and democratic, determined by a body of citizen voters made up of all Palestinians eighteen years and older.

The Oslo Accords were interim agreements intended to build confidence between the parties. The Palestinians would obtain more freedom, land, and responsibilities in other parts of the West Bank if all terms were implemented and adhered to as agreed. Israel was supposed to become more secure. The PA was to consider Hamas and Islamic Jihad as threats to its own existence and would work with Israeli forces to combat terrorism perpetrated by these organizations. The agreements, therefore, would assuage Israeli fears.

But Oslo I and II were fiction, never to be realized.

As Israel became more accessible because of the agreements, it also became more vulnerable. The Palestinians had what they wanted: havens for themselves and their stockpiles of weapons. The "police force," limited by agreement to thirty thousand, became, according to one estimate, sixty thousand—its arsenals swelling with artillery and rockets intended for war, though these were forbidden by the agreement. (Ironically, the small arms provided to this force were supplied by Israel under the assumption that Israel would be relieved of keeping order in the territory it was ceding. However, heavier additional weapons were later smuggled in from Arab countries.) The PA was run more like a syndicate than a democracy. It gained monopolistic control over sectors granted to individuals or institutions in return for officials being paid percentage kickbacks. The pyramid went all the way up to Arafat's office, and no transactions were carried on in a transparent manner.

Most noteworthy, the PA made no effort to change the culture of hatred against the Jewish people and the State of Israel. The belligerent speeches, the Arab school curriculum, and the whole ideological underpinning of Palestinian thought remained anti-Semitic and anti-Zionist. In fact, it became even more intense, becoming an incessant drumbeat on Palestinian radio and television. David Horowitz of the Center for Study of Popular Culture writes that during the peace process between 1993 and 1999, Palestinians committed four thousand terrorist incidents against Israelis, and more than one thousand Israelis were killed as a result of Palestinian attacks—more than had been killed in the previous twenty-five years.[20] Thievery of Israeli cattle, machinery, vehicles, and farm products became a Palestinian sport. The Palestinian "police force" was a law-enforcement group only insofar as it concerned the protection of Arabs. In reality it was an army and a violation of the agreement. Arafat determined that Gaza and the West Bank would be staging grounds for attacks against Israel and said so to Palestinian audiences. "O Haifa, O Jerusalem, you are returning."

Implementation of Oslo I and II had slowed down, and the accords were no longer effective. Israel's settlements on the West Bank, though not against the provisions, gave the Palestinians a pretext for more terrorist activity. Although new settlements were subsequently halted, Arafat was now in an intransigent mode. He released Hamas terrorists from Palestinian jails and suspended security cooperation with Israel. This halted Israeli support for any further interim steps.

Daniel Pipes, director of the Middle East Forum and a former instructor at Harvard University, when asked what went wrong with Oslo, answered:

> Many things, but most important was that the deal rested on a faulty Israeli premise that Palestinians had given up their hope of destroying the Jewish state. This led to the expectation that if Israel offered
> • sufficient financial and political incentives, the Palestinians would formally recognize the Jewish state and close down the conflict. [The

concessions by Israel] made matters worse by sending signals of apparent demoralization and weakness…Each concession further reduced Palestinian awe of Israeli might, made Israel seem more vulnerable and incited irredentist dreams of annihilating it…When intermittent Palestinian violence turned in September 2000 into all-out war, Israelis finally awoke from seven years of wishful thinking and acknowledged Oslo's disastrous handiwork.[21]

The Palestinian leaders did not want peace; they wanted the annihilation of Israel and the "cleansing" of Islamic holy places.

CAMP DAVID 2000

In May 1999, Ehud Barak, a retired general and the Labor Party candidate, became Israel's new prime minister. During the election campaign, he had promised a renewed and vigorous drive for peace. In a July meeting with President Bill Clinton, the prime minister's eagerness for a comprehensive peace agreement was evident. He wanted to accomplish this goal before the end of Clinton's presidency. Indeed, at this point he was ready to present details regarding his strategy, a timetable, and the assistance that would be needed from the United States. The thorniest issues, such as the status of Jerusalem and the future of the Palestinian refugees, were not outside his purview. Simultaneously, Clinton was anxious to establish for himself a legacy as a Middle East peacemaker. His delight at the election of Barak was no secret. The two of them were zealous partners for peace.

Yassir Arafat, the man who was still proving himself to be the leader of an anti-Semitic terrorist organization, was entreated to join Clinton and Barak in negotiations. The language used at that time in literature about Middle East peacemaking described the initial stages of Israeli and US negotiators as efforts to "induce the Palestinians to participate in the talks." Could Arafat be induced? Was he a leader who would relish the prospect of negotiating peace and establishing autonomy for the PLO, thus giving the people under him new opportunities? It turned out that he was not. Aaron David Miller's *The Much Too Promised Land* recounts the events of peace talks as Miller worked under six US secretaries of state. Miller describes Arafat's approach to the Camp David 2000 talks as follows: "He came neither to make sweeping concessions nor to negotiate in any meaningful sense of the word." He was there "with no real strategy, little flexibility, and a suitcase full of complexes, including fear of an Israeli-American trap and a desire to get even with Barak for chasing Syria." (Barak had been eager to negotiate with the Syrians on the Golan Heights border, in spite of President Assad's intransigence.) Miller calls Arafat's attitude "aggressively passive," his strategy "hyper-passive."[22] It should be noted that by this time, as the result of Oslo and succeeding talks, 98 percent of the Palestinians in the West Bank and Gaza were already under the rule of the PA.[23] Arafat had his kingdom, his army, and absolute authority.

Barak was angered at "Arafat's lack of responsiveness and was also beginning to realize that the price for a deal was much higher than he was willing or able to pay."[24] Nevertheless, Barak conceded so much that it went beyond anyone's anticipation of how much Israel was willing to relinquish to achieve a permanent agreement. Saul Singer, in the *Middle East Quarterly*, puts Barak's position in perspective: "Barak apparently thought that the Palestinians, if presented with a sufficiently attractive proposal and an appropriately unattractive alternative, would have no choice but to say 'yes.' In effect, each successive Palestinian 'no' led to the next best Israeli assessment of what the Palestinians couldn't turn down…Barak's approach, from a Palestinian perspective, was ideal. Barak did not present the Palestinians with one final, all-or-nothing offer. He was clearly working to find an offer that was too generous to refuse."[25]

So what exactly was offered? At a decisive point near the end of the July 11–25 summit at Camp David, the Palestinians were offered a state with Arab Jerusalem as its capital and with control over the Temple Mount, the most sacred site in Judaism. They would be given 94–96 percent of the West Bank plus 1–3 percent of Israel's possession. (This included the Jordan Valley, which the Israelis considered necessary to own in order to intercept attacks from the East.) Israel would dismantle sixty-three of their settlements because, of course, the Palestinians would require that their nation be free of Jews. Some but not all of the Palestinian refugees who had left Israel would be permitted to return. (Were that offer accepted, Israel's very survival would be at risk.) Refugees would be given $30 billion in reparations. The only concession by the Palestinians would be to give the Israelis sovereignty over certain parts of the Western Wall, especially those parts sacred to Judaism, plus three early-warning stations in the Jordan Valley from which Israel would withdraw after six years. No compensation was offered for the approximately seven hundred thousand Jews that were driven out of Arab countries *without their personal property* following Israel's independence.

This was unequivocally the greatest offer the Palestinians had ever had for a nation of their own. Neither the Ottomans (a Muslim empire) nor the Jordanians (a Muslim nation) had opened up any such an opportunity for their own Palestinian brothers and sisters.

To the Barak government and many Israelis, the actuality of final peace negotiations was a great accomplishment. For the Palestinians, being involved in such discussions on crucial points meant that they were recognizing Israel's legitimate existence. Historically, the Israelis had opposed a Palestinian state. But under former Prime Minister Yitzhak Rabin, the PLO had been recognized, and the Israelis had undergone a change of mind. Most were now ready for a Palestinian state. They viewed its coming as not only inevitable but also desirable as a stepping-stone toward peace and cooperation.

But to the Palestinians, the process was an opportunity to show the world their importance and their victimhood status. Many of the Muslim participants could not abandon the doctrine of jihad. As for Arafat, he knew that he could not get away with offering security to Israel based on his familiarity with Islamic decrees that the Jews should forever be disgraced and debased. The Palestinian Charter had called for annihilation of the Zionist entity, specifying that "armed struggle is the only way to liberate Palestine." Oslo called for the deletion of the offending articles in the covenant, but though the PLO council voted to do so, there were leading Palestinians who later insisted that the articles should remain as originally composed. Today those articles still stand.

Though Arafat initially signaled acceptance, he later added modifications that negated what he had previously agreed to. He would not allow Israeli control over Jewish holy sites, the security arrangements were unacceptable, and the Israelis would not be allowed to fly through Palestinian air space. According to US Special Envoy Dennis Ross, the reason for Arafat's rejection of the peace plan was that to accept it meant he would have to give up fighting. And to end the conflict would be to end his *raison d'etre*. Furthermore, violence had been working for him in that it portrayed the Palestinians as victims in the eyes of the world. Why change that image and let the world avert its gaze from "Palestine"? Thus, Ehud Barak's offer of greater than 90 percent of the West Bank—Samaria and the Galilee—was rejected in favor of returning to open warfare. Mr. Singer in the *Middle East Quarterly* reports that "Malley, Agha, Abu Mazin [Mahmoud Abbas] Ben Ami, and Ross [the negotiators] all confirm that the Palestinians never really engaged in negotiations at Camp David and, despite massive pressure from President Clinton, never presented a counteroffer to Israel's proposals. But Ben Ami and Ross argue that the Palestinians actually went beyond intransigence, by introducing new obstacles to an agreement."[25]

THE FAILURE OF THE OSLO ACCORDS AND CAMP DAVID
Arafat's approach to negotiations was akin to that of the prophet Mohammed. Mohammed made a treaty with the enemy tribe, Quraysh, over the objections of some of his henchmen. The agreement was beneficial for Mohammed's army because it anesthetized his enemy, prompting them to let up on battle readiness. The treaty didn't put an end to the state of war; it only postponed it. It enabled Mohammed's army to continue the build-up of their military power. When Mohammed was fully prepared, his army returned to battle,

breaking the treaty. That treaty is termed *hudnah*, meaning "ceasefire," and is still, for the most part, the only kind of agreement entered into by Muslim countries today with non-Muslims.

Dr. Kenneth Levin, graduate of Oxford and Princeton Universities, says in his book *The Oslo Syndrome*,

> For any Oslo enthusiasts paying attention, there was within hours even more reason to feel crushed. Shortly after the signing of the Declaration of Principles and the famous handshake between Arafat and Yitzhak Rabin on the White House lawn, Arafat was declaring to his Palestinian constituency over Jordanian television that Oslo was to be understood in terms of the Palestine National Council's 1974 decision. This was a reference to the so-called Plan of Phases, according to which the Palestine Liberation Organization would acquire whatever territory it could by negotiations, then use that land as a base for pursuing its ultimate goal of Israel's annihilation. But not many people were paying attention.[26]

Yasser Arafat was not out of touch with his people in rejecting any feasible plan for coexistence. The Palestinians never rejected Arafat's leadership during his tenure, despite his corruption. They never rejected the PLO despite its terrorism. They didn't reject Saddam Hussein either when he lobbed missiles into Israel during the First Gulf War, even though Israel was populated by Arab Israelis as well as Jews; they danced gleefully in the streets. When they were offered democracy in the form of an election in January 2006, they chose Hamas, the terrorist organization whose charter denies Israel's right to exist. What they reject and what they elect should clearly tell the world what they want. More than anything else, they want the destruction of the State of Israel. Any offers they might accept are agreed to only with an eye toward gaining a foothold that will aid them in attaining their ultimate goal of wiping the State of Israel off the map.

The Palestinians profess to be interested in their own nation. They are one of the last peoples on earth, along with the Kurds, who wish to have a nation but who, as yet, live under the rule of other regimes. Yet in spite of the offers—the ones enumerated here in this book, as well as others—in the crucial hour of decision making, their leaders have responded with rejection. By contrast, the Zionists, even in response to the Peel Commission's decision of 1936, were willing to take the sliver of land offered, believing that history would be kinder to them if they had a haven for their persecuted people. But even that was undermined by the violent protests of the Palestinians.

Thus, since Oslo and Camp David, many observers and most Israelis are skeptical about further efforts in the peace process. Other less ambitious plans have been given some attention. Leaders of the United States and Israel feel the obligation to continue the peace process. But many have concluded that hopes for a viable agreement are an illusion. Israeli troops have had to return to much of the West Bank to gain on-the-ground intelligence to deter terrorism. Giving back full control of this area to the Palestinians would threaten Israel's very existence by means of the PLO, Hamas, or whatever Palestinian group would gain power.

Following the realities of Camp David, left-leaning Israelis were mortified. They had pinned their hopes on Yasser Arafat, believing he was really interested in peace and that if Israel was willing to give up the West Bank, he would be a good partner in that peace. Their assessment of the Palestinian Arabs was that they yearned for a homeland and that an offer such as the one Ehud Barak made could not be refused. "We want peace; they want peace." So the saying went among those who voted for the Labor Party. But following Camp David, most of them made an about-face, seeing and acknowledging that the Palestinians simply hated them and wanted them out—not just out of the West Bank and Gaza but out of Palestine and the Middle East.[27]

As stated, there have been other peace efforts along the way. For example, there was the Bush Administration's "road map," a performance-based agreement containing three parts. The Palestinians failed the first one, which was to dismantle terrorist groups and their infrastructure. In 2008 Israel offered nearly *100 percent* of the West Bank and Gaza after land swaps, *and a shared Jerusalem*! The offer was rejected, and one month later Israel was forced into another defensive war in order to stop Gaza's shelling of Israeli residential territory. All the negotiations for peace have assumed that what the Palestinians want is a state of their own. But indeed they have their own state now in Gaza, and they have turned it into an armed camp.

If the Palestinians are ceded the West Bank or any part of it, no Jew will be permitted to live there. None. Official spokespersons of the PLO have repeatedly stated this to their constituents. Abbas shamefacedly speaks out of both sides of his mouth, telling Westerners of his interest in peace while, in Arabic, boldly spewing forth hatred against the Zionist entity. Throughout the Middle East, the terrorist organizations such as Hamas, Hezbollah, Islamic Jihad, and others reject the creation of a two-state solution. They vow to continue their vicious attacks until Israel is wiped out and the Palestinians are in total control of the whole of what they term "Palestine." In 2015–2016 the terrorism inside Israel and Judea and Samaria (the West Bank) turned from suicide bombing to stabbings. The Palestinians have expressed their admiration for these "martyrs" and "freedom fighters" and, when Israeli police move in, deny that anyone has committed a crime. The Palestinian press joins in the cheering, as helpful hints are given in ISIS videos about how to skillfully do this work.[28]

Meanwhile, most Arab states in the Middle East refuse to establish open trade relations with "the Zionist entity." They reject the visa applications of Israelis and ban them from international and regional competitive sporting events as well as academic and professional conferences. Arab governments refuse to permanently end state-sponsored propaganda campaigns that demonize Israel and foment hatred toward Jews among the Arab populations.

It is not only the leftists, Labor Party, and drivers of the Peace Movement in Israel that want peace and are willing to make great sacrifices for it. The vast majority of Israelis yearn for peace and would yield to most of the territorial demands of the Palestinians. Israel doesn't need to be prodded to go to the negotiating table; from 1936 to the present, they have shown that they are willing to sit down with those who threaten to destroy them. To attain security, they are ready to make concessions that few nations would be willing to make: offering the land (much of which was never Palestinian owned) they gained in repeated wars—wars initiated by their enemies.

Listen! The valiant cry in the streets;
The envoys of peace weep bitterly.
The highways are deserted,
Travelers have quit the road.
The treaty is broken,
Its oaths are despised,
Its obligation is disregarded. (Isaiah 33:7–8)

1. Reinhold Niebuhr, *Love and Justice: Selections from the Writings of Reinhold Niebuhr* (Louisville: Westminster/John Knox, 1992), 132–133.
2. Howard M. Sachar, *A History of Israel from Zionism to Our Time* (New York: Knopf, 1996), 189.
3. Ibid., 196–197.
   Sachar states, "It was a fateful irony...that transformed Nazi Germany, self-appointed patron of the Arab world and inspiration for Arab right-wing nationalism, into an involuntary benefactor of Zionist growth and expansion in Palestine...As the tempo of persecution mounted in Germany itself, Jewish emigration to Palestine and other lands grew correspondingly." In all the countries of the Middle

East, the Nazis were widely publicizing their anti-Jewish policies and spreading their anti-Semitic propaganda.

4. Joan Peters, "Official Disregard of Arab Immigration," in *From Time Immemorial* (Chicago: JAKP Publications, 2002), 296–325.

5. Ibid., 300.

6. Walter Laqueur, *A History of Zionism* (New York: Schocken Books, 1972), 511.

7. Efraim Karsh, *Palestine Betrayed* (New Haven: Yale University Press, 2010), 8.

8. Michael Makovsky, *Churchill's Promised Land* (New Haven: Yale University Press, 2007), 15–156.

9. Benny Morris, *Righteous Victims: A History of the Zionist-Arab Conflict, 1881–1999* (New York: Alfred A. Knopf, 1999), 144–145.

10. Walter Laqueur, *A History of Zionism*, 559–560.

11. Ibid., 561-562

12. Benny Morris, *Righteous*, 177.

    By this time, in March 1946, the committee found that "The Jews in Poland lived in an 'atmosphere of terror...' (Indeed, Poles had murdered over a thousand Jews since the end of the war.)"

13. Howard M. Sachar, *A History of Israel*, 263–264.

14. Ibid., 284

15. Mitchell Bard, *The Complete Idiot's Guide to Middle East Conflict* (Indianapolis: Macmillan USA, Inc., 1999), 151.

16. Benny Morris, *Righteous*, 459–460

17. Ibid., 473.

18. Ibid., 621–622

19. Ibid., 623.

20. David Horowitz, *Why Israel Is the Victim* (Los Angeles: Center for Study of Popular Culture, 2002), 16.

21. Daniel Pipes, "Why Oslo's Hopes Turned to Dust," *New York Post*, September 9, 2003, www.danielpipes.org/article/1242.

22. Aaron David Miller, *The Much Too Promised Land*, (New York: Bantam Books, 2008), 297–301.

23. Neal Kozodoy, *The Mideast Peace Process: An Autopsy* (San Francisco: Encounter Books, 2002), 99.
24. Saul Singer, "Camp David, Real and Invented," *The Middle East Quarterly*, Spring 2002., http://www.meforum.org/169/camp-david-real-and-invented.
25. Ibid.
26. Kenneth Levin, *The Oslo Syndrome: Delusions of a People Under Siege* (Hanover: Smith and Krause, 2005), ix.
27. Daniel Gordis, *Home to Stay*, New York: Three Rivers Press, 2003), 144.
28. Matti Friedman, "A Walk in Jerusalem," *Jewish Review of Books*, Winter 2016, 9–10.

CHAPTER 8

Land Forfeiture

§

O God, the nations have come into your inheritance;
They have defiled your holy temple;
They have laid Jerusalem in ruins...
We have become a taunt to our neighbors,
Mocked and derided by those around us...
They have devoured Jacob
And laid waste his habitation.

—PSALMS 79:1, 4, 7

UNDER THE BRITISH MANDATE, WE have seen that Palestine was to be open to Jewish immigration and settlement. Yet in between the allied nations' endorsement of the Mandate in 1920 and the ratification of it by the League of Nations in 1922, the British began to reverse its position. To propitiate the Arabs, *75 percent of the original territory was carved out of the whole* and awarded to Abdullah bin Hussein, who became leader of the nation named Transjordan. It formally remained part of Mandate Palestine until the end of the Mandate in 1947, but under Abdullah it was closed to the Jews. Accordingly, under Arab rule, it would be *"Judenrein"*—free of the detested Jewish people. No Jew could purchase property or live there, and the effects of that ban were what we now term "apartheid." But on the other hand, concerning the remaining 25 percent of the mandated land where the Jews had settled, during the 1920s and 1930s, the British administration was indulgent with the Arabs, permitting Arabs from Transjordan and other surrounding Arab countries to move in, both legally and illegally, where the Jews were developing the land.[1]

These Arab immigrants, later called "Palestinians," were counted from the time of their arrival as "original settlers" of the Jewish-settled area. In time they would claim to be descendants of ancient farmers and argue that the Jewish refugees were replacing them. Joan Peters, award-winning author and White House consultant, summarizes the situation: "All the myths surrounding the Arab 'Palestinians' are based on the same premises: 1) the 'Palestinian people' have had an identity with the land; 2) that identity has been present for 'thousands of years'; 3) the alien Jews 'returned after 2000 years' in 1948 to 'displace' the 'Palestinian Arabs' in the 'new' Jewish state; 4) the Arabs were there first—it was Arab land; 5) the Jews 'stole' the Arabs' land; 6) the Jewish terrorists forced the peaceable Arabs to flee from 'Palestine.'"[2]

In reality, says Peters, "the land of Palestine proper had been laid waste, causing peasants to flee…Jews and 'Zionism' never left the Holy Land, even after the Roman conquest in AD 70…Imbued with religious prejudice, the Muslims of Palestine erupted into anti-Jewish violence often, and at the call of the Muslim leaders long before Israel…The bulk of all 'Arab' peasantry in the area—East-Palestinian, Syrian, Iraqi, Egyptian, and others—were rendered 'landless' by feudal-like societal structures, natural disasters, extortionate taxation, and corrupt loan sharks. Yet the Jews were cynically charged with creating 'landless' Arabs in 'Palestine.'"[3]

Thus, almost immediately following the opening of Palestine to the Jews, the area's dismantling began through political gerrymandering and modifications. As historian Howard W. Sachar states in his mammoth tome on the modern history of Israel, "It was plain, then, from beginning to end, that the League [of Nations] award was framed to protect the Zionist redemptive effort."[4] That was true even though, both early and later on, there were onerous restrictions placed on Jewish immigration and, finally, the grotesque partition. When the time of crisis in the late 1930s came and Jews were rushing to gain access to what was left of the mandate to escape the holocaust, *most were shut out.* It was said by the Arabs and seconded by the British that there was no room! *Yet all the while, large numbers of Arabs were moving in, legally and illegally.* So for the Jews, the land that carried the hope of escape from destruction could not be freely accessed until the Jewish nation was reborn in 1948.

The occupying British were soon frustrated. Their motives for opening up Palestine to the Jewish people were mixed: compassion for the Jews, on the one hand, and foreign policy favoring the huge Arab Middle East on the other. For the British leaders in the '30s and '40s, Palestine had become a burdensome weight, a millstone hanging from their necks. The leaders who had honored the biblical promise of God to recover the Promised Land for the Chosen People were gone. In their place were men who had no regard for the biblical claims they judged to be obscure. The British administration, enamored with Arab culture and greedy for Middle East oil, came to politically favor the Arabs over the Jews. Simultaneously, the British Empire's power was on the decline. It was no accident that it was declining at the same time it was slamming the door on the afflicted Jewish Diaspora who were desperate to escape Europe's growing anti-Semitism. This action against the Chosen People would contribute to the Empire's weakening. Quoting from Benjamin Disraeli, Churchill warned the House of Commons: "The Lord deals with the nations as the nations deal with the Jews."[5]

The decline of British power and influence was now destined to continue and accelerate as it played fast and loose with the welfare of God's chosen.

THE AMERICAN INITIATIVE

America's support for the restoration of the State of Israel was more consistent and widespread than that of Great Britain. George Washington and Abraham Lincoln both affirmed the Jewish people in America and welcomed those who immigrated to the United States, especially those who were escaping persecution. In taking this stance, their eyes were on biblical Israel. President Washington wrote to the Jewish congregations in Newport, Rhode Island, addressing them as "children of the stock of Abraham" and expressing his delight in affirming their citizenship under the protection of the United States.

The time would come when America's affirmation of the Jewish people would be needed. In nineteenth-century Russia, the Jewish population was rapidly increasing. For generations the Czarist governments had restricted Jewish employment, education, real-estate purchases, and movements while also permitting Jewish persecution at the hands of local anti-Semites and the Orthodox Church. It was in the latter part of that century that the Jews became panic-stricken by the pogroms and harsh laws. A worldwide outcry ensued.

As the American people became aware of the condition of Jews in Russia, they rose up in protest. Churches united to support a plan of rescue. Into the leadership gap strode William E. Blackstone, a successful businessman who became a prominent evangelist and author of the book *Jesus Is Coming*. He reported the plight of these harassed Jews and published his vision of a renewed Palestinian homeland.

In 1890 Blackstone chaired a conference on Israel's place in history. America's leaders, both religious and political, were present and sent resolutions to the Russian Czar on behalf of the Jewish plight. Then, following a meeting with President Benjamin Harrison, Blackstone promoted his famous document "What Shall Be Done for the Russian Jews?" which came to be known as "The Blackstone Memorial." In it he wrote, "A million of exiles, by their terrible suffering, are piteously appealing to our sympathy, justice and humanity. Let us now restore to them the land of which they were so cruelly despoiled by our Roman ancestors." He stressed that the Jews had never abandoned their land. "They made no treaty; they did not even surrender. They simply succumbed, after the most desperate conflict, to the overwhelming power of the Romans."[6]

Blackstone personally obtained the signatures of highly regarded notables such as J. P. Morgan, John D. Rockefeller, William McKinley (congressman and later US president), additional members of Congress, mayors, governors, publishers, business leaders, Robert R. Hitt (chairman of the House Committee on Foreign Affairs), and prominent Jewish and Christian religious leaders.

America now awakened to the need for world Jewry to recover its land. Faith-based Americans were now asking for something that, at the time, looked impossible: restoration of the land. Because the Ottoman Empire ruled Palestine, there was little hope of the doors being opened to Jewish immigration. Because the suffering was so severe, the American government had already been acting, opening its doors and admitting Russian Jews, and it would admit over two million of them by 1920.

In 1883, just a few years previous to this movement, American Jewish woman Emma Lazarus penned the words inscribed on the Statue of Liberty: "Give me your tired, your poor, your huddled masses yearning to breathe free...Send these, the homeless, the tempest tossed to me." In 1904 President Teddy Roosevelt pressured the Russian Czar Nicolas II to take measures to end the harassment of the Jews. Following World War I, when Britain became the overseer of Palestine, President Woodrow Wilson signed a convention with Great Britain that included the complete text of the "Mandate for Palestine," making immigration to Palestine possible. Later, the United States was the first nation to recognize the new state of Israel in 1948, at the insistence of President Harry Truman.

With some exceptions, America has stood with Israel when that nation's existence was threatened by war and whenever her case has been presented at the United Nations. It is noteworthy that Israel has never requested that the

United States fight her wars. But from the very beginning of Israeli statehood, America has provided economic grants, military assistance, guaranteed loans, and aid for rebuilding military bases when Israel relinquished territories under the policy of "land for peace." Polls show that the American public has supported this assistance and thus shown its appreciation for the only true democracy in the Middle East.

However, America's support for the new nation wavered when her commitments clashed with Israel's needs in the 1960s and early 1970s.

Following the defensive Six-Day War of 1967, when Israel's victory placed within its hands an expanded stretch of the land, Colonel Abdul Nasser of Egypt saw that he would have to change his strategy. Instead of declaring war against Israel, he began to support a campaign of ongoing terrorism.

Three years before the Six-Day War, at the Arab Summit in Cairo, Nasser had initiated the formation of the Palestine Liberation Organization, later led by Egyptian-born Yassir Arafat. Arafat inaugurated his rise to power with acts of terrorism against Jews in Israel and other countries. His aims were to disrupt Israeli society and gain notoriety in the Arab world. In order to reduce the risk of bombings in their own countries, leaders of the Western world began to appease Arafat by allowing him his terrorist acts so long as he didn't target their own citizens.[7] Eventually, some Westerners, especially members of the press, came to accept him (albeit wrongly) as a legitimate freedom fighter. In fact, at a meeting of his legislative body in 1988, he intimated that he would renounce terrorism; this was a tacit admission of the strategy he had, in fact, been using. (However, in the same year, Hamas was formed, with its charter stating that no negotiations with Israel would ever be held for any reason, in view of the fact that the organization's stated goal was the annihilation of the Jewish people.) Acceptance of Arafat and the PLO became so solid among American and most Western leaders that they announced their readiness to talk with the Palestinians. Later, the United States began to exert pressure on Israel to return much of the land for which she now had responsibility as a result of her victory in the Six-Day War of 1967. In the 1970s the term *peace process* was coined for Middle East talks. It must be remembered that *because the Arab nations refused to recognize Israel or negotiate with her, the lines of the cease-fire became the boundaries delineating the territories for which Israel would be responsible to govern, pending future talks.*

AMERICA CHASTENED

Beginning in 1991 consecutive US Administrations began in earnest to urge Israel to give up some of the land acquired in 1967, in the interest of peace. The assumption was that if Israel would surrender land, the Palestinians would form their own nation and finally recognize Israel. But this approach assumed far too much.

We begin here with the Madrid Peace Conference of 1991, which was seen to be a major breakthrough. Included in the talks were the nations that had fought to drive Israel into the sea. Then US President George H. W. Bush determined that the State of Israel would have to relinquish territory. In his address to the nations gathered, he said, "Throughout the Middle East, we seek a stable and enduring settlement. We've not defined what this means. Indeed, I make these points with no map showing where the final borders are to be drawn. Nevertheless *we believe territorial compromise is essential for peace.*"[8]

The Egyptian Foreign Minister echoed Bush's call for Israel to give up land. This was the beginning of numerous such entreaties hereafter called "land for peace." At the time, no peace treaty resulted—only continued letters and negotiations.

At this point, it is helpful to turn once again to viewing the land as a divine gift. If God in His sovereign wisdom and goodness has been behind the restoration of this state, will those who pressure Israel to give up a portion of the sacred land suffer for it? Will they pursue this course without being subject to correction or chastening? John P. McTernan, former US treasury agent, has written about what might be the consequences of America's initiative in the peace process. In his book *As America Has Done to Israel*, a chapter titled "America on a Collision Course with God" contains an argument that the pressure on Israel to give up land is a position at loggerheads with the prophets' promises found in the Old Testament. It is there that the Word of God gives solemn assurances that the land will be restored to the Jewish people. As just one of many prophecies puts it, "I will take the people of Israel from the nations among which they have gone, and will gather them from every quarter, and will bring them to their own land" (Ezekiel 37:21).

An examination of many such scriptures will be made in the last chapter of this book. Turning back to Mr. McTernan's contentions, we note that he compiled a list of meetings throughout the peace process during which American leaders urged Israel to give up land. McTernan sees immediate consequences for America's stance, consequences that have come mostly in the form of natural disasters and, secondarily, in steep market declines.[9]

COINCIDENCES OR DIVINE INTERVENTION?

The aforementioned Madrid Peace Conference of 1991 took place from October 30 to November 4. With careful planning by Secretary of State James A. Baker and the urging of President George H. W. Bush, the delegates gathered to finalize a plan for Israel to make concessions in exchange for a Palestinian promise of peace. As this conversation occurred, anti-Israel terrorism was being perpetrated by Arab Muslims whose commitments to Islamic Jihad were well known. Nonetheless, the planning continued. The sequence of steps was important: Israel would cede control of the land, the Arabs would make a pledge of peace, and then Israel would make the promised withdrawal.[10] McTernan observes what happened concurrently with this conference:

A powerful storm developed off Nova Scotia, catching the National Weather Bureau completely by surprise….The storm was extremely rare because it traveled for one thousand miles in an east to west direction....Meteorologists called the storm 'extra-tropical' because it did not originate in the tropics, as most hurricanes do.[11]

It became commemorated as "the Perfect Storm." The peak intensity of the storm came on October 30, the opening day of the conference. The National Climatic Data Center relates that "an interesting aspect of the huge system was its retrograde motion not away from the New England Coast, but toward it....Not too many people could fathom—or believe—100-foot waves and hurricane force winds, 70-80 miles-per-hour plus, in a storm that was heading from east to west. 'You were looking at a set of meteorological circumstances that come together maybe every 50-100 years,' said Bob Case, NOAA National Weather Service meteorologist at the Boston, Mass. Forecast office. [12]

The most extensive damage occurred in New England, where federal disaster areas were declared for seven counties in Massachusetts, five in Maine. Former President Bush's home in Kennebunkport, Maine suffered damage as windows were blown out, water flooded the building, and some structural damage also occurred." It was a monster storm that traveled down the East Coast from Maine to Florida, creating ocean waves over one hundred feet high, among the highest ever recorded. McTernan says, "The President's land was touched the day he attempted to touch the covenant land of Israel."[13] A coincidence? Possibly. But after researching this pattern, McTernan lists many more such concurrences, and as the list grows, the likelihood of these events being only coincidence diminishes.

Recall that this was the first major attempt to structure a land-for-peace arrangement between the Israelis and Palestinians following the Six-Day War of 1967. The pressure placed upon Israel to cede land it had rightfully obtained in a defensive action occurred simultaneously with the devastating hurricane of the century dubbed "the Perfect Storm."

In September and October of 1999, events in Middle East diplomacy again coincided with natural disasters. The "final status" of land for peace was to be negotiated. On September 3, Secretary of State Madeline Albright met with Israeli Prime Minister Ehud Barak to restart the stalled Wye Agreement and thus give more authority over the West Bank to the PLO. These negotiations had been taking the form of partial, step-by-step agreements and withdrawals to get the Israeli public accustomed to the idea and process of ceding land to the Palestinians. Albright was hoping to move the process along.

On that very same date, after moving slowly off the coast of North Carolina, Hurricane Dennis reversed course and went ashore. McTernan says, "This hurricane was literally doing circles in the Atlantic Ocean until the meeting in Israel." Dennis itself did not do major damage, but it left tremendous amounts of rain in its wake. By September 13 the Israeli foreign minister and one of Yassir Arafat's deputies were in meetings to work out arrangements for the "final status."

While these leaders proceeded to arrange for the land to be given away, yet another storm, Hurricane Floyd, was on the move, and ultimately led to the third greatest evacuation in American history. Floyd ran parallel to the East Coast, causing further damage from tornados and widespread flooding. Dennis and Floyd together resulted in almost every river basin in eastern North Carolina exceeding five-hundred-year flood levels. It continued up the coast to Maine and the Atlantic Provinces of Canada. Wikipedia's summary of the event states, "It was among the largest Atlantic hurricanes of its strength ever recorded....Nearly every river basin in the eastern part of the state exceeded 500-year flood levels."[14] Some observers said that Dennis and Floyd together knocked out many sewage and water systems, resulting in sewage, chemicals, and dead animals all flowing into the rivers.

On September 21—the same month as the above-mentioned hurricanes--the stock market took a dive, falling 225 points—the steepest slide in four months. On September 22 Arafat paid a visit to President Clinton to go over the stipulations of the agreement. Another telling occurrence followed. On

September 23, the stock market dropped another 205 points. The total drop for the three days before, during, and after the meeting between Clinton and Arafat on "land for peace" was 504 points—the first time in the history of the stock market that it suffered two two-hundred-point losses in the same week.[15]

Are these distressing events signs of a jealous God protecting and assuring this land for His Chosen People? Is He even today watching over Israel? Benjamin Disraeli, who, in the nineteenth century, served twice as prime minister of Great Britain, argued before Parliament in 1854 regarding Jewish emancipation: "There is no country, in which the Hebrew race has been persecuted which has not suffered, whose energies have not been withered, whose political power has not decayed, and where there have not been evident proofs that the Divine favour has been withdrawn from the land. The instances of Spain, and Portugal, and Italy are obvious."[16]

Many observers think it odd that a world leader would argue for Jewish rights from a religious perspective. So convinced have US church-going presidents been that a two-state solution is a proper and fair one, that the idea of America being punished for its support of such a plan is unthinkable. But America has not been serious enough in this regard: the Chosen People are a covenant people selected as witnesses to a holy and sovereign God. It doesn't matter that it has been four millennia since God first assigned this land to them. They are His own, and the land is covenant land. The prophets prophesied of the return of His People to the land of promise. Looking at what we call natural phenomena—the movements of Mother Nature—are we in fact looking at the work of the God of all creation and the sovereign Lord of history? The reader might ponder this question.

In all, Mr. McTernan lists thirty instances of a specific US Administration proposal for a giveaway of the covenant land being accompanied by a disaster in America. It will suffice to cite one more such incident.

Yassir Arafat's death occurred on November 11, 2004, and in January he was replaced by Mahmoud Abbas. In spite of Abbas's calls for the destruction of the State of Israel and for a major jihad to immediately begin, he was invited by President George W. Bush to the White House to discuss the road map for peace, Bush said, "We look forward to working with [Abbas] and the Palestinian people to advance the cause of Middle East peace."[18] One can only wonder on what such a hope was based, given Abbas's call to destroy Israel!

Three months later, on April 11 and 12, President Bush and Israeli Prime Minister Ariel Sharon met to formulate the road map for peace. The focal point was the "Disengagement Plan," the abandonment of Jewish settlements—five in the West Bank and twenty-one in the Gaza Strip—and cancellation of plans for a residential complex in the Maaleh Adumim section of East Jerusalem. During the week of these discussions, the stock market experienced a stunning downturn, with the Dow Industrials, NASDAQ, and S&P 500 reaching their lows for the year.[19]

As the weeks rolled on, McTernan says, "President Bush and Secretary of State Condoleezza Rice put enormous pressure on the Israeli government to carry out the removal of these twenty-five settlements," beginning with Gaza. On August 16, 2005, the destruction of the settlements began, and by August 23 it was complete. About ten thousand Jews left their homes and businesses in the covenant land. The Israeli Defense Forces demolished the Jewish homes, leaving twenty-one synagogues and a number of vegetable greenhouses standing for Arab use. The Israeli military presence was then withdrawn. "President Bush was extremely happy," says McTernan, and the president congratulated Prime Minister Sharon and the Israeli people for their courage. Meanwhile, the Palestinians moved in, looting the greenhouses and synagogues, following the pattern of the Bedouins and many Palestinian Arabs preceding them.[20]

The repercussions began immediately. McTernan reports, "On August 23rd, just as Israel removed the last settler, tropical depression twelve formed over the Bahamas and upgraded to a tropical storm named Katrina. Katrina grew rapidly in power and on August 24th became a Category 1."[20] On August 27 Katrina reached Category 3 intensity, thereafter gaining size and entering the Gulf of Mexico to become a Category 5. On August 28 it exhibited unusually rapid growth, sustaining winds of 175 miles per hour. It was the costliest natural disaster—as well as one of the five deadliest hurricanes—in American history. The greatest number of the 1,833 deaths occurred in New Orleans, where the levee system gave out. The national spokesperson for the Red Cross said at the time, "We are looking now at a disaster above any magnitude that we've seen in the United States."[21]

Both Hurricane Katrina and the Gaza giveaway dominated the news. President Bush, who had exulted in the "breakthrough" with the Israelis, was now widely criticized for failing to show up on the ground in the Gulf region that was devastated by the hurricane. McTernan lists thirteen similarities between the abandonment of Gaza and Katrina. Here are six of them:

1. The residents of Gaza were required to evacuate their homes. Residents living in the path of the hurricane were called on to evacuate.
2. Israel sent 40,000 troops to enforce the evacuation mandate. The U. S. sent 80,000 soldiers to the affected areas of Katrina.
3. Israeli citizens went to their roofs to demonstrate their determination to remain in Gaza. American citizens also went to their roofs, in their case to stay above the rising floods.
4. The Israelis in Gaza dug up their dead to carry them to their new place to be reinterred. The Americans found hundreds of bodies from the graveyards in the Gulf Coast.
5. Many Israelis felt abandoned by their government in being forced to move out of their homes. Likewise, many Americans in the affected areas felt abandoned by their governments in the failure to respond quickly to the hurricane.
6. Gush Katif, the area in Gaza out of which the settlers moved was a major agricultural center. The Port of New Orleans was a major center of agricultural distribution and shipping.[22]

Close on the heels of Hurricane Katrina came Hurricane Rita, which headed into the Gulf and quickly grew into another Category 5. The timing of it coincided with the giving up of sacred land. On September 21 the resident settlers in Samaria completed their withdrawal as Rita's winds reached their peak of 175 miles per hour and headed for Texas after the storm surge flooded New Orleans for the second time in thirty days.[23]

The abandonment of covenant land was accompanied not only by these disastrous hurricanes but also by personal crises for the two leaders. President Bush suffered devastating criticism after Katrina for what was seen as his aloofness during the confusion that followed, and that perception deeply affected his standing as a compassionate leader. Following the Israeli disengagement from Gaza and five West Bank settlements, Prime Minister Sharon, under the pressure of his autumn reelection campaign, decided to continue the process of land for peace. In a brazen maneuver, he endorsed a plan to surrender large areas of land in Judea and Samaria to the Palestinian Authority. It was not to be. On December 18 he suffered a minor stroke, which was followed by a major hemorrhagic stroke on January 4, putting him into a coma from which he never awakened.[24]

As previously stated, there are many more instances by which McTernan correlates the tragic causes and effects of the land-for-peace policy. Those cited alert us to the consequences of dealing away the land that has been sanctified as a gift for the Chosen People. The repeated attempts to use the land as an enticement to the Palestinians in exchange for peaceful coexistence have failed every time.

We see what happens when the Israelis simply give the land away without meaningful negotiations or hope of reciprocity. In 2005 Israel withdrew every resident and soldier from Gaza in an effort to obtain peace, leaving the territory to the Palestinians with trade and travel agreements. That same territory was shortly thereafter transformed by a newly elected Hamas leadership into an arsenal of rockets, missiles, and mortars for the purpose of terrorizing Israel. An increasing number of Israelis came within range of that firepower—at first, just twenty-five thousand. But by 2012 those living within range grew to 3.5 million.[25] The Hamas governing charter provides the rationale for such fearful terrorist activity: eradication of the State of Israel.

Peace will not come by way of real-estate concessions, for the land is a sacred holding. The often-repeated and relevant phrase in the Book of Devarim/ Deuteronomy states, "the land which the Lord your God is giving you."(e.g. 4:1) It will not be taken away except by divine intervention. That is the promise in the Torah. Furthermore, the Lord specified, "The land shall not be sold in perpetuity, for the land is mine; with me you [the Chosen Nation] are but aliens and tenants" (Vayikra/Leviticus 25:23). American administrations have wanted Israel to exchange the land for peace in treaties that could be broken or nullified. It is well known that Muhammed and his followers have historically ignored such agreements. The Palestinians themselves habitually ignore treaty articles.

All this would indicate that it is a risky policy for heads of foreign nations to pressure Israel to relinquish a land acquired with divine assistance. But American presidents, like others in the American State Department and security councils, are oblivious to such a perspective on Middle East policy. This is no surprise. But recently the US administration has gone further: in its disregard for the security of Israel, it has concluded a nuclear-arms agreement with Israel's archenemy, Iran. In July 2015, under American leadership, the leaders of the world's most powerful nations (called the P5+1), put into place a plan to pacify the nation of Iran. This Joint Comprehensive Plan of Action will enable Iran to retain its huge stockpile of uranium and continue to multiply the supply of its centrifuges. This is the nation most guilty of sponsoring terrorism throughout the world and most belligerent in its calls for Israel's destruction. The enforcement of rules for this agreement will depend on the cooperation of Iran itself! Furthermore, the restrictions on Iran's nuclear ambitions will end within a decade.

In the meantime, this agreement provides help for the safety of Iran's uranium mines, storage sites, nuclear power plants, covert uranium enrichment facility, and research sites. It does it in this way: it stipulates that America, the United Kingdom, France, China, Russia, and Germany (the P5+1) will all cooperate to strengthen Iran's ability to protect against any sabotage of Iran's nuclear facilities. Article 10 stipulates that the P5+1 powers and Iran will foster "cooperation through training and workshops to strengthen Iran's ability to protect against and respond to, nuclear security threats, including sabotage." Thus, these nations pledged to help defend the arsenal of the nation that, for years, has repeatedly pledged the annihilation of Israel!

Iran is now back in the community of nations. All sanctions now having been lifted, global corporations are now scrambling to collaborate with this repressive and criminal regime for a share in the commerce generated. With the Iranian economy rebounding, Iran soon promises to reach the goal of national prosperity.

Meanwhile, the Iranian leadership views Israel as "a one-bomb state," meaning it can be wiped out with one atomic bomb.

With all this in mind, one might ask, "What can Israel do? Can they rest at night, knowing these things?" And the alternate question is this: "How might the Lord of history react against those nations that have endorsed this horrifying treaty?"

Understand, O dullest of the people...
He who disciplines the nations,
He who teaches knowledge to humankind,
Does he not chastise?...
For the Lord will not forsake his people;
He will not abandon his heritage. (Psalms 94:8a, 10, 14)

1. Joan Peters, *From Time Immemorial: The Origins of the Arab-Jewish Conflict over Palestine* (Chicago: JKAP Publications, 2002), 296–330, 392

2. Ibid., 392.

3. Ibid., 392.

4. Howard M. Sachar, *A History of Israel from the Rise of Zionism to Our Time* (New York: Alfred A. Knopf, 2003), 129

5. Gertrude Himmelfarb, *The People of the Book* (New York: Encounter Books, 2011), 139.

6. John P. McTernan, *As America Has Done to Israel* (New Kensington: Whitaker House, 2008), 76–78.

7. Caroline Glick, *The Israeli Solution* (New York: Crown Forum, 2014), 58–59.

8. John P. McTernan, *As America*, 147–222.

9. Ibid.

9. Neal Kozodoy, *The Mideast Peace Process* (San Francisco: Encounter Books, 2002), 28.

10. John P. McTernan, *As America*, 156.

11. John P. McTernan, *As America*, 156–157.

12. "The Perfect Storm, October, 1991," National Climatic Data Center of the National Oceanic and Atmospheric Administration, Ashville, NC. www.noaanews.noaa.gov/stories/s444htm.

13. Ibid., 172–173.

14. "Hurricane Floyd," Wikipedia, https://en.wikipedia.org/wiki/Hurricane-Floyd.

15. John P. McTernan, *As America*, 173

16. Michael Makovsy, *Churchill's Promised Land: Zionism and Statecraft* (New Haven: Yale University Press, 2007), 42.

17. John P. McTernan., 190–192.

18. Ibid., 188.

19. "Hurricane Katrina," Wikipedia, https://en.wikipedia.org/wiki/Hurricane_Katrina.

20. John P. McTernan, *As America*, 194.
21. Ibid., 194.
22. Ibid., 196, 197.
23. Ibid., 197, 198.
24. Caroline Glick, "Sharon's Final Road," Glick Blog, January 14, 2014, carolineglick.com/sharons-final-road/

CHAPTER 9

The Acceptance

§

You shall also love the stranger, for you were
strangers in the land of Egypt.

—Devarim/Deuteronomy 10:19

Anxious as they were for an orderly and peaceful transition to
statehood, the Jewish authorities did what they could to arrest the
exodus [of Palestinians]. Israel's Proclamation of Independence called
upon "the sons of the Arab people dwelling in Israel to keep the
peace and to play their part in building the State on the basis of full
and equal citizenship and due representation in all its institutions,
provisional and permanent." Appeals in similar phrase were circulated
by every available means—radio, handbills, sound-trucks.

—Abraham Joshua Heschel[1]

During the Middle Ages and up until the modern growth of the Jewish
community in Palestine, the Jews who resided there were subjected to harassment and humiliation by Muslims. During certain periods, Jews experienced
relative calm, but, as the Israeli historian Benny Morris puts it, they were "extremely submissive toward the Turkish authorities and deferential toward the
large Muslim communities among which they lived...Arabs in Palestine in the

nineteenth and early twentieth centuries often referred to Jews as awlad al-maut (children of death)...Jews were forbidden to bear arms; were permitted to ride asses only, not camels or horses, and only sidesaddle rather than astride; and were obliged to wear distinctive garb. Other restrictions had nothing to do with security and everything to do with religious and economic discrimination."[2]

By contrast, from the beginning of the Zionist movement, some thinkers in the movement were giving thought to the role and was welfare of the resident Arab population.

As previously noted, the numbers of these Arabs were small, about a half million. Many of them were transient laborers. All of them considered themselves as part of the greater Arab nation and had little if any identity as Palestinian. Many early Zionists were confident that Jewish settlement in the land, far from being a problem for the Arab inhabitants, would be beneficial. The early Russian Zionists in the 1880s clearly anticipated that there could be harmony. Theodore Herzl, Zionism's founder, met with prominent Arab leaders and carried on a correspondence with some of them, leading him to this conclusion.

There was, of course, apprehension during Jewish immigration. As new Jewish settlements were established after the turn of the century, armed attacks by Arab gangs were not uncommon. Some Zionist leaders issued grave warnings about the difficulties they could foresee in trying to coexist. In fact, tensions did arise as the newcomers became established and began to prosper. The rich effendis had sold large parcels of the land to Jews at exorbitant prices, thereby forcing some peasants off their land. However, the new settlers, though concentrating on their own efforts to survive, offered assistance to their Arab neighbors by hiring workers, giving free medical assistance, and lending agricultural machinery.[3] Further, when the Jews realized the potentially explosive situation that land purchases were creating, they took action. They gave assistance to the small peasant farmers in purchasing other land or finding employment elsewhere. This development by the Jewish Yishuv resulted in economic opportunities for the Arab population, which, in turn, brought about a large increase in Arab immigration.[4]

In spite of numerous brush-offs from the Arab leaders, most of the Zionists remained hopeful in the early 20th century that the two sides could establish close communication. At the first Zionist Congress following WWI (1921), the conferees announced their intention to "live with the Arab people in friendship and mutual respect, and together with them to develop the homeland common to both into a flourishing community which would ensure to each of its peoples an undisturbed national development."[5] Arthur Ruppin, a Zionist leader and sociologist, contended that the Jewish influx into Palestine would be a means of improving conditions within the surrounding Arab states. Ruppin envisioned a common currency and cooperation in educational endeavors.

As David Bur-Gurion (later the Israeli state's first prime minister) began to rise in positions of leadership within the Yishuv, he agonized over the issue of Jewish-Arab relations. At the fourteenth Zionist Congress in Vienna (1925), he insisted on the necessity "to find the way to the heart of the Arab people."[6] Though he perceived the difficulties in dealing with them, he spoke out against a population transfer and insisted that the movement for Arab nationalism among the Arab notables was legitimate even though ill-defined. He wanted them to stay, to have some form of self-government, and to prosper with the help of the Jews. In a letter to his son dated October 1937, he wrote, "We do not wish and do not need to expel Arabs and take their place. All our aspiration is built on the assumption—proven throughout all our activity— that there is enough room for ourselves and the Arabs in Palestine."[7]

On numerous occasions Ben-Gurion reminded his audiences that the Jews were called to be a "light to the nations"[8]—that the coming Jewish state should be exemplary, one that would even lead to universal redemption! Later, when armed force was necessary, Ben-Gurion exhorted his army to show self-restraint, embody the messianic ideal, and be morally impeccable in defending against Arab violence. In an address to the Knesset as prime minister in August 1952, he expressed his longstanding fervent desire: "All my life down to today—as a Zionist and a Jew—I regarded peace and understanding with the Arabs as a basic and primary value...I would regard it as a grievous sin not only against our generation but also against future generations were we not to do everything possible to reach mutual understanding with our Arab neighbors."[9]

Credible historians do not place responsibility at the feet of the Israelis for the flight of much of the Palestinian population during the Israeli War of Independence. The British had intended that Palestine provide a homeland for the Jewish people, as the British Mandate from the League of Nations indicated. In November 1947, the United Nations recommended the partition of Palestine into a Jewish state and an Arab state. Immediately, the resident Palestinians began to make war on the Jews, followed by attacks from the armies of the neighboring Arab states. They unashamedly referred to their action as an intended massacre of the Jews. So for the Jews, it was a war of survival. It was not fought, as other wars of independence have been, to gain freedom from an occupier. Nevertheless, despite the murderous intent of the Arabs, Ben-Gurion and other leaders of the Yishuv publicized their hope that the Palestinian families would stay in their homes. Through flyers dropped from aircraft and loudspeakers on vehicles driving through Arab neighborhoods, the Jews urged the Arabs to remain.

GENERAL BENEFITS FOR ARAB ISRAELIS

Within five years of the war's end in July of 1949, the Arabs who did stay were given full rights as citizens in the new Jewish nation. Their enduring communities in Israel today indicate they have preferred to live there. Israel's Bureau of Statistics reported in 2001 that the rate of growth of the Arab population in Israel has been 3.4 percent per year, on average, a very high number exceeding the rate of growth among Arabs in the neighboring countries. For example, the Arab annual growth rate was only 2.8 percent in Syria, the same in Jordan, and 2.1 percent in Egypt. (In the Palestinian Authority, it was even higher than in Israel, an amazing 4.3 percent per year![(10)]) Thus, even though many of these Arabs chafe under the security regulations of Israel and real or perceived neglect by the Israeli government, the numbers show that they feel some degree of acceptance in the Israeli state. Clearly, this nation and culture is tolerable enough to make a home within it and create large families there. Indeed, a poll taken by Harvard's John F. Kennedy School of Government in conjunction with Haifa University strongly indicated such (reported June 23, 2008). The poll's survey item stated: "I would prefer to live in the State of Israel than in any other country in the world." 48.8 percent of Israeli Arabs agreed, and 28.1 percent tended to agree for a total of 76.9 percent.[11] So what is it about Israel that creates a feeling of sufficient acceptance and security that causes Arab citizens to multiply faster there than in many Arab nations?

ISRAELI LAW

Israel's Declaration of Independence specifies that the Jewish State "will uphold the full social and political equality of all its citizens, without distinction of religion, race, or sex; will guarantee freedom of religion, conscience, education and culture; will safeguard the Holy Places of all religions; and will loyally uphold the principles of the United Nations Charter." Accordingly, from the beginning of the Israeli nation, Arabs have enjoyed the right to form their own political parties. The voting franchise was extended to them, as to all residents; all citizens vote on the uniform roll in regular multiparty elections. Arabs hold seats in the Israeli Knesset. Religious freedom means that non-Jews observe their own days of rest and holy days. Every religious community has its own councils and courts. From the beginning, Muslim religious courts were given jurisdiction over such issues as marriage, divorce, burial, inheritance, and religious sites. Their *qadis* (Muslim judges) became paid employees of the state.

While these rights are guaranteed, pluralism is still established in Israeli society, as it is multiethnic, multicultural, multireligious, and multilingual.

Groups are not separated by regulation but are free to live in various segregated areas and live in varying lifestyles. Arabs and Druze have their own schools. Both Arabic and Hebrew are official languages.

Due to the hostility of the Arabs on both sides of the Israeli border in the early years following independence, it was necessary for the Israelis to establish certain firm policies. At times the army evicted residents within small "security zones" located on border areas with hostile Arab nations. These areas had concentrations of militants, many of whom had connections—familial or military—with people in the border country. Therefore, Arabs living in these areas could be searched, detained, or evicted on short notice. Obviously, since Israel is surrounded by nations who have demanded Israel's dissolution and even annihilation, security was a high priority for the fledgling state. Even then, the Israeli military acted with restraint. Furthermore, the Israeli Supreme Court frequently reversed the rulings of the military, even where there was proof of subversion.

Concerning the ownership of land, in 2005 the attorney general of Israel ruled that Israeli Arabs must have equal purchasing access to Israeli land parcels under the control of the Jewish National Fund and the Israel Lands Administration.[12] The property laws in Israel are somewhat complicated, but a summary of my understanding is that while most of the land is government owned, property "is equally available to all Israelis, whether Jewish or Arab" through lease agreements.[13] This stands in contrast to life under the Palestinian Authority, where, at least some of the time, Arabs who've sold land to Jews have faced the death penalty if apprehended.

The Supreme Court of Israel has come to be known as one of the most liberal courts in the world. Alan Dershowitz, Felix Frankfurter professor of law at Harvard Law School, points out that "Israel is the only nation in the world whose judiciary actively enforces the rule of law against its military even during wartime."[14] Palestinians as well as Arab Israelis have rapid access to the Supreme Court.[15] Contrast this with the nations around Israel, including the

Palestinian Authority, that routinely torture suspected terrorists and their relatives. "Khalil Shikaki, a Palestinian political scientist who has been polling Palestinians since 1996 about 'what governments they admire,' found the following: 'Every year Israel has been the top performer, at times receiving more than 80 percent approval. The American system has been the next best.'"[16] This is largely due to the experience of the Palestinians with Israel's judiciary.

It is common practice (and knowledge) that Arab and Palestinian propagandists will criticize Israel whenever, from necessity, its security measures deviate the slightest degree from liberal human-rights standards, but, as Dershowitz points out, the same people "are quick to praise and support every tyrannical destroyer of human rights, ranging from Saddam Hussein to Muammar Khadafi to Fidel Castro."[17]

HEALTH BENEFITS OF LIVING IN THE STATE OF ISRAEL

Subsequent to the rise of Jewish settlements in the early twentieth century, health care for the Arabs improved dramatically. Infant mortality was reduced, and adult life expectancy was increased. In fact, it was partially due to the improved health services in Jewish areas of Palestine that the Muslim population was exploding long before Israeli independence. Dershowitz quotes a British official, reporting in 1937 that "the growth in [the numbers of the Arab fellahin] had been largely due to the health services combating malaria, reducing infant death rates, improving water supply and sanitation." Dershowitz adds, "These improvements began with modern hospitals and water and sanitary systems introduced into Palestine by the Jewish refugees from Europe."[18]

As time went on, Arab Israeli infant death rates plummeted. From 1961–1996 they went from 46.4 per thousand births to 10.0 in the Muslim population; among Christians it was reduced from 42.1 to 6.7.[19] The life-expectancy indicator should also be noted: David Bar-Illan of the *New York Post* reported in 1999 that "average life expectancy among the Palestinian population under

Israeli rule…increased by twenty-five years."[20] It was reported in the *Times of Israel* in August, 2013 that Israeli Arabs have access to a health-care system that is rated the fourth best in the world based on life expectancy, per capita cost, and absolute per capita cost (including preventative and curative services, family planning, nutrition, and emergency aid).[21]

EDUCATION IN ISRAEL FOR ARABS

In nineteenth-century Palestine, what little educational progress was being made was due to European Christian missions.[22] The Ottomans made little or no effort to lift the standards of its subject population. With the commencement of aliyah and development of the Yishuv, education came to the land. Finally, with the establishment of the Jewish state, universal education was introduced with unparalleled and previously unseen benefits accruing for its Arab inhabitants.

In Israel both Hebrew and Arabic became the official languages. Arabic is taught not only in the Arab schools but also in Jewish high schools. Israeli educational policy is inclusive and promotes both the culture and traditions of the Arab minority.

More than three hundred thousand Arab children attend Israeli schools. In 1948, at Israel's independence, there was only one Arab high school in all of Palestine. To see the astonishing advances in and growth of education among Arab Israelis, one must look at the statistics showing the number of years Arab children have been in school. Over a thirty-five year period, from 1961–1996, the median number of years for the schooling of Arab Israelis rose from 1.2 to 10.4 years. The literacy rate for Arab Israelis is 95 percent, almost the same as for Israeli Jews.[23]

Benefits to Arabs of living in Israel were exemplified in a poll conducted by Professor Sammy Smooha of Haifa University about life within the Jewish state. The poll showed that in 2013, the percentage of Israeli Arabs accepting

Israel's right to exist as a Jewish and democratic state was 52.8 percent, which was much more than the previous year's 47.4 percent. In 2013 63.5 percent of these people considered Israel to be a good place to live, which showed an increase from 58.5 percent in 2012.[24]

BENEFITS OF PALESTINIANS LIVING IN THE TERRITORY OF THE WEST BANK

When Israel defeated the Arab nations that had vowed to exterminate it in the Six-Day War of 1967, the Israeli government expected that formal negotiations for peace would follow. But the Arab League refused to talk, because sitting down at a table with Jews was for them unthinkable. Likewise, on October 15, 1968, the Palestinians flatly rejected UN Resolution 242, which called for a just settlement of the refugee problem. Israel, however, refrained from annexing the conquered land—the West Bank and Sinai Desert—that had been used as a staging ground for the Jordanian army and instead created a military administration in the West Bank. The Israeli government was anticipating future negotiations that would result in their returning much of the conquered land as a quid pro quo for recognition of Israel's right to exist and formal peace. But as time went on, all signals from the Arab parties were rejectionist and all actions hostile. Egypt began a war of attrition, and the PLO instituted guerilla warfare against Israel. Lebanon, Syria, and Jordan soon joined in the strategy.

The Israeli government, seeing no end to hostilities, resolved to remain in the acquired territories for the time being and set about improving the degraded conditions under which the Palestinians had lived while under Jordanian occupation. Hospitals were built, universities were founded, and the standard of living began rising with increased employment. The Israelis enlarged their electrical grid, extending its power to the territories just conquered in the 1967 war and providing its benefits to villages that were without electricity[25] According to Mitchell G. Bard of the American-Israeli Cooperative Enterprise, "When Israel captured the West Bank and Gaza Strip in 1967, officials took measures to improve the conditions that Palestinians had lived under. More than 100,000 Palestinians were employed in Israel, and were paid the same wages as Israeli workers, which stimulated economic growth." (Later, that number decreased because of stringent measures taken to increase security in Israel during the Intifadas but eventually rebounded. More recently, "the West Bank economy grew by more than 7 per cent representing the 26th best growth rate in 2009 out of 212 countries and territories in the world...*double the rate of Israel*."[26] (emphasis added)

Illiteracy among Arabs, which had been the norm, dropped to 14 percent of adults over 15 (compare Egypt's at 61 percent) by the early 1990s. Per capita Gross National Product increased between 1969 and 1991 from $165 to $1,715. Life expectancy rose from forty-eight years old in 1967 to seventy-two in 2000. Israeli health programs were introduced, which reduced infant mortality from sixty per one thousand live births in 1968 to fifteen per one thousand live births in 2000. A network of hospitals for Palestinians was built, not by the UN or the United States but by Israel. In addition, Israel's own hospitals are currently available and used by Palestinians, even by the families of terrorists, and patients go without fear of the Jewish medical personnel.[27]

Inoculation efforts in the territories resulted in wiping out polio, whooping cough, measles, and tetanus. Under Jordanian rule, modern conveniences were owned by only a small minority, but by 1986, 92.8 percent of the population had electricity and 85 percent had running water. A comparable percentage owned major appliances and at least one automobile. The material standard of living increased enormously under the occupation of the hated Jews.[28]

By 1979 the standard of living in the West Bank had risen dramatically since the War of 1967, when Israel began its administration. Many Arabs had become salaried blue-collar workers, laboring in an Israeli-Palestinian common market. Many were becoming skilled workers. In the years between 1973 and 1980, the territories of the West Bank and Gaza experienced an annual Gross National Product increase of 13 percent, *far more than Israel's*. Universal health care for Palestinians was established by Israel, with the government establishing 146 clinics in the West Bank and 20 in Gaza. The education of Palestinians was also greatly improved under Israeli administration. By 1980 six universities and twenty community colleges and teacher-training seminaries were founded. Literacy rates were rising significantly. Palestinian youths and women were finding newfound opportunities in the economy and society.[29]

In a recent report of the United Nations High Commissioner for Refugees, the number of worldwide stateless peoples was ten million. Not one Palestinian was listed as being stateless. Unlike refugees of the rest of the world, most Palestinians in the West Bank live in towns comprised not of tents but of houses or apartments, and they have schools, electricity, running water, and all the other amenities of modern life.[30]

Kenneth Levin, in his book, *The Oslo Syndrome,* reports that in this time period following the 1967 war, the Israelis went to work on building housing units for the Palestinians living in squalid areas. "By 1983," he says, over 3,000 Palestinians families had moved into Israeli-built houses and about 3,500 families had moved into houses they had built themselves on lots prepared and provided by Israel." But that kind of assistance was not appreciated by the Palestinians who realized that continued provisions of this sort would reduce their effectiveness in pushing for the return to their previous residences and in recruiting the men into PLO cadres. [31]

The West Bank economy grows when there is no sustained terrorism and business feels secure in establishing and investing. But when terrorism is rampant, the economy plunges, unemployment rises sharply and Israel is blamed. So then, with security comes prosperity, with lawlessness want.

PERSISTENT ENMITY

Even given all the aforementioned benefits and advances, the attitude of many Israeli Arabs and Palestinians in the West Bank is summed up in this statement: "We like what you can do for us, but we hate you." In a speech delivered at the Conference Against Racism in Durban, South Africa, in August 2001, Hanan Ashwari, a Palestinian leader during the First Intifada, made this accusation:

Levin, 241
Those of us who came under Israeli occupation in 1967 have languished in the West Bank, Jerusalem and the Gaza Strip under a unique combination of military occupation, settler colonization, and systematic oppression. Rarely has the human mind devised such varied, diverse, and comprehensive means of wholesale brutalization and persecution.[32]

Facts, however, belie Ashwari's statement. Howard Sachar, in his monumental *A History of Israel: From the Rise of Zionism to Our Time*, states that the Israeli pound was immediately made legal tender, yet local monies were accepted at the Zurich exchange rate such that banking activity increased. More significantly, freedom of movement between Israel and the West Bank became a priority; curfews were cancelled and road barriers removed soon after the war ended. The Israelis began shopping in the Arab bazaars, and the Palestinians were free to travel to Israel's beaches and cities. Palestinian farmers could drive their trucks wherever they desired to sell their produce.[33]

The Arabs under Israeli administration of the territories were, of course, without many of the political rights that Israeli Arab citizens possessed. However, they did have some rights. Jordanian law, familiar to the Palestinians, remained in force. Jordanian currency remained the legal tender for some time and still is accepted along with the U. S. dollar and the new Israeli shekel. (The exception to this was East Jerusalem and its environs. There, the Israeli government was established, which, in effect, was an annexation.) On the Temple Mount, the Muslim Waqf, appointed by Jordan, was retained as the authority. Local government was left in place. Bridges to Jordan were opened up to facilitate traffic between the Palestinian Arabs and the Arab world beyond the Jordan River. There was an increase in freedom and relative prosperity compared to the limited amount that had been achievable under Jordanian rule. It is not too much to say that the Israelis were working for the good of their Arab neighbors.

This was not colonialism, *for Israel had not sought to expand its borders and did not initiate hostilities*. Indeed, the Israeli government had begged King Hussein of Jordan not to join forces with Egypt and Syria in the War of 1967. (Jordan itself was an illegal occupier of the West Bank; it laid claim to it after Israel's War of Independence.) As stated previously, Israel was more than ready, following its victory in 1967, to enter into negotiations for a quid pro quo of land for formal peace. In fact, it was reported that early in their administration of the territories, Israeli government officials explored the possibility of establishing a Palestinian Arab government in areas that, with negotiations, would probably be offered to Palestinians. Eighty-eight Arab notables were interviewed at the time, but there was little agreement as to what type of government should be established. In addition, opposition to any such proposals was fierce, coming from King Hussein of Jordan, Nasser of Egypt, and Palestinians outside of the territories.[34] So when these efforts failed, the Israelis took the logical course: they became beneficent overseers of the territories.

But later, under the Gaza-Jericho Agreement of May 4, 1994 (a follow-up agreement to Oslo I), the majority of Palestinians came under limited control ("interim empowerment") of the new Palestinian Authority with Yassir Arafat as its president. Drastic changes occurred. The economies of the West Bank and Gaza were quickly damaged due to corruption and the establishment of a police state. Many who had done business with any Israeli person or business were murdered. Arafat and his inner circle formed monopolies, took control of banks, and demanded protection money from business people. The Palestine Authority became the largest employer in the areas it governed. In addition, given the frequent use of suicide bombers with the backing of the PLO, Israel initiated a closure policy, which disrupted business activity and led to widespread unemployment. In 1997 Israel was able to lift those safe-guards or penalties, and the economy rebounded slightly. However, little has changed, even with the ascendancy of Mahmoud Abbas to the PLO presidency. The refugee camps have been ignored; their residents have not been moved to better housing. This continues in spite of vast sums being poured into this cause by UNRWA—the UN agency created for this purpose, funded mostly by Western nations. No, the refugees are not being served, because the PLO needs them to maintain the sympathy of the world.

The benefits of freedom and capitalism established during Israeli control vanished when the Palestinian Authority entered the picture. Freedom of the press ceased to exist; freedom of religion morphed into the persecution and emigration of Christians; and all nongovernmental organizations (NGOs) were shut down. The Palestinian Authority became master.[35]

Yet, to Israel's credit, her High Court sometimes rules in favor of the Palestinians. In 2006, it ruled that in some cases, Palestinians may sue over damages done by the Israeli army in the territories. [36] This in itself indicates that the West Bank does not have apartheid, as is too often claimed, and is not a place without recourse and hope for Arabs.

Do the Palestinians appreciate Israel's contributions to their lives? Do they not chafe under the repression of the Palestinian Authority? Probably so. But those who desire a return of freedom and democracy dare not express such thinking publicly or too loudly. While many may prefer living under Israeli law, it is difficult and dangerous to admit so, even among relatives, because the enforcers of the Authority are close at hand.

No-Cost Medical Assistance

As I write this, Israelis are giving free medical help to any Syrian or group of Syrians who make it over the northern border of Israel to one of the hospitals there, staffed with Israelis. This is truly exemplary when we look at Syrian treatment of their former Jewish population and of the state of Israel. In the late 1930's and 1940's, the Jews were experiencing severe hardship and persecution from the Syrians. Jews were being squeezed out of the professions. Half the Jewish population living in Damascus was living in poverty and could only exist there because of contributions sent into the country by Jews who had already emigrated. In spite of the efforts of Syrian Jews to prove their loyalty to the Syrian government, the Jews were blamed for an outbreak of cholera, for poisoning the water and other such adversities. Mob violence broke out in 1948, the year of the state of Israel's birth. The Syrian government then made it extremely difficult to leave the country, many Jews being imprisoned and some receiving death sentences for trying.[37] Syria was an instigator in the Israeli War of Independence, the Six-Day War of 1967 and the Yom Kippur War of 1973. It continues to be a participant in the Arab boycott of Israeli goods, and there have never been diplomatic relations between the two countries.

In spite of this poisonous relationship, Jewish medical teams and hospitals are showing kindness to the wounded in the Syrian civil war. Suffering from war trauma and from all manner of injuries, they manage to cross the border to the place where they can get expert treatment—Israel's hospitals. The same is true of the injured from Gaza. Hundreds of Palestinian patients from Gaza are treated every year in a Haifa hospital. After being treated at an Israeli hospital, some are fearful of returning home. Yet the stream of patients continues to check into Israeli hospitals.[38, 39] Israel Prime Minister, Benjamin Netanyahu declared Israel's willingness to find ways to move injured Syrian civilians from the city of Aleppo, Syria to Israeli hospitals.[40]

THE QUESTION OF ISRAEL'S BENEFICENCE

What is behind this Israeli acceptance considering the rejection they have received from these peoples? What moves this chosen nation to accept the Arab Palestinians and provide them with human rights and political status? What has prompted the Zionist leaders and Israeli governments to extend the benefits of medical, educational, and economic progress as well? This human-itarian effort is not at all like what the Jews experienced in Arab countries. To the contrary, the Jews there were offered nothing under Muslim law except state protection. Otherwise, they were *persona non grata*—accepted, for the most part, *only if* they kept their ignominious position. The answer to the Israeli nation's generosity, by my understanding, is the influence of the Torah and the Old Testament prophets on key leaders of the Yishuv and the emerg-ing state. One of the key themes of the Tanakh is righteousness and the pro-motion of justice in the world. Ben-Gurion, perhaps the best example, was a great lover of the Tanakh, voraciously studying it alone and in group settings. (He eschewed the Talmud and gave full attention to the law and prophets.) One of his great themes came from the prophecy of Isaiah: the servant of the Lord will be "a light to the nations." (He took "the Servant" to mean "the Jewish people.")

A prime consideration for the Zionists was the drive for a separate nation that would be the defender of the persecuted Jewish people and promoter of their culture. (For some, like Ben-Gurion, socialism provided a political framework.) But one cannot help but notice, within the opinions and writings of Ben-Gurion and other Zionists, the question of the welfare of their Arab neighbors. In a meeting of the Jewish Agency Executive in June of 1938, Ben-Gurion said, "The question of the Arabs in the Jewish State is not an ordi-nary minority question—but one of the fundamental questions of our Zionist policy. The State will of course have to enforce order and security and will do this not only by moralizing and preaching 'sermons on the mount' but also by machine guns should the need arise. But the Arab policy of the Jewish State must be aimed not only at full equality for the Arabs but at their cultural, social, and economic *equalization*, namely, at *raising their standard of living to that of the Jews.*"[41] (emphasis added) A generation before, Simon Magnes (1877–1948), reformed rabbi and president of Hebrew University, had helped set the humanitarian tone: "We can establish a Home here only if we are true to ourselves as democrats and internationalists, thus being just and helpful to others, and that we ask for the protection of life and property the while we are eagerly and intelligently and sincerely at work to find a *modus vivendi et operandi* with our neighbors."[42]

Has any nation been as accepting as Israel has to a people who have harassed her from the beginning and who have cheered Arab leaders who made war against Israel? The overriding reason for the momentum behind and the success of the Zionist movement was that world Jewry was threatened with extinction and needed a place of refuge. This is the issue that was faced by Theodore Herzl and his Zionist brethren as they observed their oppressed people throughout Europe in the late nineteenth and early twentieth centuries. The preservation of their race was at stake. But as Zionism developed and Jewish immigration to Palestine began, the collective conscience of these leaders led them to consider the proper and beneficent inclusion of their Arab cousins in this new community. A generation later, during the Israeli War of Independence, the loudspeakers of Jewish troops were urging the Palestinian Arabs in their towns and cities to stay in their residences. One would be hard pressed to come up with an example of any other nation that urged the communities of an enemy bent on her destruction to stay and keep its residences—but Israel did just that in her War of Independence. For that she should be praised.

Though there were a few voices in Zionism that gave contrary opinions, the ones that prevailed advocated inclusion. The residents of Palestine were looked upon as the descendants of Ishmael and Esau and so were relatives to be received kindly. Though some Zionists were socialists and religiously non-observant, the biblical tradition was nonetheless influential in their actions. They were not coming to just any land; this was the land of their forefathers, and the ethos of their progenitors bore down on them. A distinguishing characteristic of the Hebrew people was that they gave place to those wanting to live with them. Though they were forced to be wary of the Arab residents, the Jewish immigrants, as a community, would not be combative. They would accept. They would be—insofar as was feasible—an inclusive society.

1. Abraham Joshua Heschel, *Israel: An Echo of Eternity* (New York: Farrar, Strauss, and Giroux, 1969), 179.

2. Benny Morris, *Righteous Victims* (New York: Alfred A. Knopf, 1999), 5, 10.

3. Walter Laqueur, *A History of Zionism* (New York: Schocken Books, 2003), 214–215.

4. Benjamin Netanyahu, *A Place Among the Nations* (New York: Bantam, 1993), 36. "President Franklin Delano Roosevelt said in 1939 that 'Arab immigration into Palestine since 1921 has vastly exceeded the total Jewish immigration during the whole period.'"

   See also Joan Peters, *From Time Immemorial* (Chicago: JAKP Publications, 2002), 223. "The various reports usually acknowledge in one place or another that the Arab population of Palestine would have remained stable at the figure—actually 300,000 to 400,000—where it had remained for the last two centuries, if it were not for the better conditions introduced by the Jewish settlements and/or the British administration."

   See also Efraim Karsh, "1948, Israel, and the Palestinians—The True Story," *Commentary*, May 2008, 24.

   The Peel Commission report in 1937. www.jewishvirtuallibrary.org/jsource/History/peel/html. "The general beneficent effect of Jewish immigration on Arab welfare is illustrated by the fact that the increase in the Arab population is most marked in urban areas affected by Jewish development. A comparison of the census returns in 1922 and 1931 shows that, six years ago, the increase percent in Haifa was 86, in Jaffa 62, in Jerusalem 37, while in purely Arab towns such as Nablus and Hebron it was only 7, and at Gaza there was a decrease of 2 per cent."

5. Walter Laqueur, *A History*, 242.

6. Ibid., 220n.

7. Efraim Karsh, "Re-visiting Israel's 'Original Sin,'" *Commentary*, September 2003, 48.

8. The phrase "light to the nations" is lifted out of Isaiah 49:6 in reference to the Servant of the Lord.

9. Benny Morris, *Righteous*, 268.

10. Israeli Central Bureau of Statistics, Statistilite, No. 27, November 2002, www.cbs.gov.il/statistical/arabju.pdf.

11. Todd L. Pitttinsky, Jennifer J. Ratcliff, Laura A. Maruskin, *Coexistence in Israel: A National Study*, *HARVARDKennedySchool*: Center for Public Leadership, https://www.jewishvirtuallibrary.org/jsource/Society_&_Culture/coexistence_poll.pdf.

12. "Land for All," *Jerusalem Post*, February 4, 2005.

13. Alexander Safian, "Can Arabs Buy Land in Israel?" *The Middle East Quarterly*, November 14, 2013.

14. Alan Dershowitz, *The Case for Israel* (Hoboken: John Wiley and Sons, Inc., 2003), 2.

15. Ibid., 183.

16. Ibid., 188. (Quoting James Bennet, "Letter from the Middle East," *New York Times*, April 2, 2003.)

17. Ibid., 186–187.

18. Ibid., 28.

19. "Israeli Arabs: History & Overview," *Jewish Virtual Library*, www.jewishvirtuallibrary.org/history-and-overview-of-israeli-arabs.

20. David Bar-Illan, "Hillary's Deafening Silence," *New York Post*, November 12, 1999.

21. *The Times of Israel*, August 27, 2013, http://www.timesofisrael.com/israel-ranks-4th-globally-in-health-care-efficiency/.

22. Benny Morris, *Righteous*, 6.

23. "Arab Israelis," *Jewish Virtual Library*, The American-Israeli Cooperative Enterprise, 2008, www.jewishvirtuallibrary.org/history-and-overview-of-israeli-arabs.

24. "Poll: More Israeli Arabs Dump Palestinian Identity, Accept Jewish State," *The Tower Magazine*, May 29, 2014, http://www.thetower.org/0352-poll-more-israeli-arabs-dump-palestinian-identy-accept-jewish-state/.

25. Kenneth Levin, *The Oslo Syndrome* (Hanover: Smith and Krause, 2005), 240.

26. Mitchell G. Bard, *Myths and Facts,* "Myth: Palestinians have the lowest standard of living in the Middle East," *Jewish Virtual Library.* http://www.jewishvirtuallibrary.org/myths-and-facts-human-rights-in-israel-and-the-territories#u

27. Kenneth Levin, *Oslo Syndrome.*, 241.

28. Ibid., 241

29. Howard M. Sachar, *A History of Israel: From the Rise of Zionism to Our Time* (New York: Alfred A. Knopf, 1996), 861–862.

30. Evelyn Gordon, "U. N. Counts 10 Million Stateless People. None are Palestinians," *Commentary/Contentions*, November 5, 2014.

31. Kenneth Levin, *Oslo Syndrome*, 241.

32. Ibid., 241

33. Howard M. Sachar, *A History*, 671.

34. Michael B. Oren, *Six Days of War* (New York: Ballantine Books, 2003), 316.

35. Caroline B. Glick, *The Israeli Solution* (New York: Crown Forum, 2014), 146–154.

36. Scott Wilson, "Court Lets Palestinians Sue Israeli Military," *Washington Post Foreign Service,* December13, 2006, http//www.washingtonpost.com/wp-dyn/content/article/2006/12/12/AR2006121200843.html

37. Joseph B. Schechtman, *On Wings of Eagles* (New York: A. S. Barnes and Company, Inc., 1961), 157-163.

38. Ben Lynfield, "The Syrian Patients," *The International Jerusalem Post,* January 20-26, 2017, 14-15.

39. "Israeli Hospitals Continue to Treat Patients from Gaza," *The International Jerusalem Post,* July 18-24, 2014, 7.

40. "Netanyahu Gives Directives to Explore Taking in Aleppo Wounded," *The International Jerusalem Post,* December 25-29, 2016, 6.

41. Efraim Karsh, *Fabricating Israeli History* (Portland: Frank Cass, 1997, 2000), 45.

42. Arthur Hertzberg, *The Zionist Idea* (Philadelphia: The Jewish Publication Society, 1997), 448.

CHAPTER 10

The Crisis of Judaism, Part I

§

AFTER [JEWISH LEADERS IN ROME] had set a day to meet with [the Apostle Paul], they came to him at his lodging in great numbers...Some were convinced by what he had said, while others refused to believe. Paul, quoting the prophet Isaiah, said:

"You will indeed listen, but never understand,
And you will indeed look, but never perceive.
For this people's heart has grown dull,
And their ears are hard of hearing,
And they have shut their eyes;
So that they might not look with their eyes,
And listen with their ears,
And understand with their heart and turn —
And I would heal them."

—ACTS 28:23–24, 27

The Gentile Christian community of every age and land is a guest
in the house of Israel. It assumes the election and calling of Israel. It
lives in fellowship with the King of Israel...Meantime the Synagogue
became and was and still is the organization of a group of men [sic]
which hastens towards a future that is empty now that He has come
who should come, which is still without consolation, which clings

to a Word of God that is still unfulfilled. Necessarily, therefore, the
Jew who is uniquely blessed offers the picture of an existence which,
characterized by the rejection of its Messiah and therefore of its
salvation and mission, is dreadfully empty of grace and blessing.

—KARL BARTH, THEOLOGIAN [1]

One generation after the life of Jesus in AD 70, Jerusalem fell, and with the
fall came the destruction of the Second Temple. The Jewish priesthood was
soon eradicated. There was no more of the Hebrew ritual system in which
animal sacrifice was the vehicle for the acknowledgment and forgiveness
of sin.

In the story of the Exodus, when the ancient Hebrews approached Mount
Sinai, God had instructed Moses to have the people sanctify themselves, separating themselves from worldly concerns. They were to approach the mount
where God would appear with reverence and godly awe. In addition, they
were required to wash their garments and abstain from sexual intercourse.

Great fear and trembling came upon the people as they approached the
mountain where the law was given to Moses. The smoke, fire, thunder, and
shaking of the mountain curbed any curiosity seekers from ascending.

Immediately following the giving of the Ten Commandments, God gave
detailed directions concerning the offering of sacrifices. Without sacrifice, the
worship and service of the Israelites would have been presumptuous, as they
were unworthy of His favor and therefore required to offer a substitute in light
of the holy nature of Hashem (see Glossary). The ordinance in the book of
Vayikra/Leviticus concerning sacrifice for sin was summed up in this statement: "The life of the flesh is in the blood; and I have given it to you for making atonement for your lives on the altar; for, as life, it is the blood that makes
atonement" (Vayikra/Leviticus 17:11). The instructions given to Moses and
the people concerning the whole system of sacrifices (the cult) and the priests

as mediators was the very essence of the Hebrew religion and the foundation of the worshippers' and nation's relation to Hashem.

For the Day of Atonement, explicit instructions were given concerning the High Priest's duties:

> He shall slaughter the goat of the sin offering that is for the people and bring its blood inside the curtain, and do with its blood as he did with the blood of the bull, sprinkling it upon the mercy seat and before the mercy seat. Thus he shall make atonement for the sanctuary, because of the uncleannesses of the people of Israel, and because of their transgression, all their sins. (Vayikra/Leviticus 16:15–16a)

Following that sacrifice, there was another ceremony prescribed for the sins of the people using a live goat:

> Then Aaron shall lay both his hands on the head of the live goat, and confess over it all the iniquities of the people of Israel, and all their transgressions, all their sins, putting them on the head of the goat, and sending it away into the wilderness by means of someone designated for the task. The goat shall bear on itself all their iniquities to a barren region; and the goat shall be set free in the wilderness. (16:21–22)

Other types of sacrifices were prescribed for such occasions as thanksgiving, vows, dedication, purification, preparation for battle, gift giving to the Lord, and covenant renewal. According to that same received plan, the tabernacle was constructed as the center of worship constituting Israel's very identity. Hundreds of years later, it was replaced by the Temple of Solomon and, still later, with the Temple Nehemiah, which, under Roman occupation, would be renovated and greatly enlarged by King Herod (and then called the Second Temple). Jerusalem was then the center of Israel's religious life, and worshipping in places other than that, even privately, was discouraged because of the insidiousness of idolatry. Throughout the ages, then, Jerusalem was the approved place of worship, and the Temple was the center of Hebrew religion.

Paul Johnson, in his volume *A History of the Jews*, describes the priestly work in the Herodian temple area in Jerusalem on the occasions of the great feasts:

At such times, the inner Temple was an awesome place—the screams and bellows of terrified cattle, blending with ritual cries and chants and tremendous blasts of horn and trumpet, and blood everywhere… Because of the huge number of animals, the slaughter, bloodying and carving up of the carcasses had to be done quickly; and to get rid of the copious quantities of blood, the platform was not solid but hollow, a gigantic cleansing system. It contained thirty-four cisterns, the largest, or Great Sea, holding over two million gallons…Innumerable pipes conveyed the water up to the platform surface, and a multitude of drains carried off the torrents of blood.[2]

All that Johnson describes dramatically came to a halt when the Roman general Titus entered Jerusalem and turned the city into a place of desolation. With the destruction of the Temple, there was no more centralized worship, and the entire priesthood became defunct. For those Jews who accepted Yeshuah/Jesus as Messiah and Savior, their approach to God came through His sacrifice for sins. But for the majority of Jews who did not, there was no more offering for sin. Judaism's sacrifices were finished, later to be compensated for by more detailed and structured prayer services.

Forty years previously, Jesus, in lamenting Jerusalem's rejection of His ministry, said, "See, your house is left to you, desolate."[3] His pronouncement was then historically and concretely verified with the devastation of Jerusalem and the Temple by the Roman army. In the wake of this catastrophe, the rabbis deposed the priests, and the ancient Hebrew religion metamorphosed into rabbinical Judaism with synagogues as local centers of worship. Henceforth, the Pharisees' concerns as seen in the New Testament were to be preeminent in Jewish life—the law, its interpretation, and elaboration. In the earliest layer of the Talmud, this is candidly confirmed: "The study of Torah is greater than building the Temple."[4]

Gone was animal sacrifice. The remedy for sin after destruction of the Temple lay with the effort to keep the law as the rabbis provided, defined, and rationalized. Judaism no longer provided sacrifice as atonement for sin. The new and permanent sacrifice for sin was, however, provided through the risen Savior. But only a minority of Jews had accepted Yeshua as the Messiah. For the Jewish establishment and the majority of the people, He was not to be considered. So then, with the destruction of the Temple and the rejection of Jesus, there was no life offered for the sins of the people, no blood shed for their forgiveness.

Consequently, Judaism became a human effort—in St. Paul's terms, "seeking to establish their own [righteousness], they have not submitted to God's righteousness."[5] The rabbis set up their own salvific scheme, presuming that observant Jews could, by their own striving, win the favor of a holy God.

Judaism's provision for sin and guilt is incorporated in the Day of Atonement, Yom Kippur, which today is observed with fasting and prayer, both public and private. In the public service, the *Musaf* (additional) prayer, named "the *avodah*," recounts the ancient sacrificial ceremonies. For Orthodox Jews, studying the ancient Temple ritual on Yom Kippur is considered an obligation. Prayers of lamentation are prayed about the absence of the Temple, petitioning its restoration. In many synagogues of strict observance, a detailed description of the Temple ritual is publicly recited in the service. Still, at the end of the day, the observant Jew considers himself or herself to be absolved from sin. No substitute and no shedding of blood is required. The seriousness of sin before God is thereby minimized.

THE TALMUD—RELIGIOUS PRESUMPTION
What followed the change from a live offering for sin to the reading of prayers in the liturgy was the development of a "do-it-yourself salvation,"

a salvation that was really nothing like that set forth in either Torah or the New Testament. Despite the rituals and liturgy of Yom Kippur, the biblical concept of sin as having fallen from God's favor was diluted and with it the concept of redemption. That drastic change in Jewish religion left little to say about the critical nature of mortal man/woman's relationship to God--God most holy, most righteous and most glorious in whose awesome presence Isaiah cried out in the temple, "Woe is me, I am lost..." (Isaiah 6:5) Emphasis then came to be placed on moral prescriptions derived from a massive literary structure pertaining to every detailed aspect of earthly life.

The law became the central focus—no, not just the law, but the human effort exerted to interpret and elaborate on that law and then conform to it. Thus, *rabbinic* law became the center of Judaism, and that law evolved into the Talmud (in Hebrew, *talmudh* means "instruction"). The Talmud itself was followed by commentaries and supercommentaries. The authority for faithful living lay in the rabbis and their *yeshivas* (academies). The study of the law became the virtue of all virtues and was reinforced by the disciplines gleaned from it. Thus, the *mezuzah* (a parchment scroll inscribed with DeVarim/Deuteronomy 6:4–9, 11:13–21 and the name "Shaddai" enclosed within a small casing) attached to door posts and the phylacteries worn on the arm and head were reminders of the greatest commandments. The rabbis were bold to declare, "Whoever has phylacteries on his head and arm, the fringe on his garment and the mezuzah on his door may be presumed to be safe from committing sin."[6]

Such legalism did not have its beginnings after the destruction of Herod's Temple but hundreds of years earlier, following the destruction of the Temple of Solomon.

Milton Viorst, noted Jewish journalist and author who has written for major publications such as the *New York Times*, *Washington Post*, and *Foreign Affairs*, elaborates:

The sages were not casual about rewriting the Torah. But like jurists throughout history, they shaped their reasoning to accommodate the desired outcome. Depending on one's viewpoint, the outcome may be applauded or deplored, but there is no doubting the willingness of the Talmudic scholars to override the Torah itself to accommodate changes in the condition or values of the society.

The Talmud explicitly recognizes the principle of rabbi-made law. Such law is designated *derabban,* and though it is lower in the legal hierarchy than Torah-based law, called *de-oraita*, both are considered valid....

But the sages also pronounced laws for which they claimed no Torah source at all. Often they imparted the force of law to existing custom, even when it contradicted Torah commands.[7]

It is certainly true that the central position and intensive study of the Talmud was a key factor in providing a sense of unity to the Jewish people in their dispersion. This was a unity, however, that was far too removed from the Torah and was constructed from analytic human reasonings with little to do with God's glory, righteousness, and gracious mercy.

Nothing extraneous was to be added to the Torah, as Moses himself instructed:

You must neither add anything to what I command you nor take away anything from it, but keep the commandments of the Lord your God with which I am charging you. (Sefer Devarim /Deuteronomy 4:2)

Rabbi Ben Zion Bokser, a renowned twentieth-century New York rabbi and Columbia University PhD, echoes Viorst in his earlier book, *The Talmud as Literature.* He states that though the Talmud originated as a commentary on the Torah, it became "an original new creation, a means by which the voices of a new age speak out in their discoveries of new truth." Thus, the rabbis "did not limit themselves to interpretations. At times they promulgated new enactments." He later quotes the famous Talmudist Rabbi Jannai: "If the Torah had been given in fixed and immutable formulations, it could not have endured." Then the rabbi says the Lord Himself said, "'There are no pre-existent final truths in doctrine or law; the truth is the considered judgment of the majority of authoritative interpreters in every generation.'"[8] This astonishing statement, put in the mouth of the Lord, places immense spiritual authority in the rabbis.

The sages who probed the law and elaborated on it gained prestige for their efforts. They were highly revered. They founded *yeshivas*, and Babylon emerged by the third century as the center of Jewish learning. These centers produced scholars willing to spend their lives on the minutiae of law concerning ethics, morals, piety, Sabbath laws, and kosher laws. Viorst says that the Talmud "reflects the habits, customs, beliefs and even superstitions of the Jews of its time," containing "biblical commentary, popular proverbs and fables, accounts of traditions and manners, narrative of folklore and moral maxims."[9]

The earlier rabbis, in the few centuries before and after Christ, prohibited the legal discussions of the growing Talmud from being written down, reserving that privilege only for the Torah itself. This meant that this vast literature had to be memorized! However, this came to an end during a time of persecution when fear arose that this literature would be lost to successive generations. The Babylonian Talmud was concluded in the fifth century and soon thereafter recorded on the printed page. This was not a fixed body of law but a protocol of the debate preceding every rabbinical decision: the rejected opinions, conflicting viewpoints, propositions of smaller parts of the main question, and scriptural support—all included in the written law of the Talmud. It consisted of what is called even today "*halakhah*," literally meaning "the way" and, for all practical purposes, meaning "the way to behave."

The development of Judaism and its vast legal literature following the destruction of the Temple and the rejection of the Messiahship of Jesus produced in Jewish people a great dependence on the law and its codification. The Torah and the Talmud became Judaism's center, and they remain so. As the great Jewish rabbi and philosopher Moses Maimonides, in the twelfth century, so emphatically exhorted, "All Israel is obliged to follow the matters in the Babylonian Talmud. Every city and every province are to be coerced to follow all the customs which the sages of the Talmud followed and to obey their decisions and follow their enactments."[10] His sense of indisputable authority led him to add another 120 rules to what became known as "The Halacha"—the part of the Talmud dealing with legal matters.[11]

This expansion of authoritative material, sanctioned and canonized by the rabbis, takes the focus off the biblical material, and in so doing, the idea and force of divine revelation is diminished. The authority of the Talmud is based on a communal tradition that, while tipping its hat to divine revelation (the revealed word of God), is supported mostly by rabbinic authority. By contrast, in The Tenakh, God the Lord speaks and His word generates a critical moment in history. The word of mortals cannot compare.

Rabbinic thought makes human reasoning prominent. This is illustrated by the Talmudic glorification of the patriarch Abraham and his powers of spiritual reasoning. The biblical version of God's election is this: hearing the call of God and responding in faith, Abraham became the father of the nation and the friend of God. ("Abraham, my friend" [Isaiah 41:8].)

Abraham was not a philosopher and did not come to his relationship with God through the powers of his own reasoning. Yet, as I understand it, this is exactly what is suggested by the rabbis' unbiblical claim promoted in some Jewish teaching. In fact, the Talmud so contends: Abraham knew and practiced the Mosaic law *in his own time* (before Moses was born!). Abraham kept all 613 commandments of the written law.

Oral law codifies the Torah, attempts to explain it, and is supplemented by the mass of interpretations from rabbis of succeeding generations. In written form it constitutes the Talmud. And amazingly, it is a fundamental teaching of at least many Orthodox rabbis that the Oral Torah (coming over a period of centuries much later) was originally transmitted from HaShem to Moses on Mount Sinai.

This brings us to the point of Yeshua's criticism of first-century Judaism: "You abandon the commandment of God and hold to human tradition"[12]—especially targeting the system of kosher foods, ceremonial washing, and Sabbath codes. He heaped scorn on tricky and esoteric religious law that obscures basic love of God and neighbor. He accused the rigorists of a hypocrisy that nurtured contempt for other classes of people while they simultaneously carried out exacting procedures for handwashing[13] and tithing every single herb plucked from their gardens.

Thus, the religion of the Jewish establishment lost the focus on divine revelation, replacing it with its own rabbinic teachings, which offered no redemptive sacrifice for sin. As a result, the Jewish world has a meager knowledge of its own Bible—the Tanakh. Proportionately speaking, few of them own and read the Bible as do Christians. Having relegated the Tenakh to a minor positon in Jewish life, it is the Talmud itself that has contributed so very much to Jewish unbelief.

MITZVOTH

Important religious obligations called *mitzvoth* (plural) are deemed to be both laws and commandments. They constitute moral prescriptions that bring one closer to God, cementing the covenant relationship with Him. All told, there are 613 mitzvoth. They were given to Moses at Sinai along with the Ten Commandments. So to the Orthodox Jew, keeping *Shabbat* (Sabbath laws) and *kashrut* (dietary regulations), for example, are acts that manifest their living faith. Also part of that living faith are *middot* (the forty-eight Jewish virtues) and *chesed* (loving kindness), the dictums to perform acts that assist other people. Mitzvoth, then, are a combination of mandatory and voluntary actions.

The rewards for mitzvoth are received both in this life and the world to come. The performers of mitzvoth will receive honor in this life known as *kavod* (Hebrew for "honorary deference"). If one desires to add merits for the next life, the recording angel is present to mark as credit the goods and services one voluntarily offers to others. Judaism states that crucial to your well-being in this life and the next is the number and value of the mitzvoth with which you are credited. If a Jewish person acts charitably to you, you might say, "May this rise up to meet you," thereby wishing heavenly credit for them. (It is noteworthy that the highest form of kindnesses or charitable acts in Judaism are those that are performed anonymously—evidence that the doing or the giving was for its own sake and not for earthly recognition.)

The rabbis of the Talmud came to believe that the destruction of the Temple, the scattering of the Jews following the Roman victory in AD 70, and the subsequent battle of AD 135—which once again resulted in the scattering of the Jews to other cities in Judea and other countries—were God-given punishments. The rabbis believed these tribulations to be the result of the Chosen People's failure to be true to their faith and give obedience to the commandments of the Torah. I believe that most Orthodox rabbis would agree that Judaism has been in a perpetual state of crisis since those events of the first and second centuries. And further, they would agree that because of the unfaithfulness of their people—from the receipt of the law at Sinai all the way through to the destruction of the Temple—they are now in a period of repairing damage they caused when they were in a state of willful rebellion. Thus, they remain in a period of restoring what was given at Sinai, and they now await the coming of the Messiah, when all Jews will return to the land, the kingdom will be reestablished, the redemption of the world will come to pass, and their sufferings will finally end.[14]

Yes, the covenant solemnized on Mount Sinai was broken by their rebellion. They acknowledge that. But it is renewed at the birth of every infant Jewish boy, when, on the eighth day following birth, the infant is circumcised in the tradition of Abraham. The ritual is designated "*brit mila*"—covenant by circumcision—whereby the male child is dedicated to Torah.

> In their daily prayers…the Jews respectfully and repeatedly remind God of the pact, of their efforts to fulfill it, and of their consequent claims upon Him. 'We are Thy people, the children of Thy covenant…Have mercy upon us for the sake of Thy covenant…remember unto us the covenant of our fathers, and the testimony we bear every day that the Lord is One. Look upon our afflictions, for many are our griefs and the sorrows of our hearth. Have pity upon us, Oh Lord, in the land of our captivity, and pour not out thy wrath upon us for we are thy people, the children of the covenant!'[15]

Concerned that the commandments might not be completely understood—that inadvertently, they might transgress and bring punishment on themselves and the community—the sages carefully worked to clarify the statutes. In addition, they constructed a "fence" around the original law, meaning supplementary regulations and prohibitions that would insure against violation of the biblical commandments. In time, these additional "fence" regulations became as binding as the original laws and were made part of the whole.[16] Not only that, but for observant Jews, all this came to be included under the title of the "Torah."

The actual physical volume of the Torah became so sacred that it was treated as a living body. It took the honored place in the synagogue and was housed in specially constructed casings and presented from the east wall of the synagogue, as it still is today. In case of fire, the men will rush to save the Torah, it being the most important thing to preserve. In some places, if it is stolen, desecrated, or mishandled by profane hands, it would be mourned and memorialized. In Jewish community celebrations, it was treated with affection and sometimes "embraced and whirled as a partner in the dance" on certain festivals and holidays.[17]

The Talmud is timeless literature, having no dates on its entries. It is also without location, as there are no differences between the entries made in Europe or in China. The same Torah and the same Talmud are being studied in every place. Discussions on laws take place concerning actions no longer being performed. Case in point: "The discussion between two Talmudists of the second century about which parts of a sacrificed lamb should go to the High Priest in the Temple have not lost their actuality even though the Temple, the sacrifices, the Priest no longer exist...To the true Talmudic scholar, it must be remembered, such a problem as correct carving of the sacrificial lamb is no abstraction but a concrete situation that has occurred and may occur again when the Temple is rebuilt."[18]

This conviction is ingrained into the strict adherent of Judaism: all issues of life, including the smallest, most insignificant ones, have answers in the Torah. Not only that, but every issue has deeper meanings than the apparent ones, and even the most humble or young student of the Torah can probe into those meanings.

This is Judaism. A concentrated effort is made in order to fulfill the law given at Sinai, aided by all its interpretations and ramifications. This constitutes a reliance on the human mortal's ability to discern the will of God and become righteous in His sight by one's own efforts. Rabbi Ariel says, "Whereas Christianity sometimes teaches that salvation is achieved through faith, Judaism believes that everything depends on our actions—the performance of the mitzvoth."[19] The Rabbi makes this statement because there is, in present-day Judaism, no mediator and no sacrifice—neither altar nor savior.

Mitzvoth vs. Faith

Very briefly, let me present what is the way of faith—what Rabbi Ariel says Christianity sometimes teaches. It is indeed the way of authentic Christianity—always. The precedent to this way of faith is the way that Abraham, the father of the Hebrew people, responded to God, the way he became "right with God"—the way that provided him life and meaning. In the Genesis story, this remarkable faith statement is made: "And he believed the Lord; and the Lord reckoned it to him as righteousness" (Bereshit/Genesis 15:6). "The Lord reckoned..." Would anyone not inspired claim to know something of divine reckoning (the mind of God)? It stands as a most astounding assertion! Abraham's God experience was based on his faith! It was not based on Abraham's adherence to the law, because Abraham lived long before the law was given. This statement in Genesis concerning God's reckoning was used by the Apostle Paul in his declaration of the Gospel (Romans 4). Once more: "And he believed the Lord; and the Lord reckoned it to him as righteousness."

This is Torah!

This point means that faith in God—and by extension, for Christianity, faith in Yeshua—is not merely received and recited as an article of a creed; *it is a life-changing act of trust, of genuine believing*, that puts human mortals into a valid relationship with God and yields the fruits of righteousness.

The Apostle Paul, having himself been a Pharisee, knew the plan of Judaism. He had tried to live it. But because of his encounter with the living Christ, he came to know the futility of attempting to satisfy divine holiness through human effort. He came to know also that the law is good but that the human effort to keep it is impossible. He declared to the church at Rome, constituting both Jewish Christians and Gentiles, "For there is no distinction, since all have sinned and fall short of the glory of God; they are now justified by His grace as a gift, through the redemption that is in Christ Jesus, whom God put forward as a sacrifice of atonement by his blood, effective through faith" (Romans 3:22b–25a). Then, turning to the example of Abraham, Paul points out that righteousness (justification) was reckoned to him not after being circumcised but rather before. "The purpose was to make him the ancestor of all who believe without being circumcised and who thus have righteousness reckoned to them" (Romans 4:11b).

And so I have reached behind and ahead at the same time to show the contrast between these two ways.to righteousness. In the following chapter, we will continue to look at the crisis of Judaism, this time in its modern expression.

1. Karl Barth, *Church Dogmatics* IV, part 3, 2 (Edinburgh: T and T Clark, 1957), 877.
2. Paul Johnson, *The History of the Jews* (New York: Harper Perennial, 1988), 116–117.
3. Matthew 23:38.
4. Rabbi Ben Zion Bokser, *The Wisdom of the Talmud* (New York: Philosophical Library, 1951), xvi.
5. Romans 10:3.
6. Rabbi Ben Zion Bokser, *The Wisdom*, 98.
      Bokser quotes from Menahot 43b in the Talmud.
7. Milton Viorst, *What Shall I Do with This People?* (New York: The Free Press, 2002), 103, 104.
8. Rabbi Ben Zion Bokser, *The Wisdom*, 6, 7.
9. Milton Viorst, *What Shall*, 100.
10. Ibid., 102.
11. The other part is known as "the Aggadah," which is commentary (or *midrash*), stories, folklore, and legends.
12. Mark 7:8.

13. William Barclay, *The Gospel of Mark* (Philadelphia: Westminster, 1975), 164, 165. "The hands, to begin with, had to be free of any coating of sand or mortar or gravel or any such substance. The water for washing had to be kept in special large stone jars, so that it itself was clean in the ceremonial sense and so that it might be certain that it had been used for no other purpose, and that nothing had fallen into it or had been mixed with it. First, the hands were held with finger tips *pointing upwards*; water was poured over them and had to run at least down to the wrist; the minimum amount of water was one quarter of a log, which is equal to one and a half egg-shells full of water. While the hands were still wet each hand had to be cleansed with the fist of the other...This meant that at this stage the hands were wet with water; but that water was now unclean because it had touched unclean hands. So, next, the hands had to be held with finger tips pointing downwards and water had to be poured over them in such a way that it began at the wrists and ran off at the finger tips. After all that had been done the hands were clean. To fail to do this was in Jewish eyes, not to be guilty of bad manners, not to be dirty in the health sense, but to be unclean in the sight of God."

The Christian reader will be aware that this mind-set is the very one that Jesus addressed in confrontations with Pharisees, priests, and scribes. "You strain out a gnat but swallow a camel!" (Matthew 24) "You abandon the commandment of God and hold to human tradition." (Mark 7:8) He heaped scorn on tricky and esoteric religious law that obscures basic love of God and neighbor. He accused them of the hypocrisy that nurtured a contempt for other classes of people while carrying out correct hand washings with absolute correct procedure and tithing every single herb that came from the garden.

14. David Hazony, Yoram Hazony, and Michael Oren, *New Essays on Zionism* (Jerusalem and New York: Shalem Press, 2006), 309.

15. Zborowski and Herzog, *Life Is With People: The Culture of the Shtetl* (New York: Schocken Books, 1952), 106–107.

16. Ibid., 108.

17. Ibid., 111.
18. Ibid., 118.
19. David S. Ariel, *What Do Jews Believe?* (New York: Schocken Books, 1995), 159.

CHAPTER 11

The Crisis of Judaism, Part II

§

They had no faith in God,
And did not trust his saving power…
Their heart was not steadfast toward him;
They were not true to his covenant.

—PSALMS 78:22, 37

Non-Orthodox Judaism is simply disappearing in America. Judaism
has long been a predominantly content-driven, rather than a faith-
driven enterprise, but we now have a generation of Jews secularly
successful and well-educated, but so Jewishly illiterate that nothing
remains to bind them to their community or even to a sense
that they hail from something worth preserving. By abandoning
a commitment to Jewish substance, American Jewish leaders
destroyed the very enterprise they claimed to be preserving.

—RABBI DANIEL GORDIS, COMMENTING ON THE PEW RESEARCH
CENTER'S "A PORTRAIT OF JEWISH AMERICANS" (2013)[1]

THE ENLIGHTENMENT AND THE EMANCIPATION

WITH THE ONSET OF THE Enlightenment in seventeenth- and eighteenth-
century Europe, the movement toward emancipation emerged, pressing for

individual freedom and the questioning of authority. This permeated the life of those in the Jewish *kehillot* (communities) in that rabbinical dominance in Jewish communities receded, and in its wake came the distinctively Jewish Enlightenment bearing the name *Haskalah*, the Hebrew term for "enlightenment." (The literal meaning is "reason" or "intellect.")

In summary, a new form of Judaism emerged out of the loss of the sacrificial system in the first century, leaving the Jewish people bereft of a system of divine redemption. In the process, the foundation of biblical authority was lost and replaced with a fixation on Talmudic legalism. This authority, controlled by the rabbis, cemented the unity of the Jewish communities in the Diaspora. Later, with the onset of the Enlightenment, Judaism lost that element of authority. Many Jews were then able to leave the kehillot and enjoy being accepted as common citizens. It was at this point that they became subject to the laws of the nation. As this occurred, the rabbis lost their control, since the laws of the nation were enforceable and, accordingly, took precedence. Since the great majority of Jews no longer cared about excommunication, rabbinic control waned. Those rabbis and congregations for whom the whole Talmud and rabinnic law still mattered began to be identified by the term "Orthodox." The Orthodox rabbis were left to preserve and enforce the legal codes that had accumulated and evolved over the preceding seventeen hundred years.

The rest of Jewry became linked to new types of more liberal and watered-down religion. Many left the Jewish faith altogether. Some of these individuals fiercely attacked traditional Judaism and adopted dogmas of radical political philosophies of the nineteenth century, such as Socialism and Communism. Some in Europe simply became enamored with the major tenets of the French Enlightenment, those being the following:

1. Man is not natively depraved.
2. The end of life is life itself, the good life on earth, instead of the beatific life after death.

3. Man is capable, guided solely by the life of reason and experience, of perfecting the good life on earth.
4. The first and essential condition of the good life on earth is the freeing of men's minds from the bonds of ignorance and of their bodies from the arbitrary oppression of the constituted social authorities.[2]

By the latter part of the nineteenth century, a great portion of European Jewry came to see themselves as having cast off the yoke of Torah. In their way of thinking, there was no more need for divine redemption or for faith in divine revelation to impart to mortals the great stories of salvation history. They celebrated their freedom—political and religious. They delighted in the increased social integration accorded to them. The nations of Europe had finally given them the rights every other citizen had, and they relished the tolerance shown and freedom offered. Such is understandable, but it left them with no internal direction. Living without the Torah for their guides and so with little comprehension of the covenant of Abraham and the Laws of Sinai left them without a foundation for their existence.

Because they rejected their moorings, their numbers diminished. They had no anchor. By the 1930s the Jewish population in Europe was in rapid decline. Mixed marriages and, in most of the major Jewish communities of Europe, an extraordinarily low birthrate were contributing factors. But behind these obvious phenomena were the prime movers of assimilation to Gentile culture and the weakening hold of the Judaic religion. Sociologist Arthur Ruppin reported in 1936 that "Vienna Jewry is moving towards extinction" and wrote of Central European Jews that "the Jews in these countries are tending to 'race suicide.'"[3]

FRAGMENTATION: ORTHODOX, CONSERVATIVE, REFORM
Not all Jews in the West who basked in the freedom of the Enlightenment became irreligious. Some converted to Christianity. In addition, a new branch of Judaism was formulated to adapt to "progressive" ways of thinking

informed by the Enlightenment. The movement of *Haskalah* adopted the liberated and rational thought of Europe and advocated integrating Judaism into it. Learning the Hebrew language was part of this. The Bible and the Talmud were taught as well but with a different slant: they were read as literature, as expressions of their own time rather than as authoritative revelation. The Haskalah Jews wanted to retain their Jewish identity while escaping rabbinic dominance. In the early nineteenth century, this led them to organize under the designation of Reform Judaism (with "reform" being, for them, both verb and adjective). The progressive Reform rabbis wanted to reformulate Judaism by casting aside what they viewed as the chaff of old nonessentials and then melding the insights of the modern world into this ancient religion to make it more "realistic and relevant." They hoped that one outcome of this process would be making Jewish people more acceptable to educated Gentile society.

Paul Johnson, in his *History of the Jews*, says, "Reform Judaism was animated less by overwhelming conviction than by social tidy-mindedness and the desire to be more genteel. Its spirit was not religious but secular... [It] was, in the first place an attempt to remove the taint of ridicule from Jewish forms of worship...a sensitivity stemming from the frequent curiosity-visits of Christians to Jewish synagogues."[4] Liturgical elements in the service were dropped, substituted with Christian church-style forms, such as the sermon. Mentions of the coming of the Messiah and the longing for a return to Zion were embarrassing to many Progressive Jews, so references to these doctrines were omitted, according to Johnson's sources.

To the rabbis who retained their Orthodoxy, these changes were the same as denouncing Judaism itself. Their core beliefs had held firm since the destruction of the Temple in AD 70, and they were not going to cede anything. Even many in the Reform movement were discomfited by the rejection of so many teachings and observances. Too much was being given up with a mind to conform to rationalism. So in the mid nineteenth century, there was a further rupture in Judaism: the Conservative movement was born. This group had been uncomfortable with both the Orthodox and Reform branches, so this branch staked out the middle ground for itself and grew rapidly in Europe and America. It retains much of the traditional liturgy and observances but includes English-language prayers and relaxes adherence to the laws of Orthodoxy.

In the meantime, Orthodoxy and ultra-Orthodoxy continue on in their unremitting analysis, and their adherents spend their lives studying some subjects that, for centuries, have had no connection with authentic modern living. They live on both in Israel and the Diaspora. The religious rigor of followers of this variety of religion have turned out layer upon layer of interpretations and commentaries—they've added volumes upon volumes to the already massive body of literature, attempting to probe every contingency of Jewish life to show that rabbinic law has the answer, often generating tricky, convoluted thinking that results in multiple answers, some patently contradictory.[5]

In the previous chapter, introduction was given to *halakhah*—the code of complicated laws, intricate interpretations, and many observances. Everything one does from the moment of awaking to the time of retiring at night is thus governed, including which shoe—left or right—should have its laces tied first. Shabbat (Sabbath) laws are spelled out to the letter so that, for instance, these observant Jews will not handle money, listen to the radio, answer the phone, or use electrical appliances on Shabbat. There is at least one elevator in every multistory building in Jerusalem that was designed to stop at every floor, taking away the need to press buttons on Shabbat. Such a rigid set of rituals covers every aspect of life and often obscures any distinction between greater and lesser rules.

The division into these three branches has provoked bitter debates up to the present. The Orthodox are contemptuous of the modernizing efforts of the other two, the Conservatives seek their desired balance between the other two, and the Reform branch believes that survival depends on accommodation and adaptation. All three have a nearly equal number of synagogues throughout the United States, though the Orthodox lag behind in membership. In Israel the Reform branch is almost nonexistent, while the Orthodox and ultra-Orthodox have great political influence.

The Crisis of Modern Judaism: Jewish Analysts

In the twentieth century, all three branches finessed their viewpoints—Orthodoxy strived to lighten the yoke of the law, while Conservative and Reform branches became, respectively, more traditional and more modern. The Reform branch became thoroughly modern and hardly distinguishable from the Unitarian Church, which stands on no faith positions. One Jewish writer observed in 1952, "It used to be fashionable for the Reform Jews to apologize for God or for a belief in Him. Our own age has taught us a great deal about the shallow rationalism that sometimes left its imprint on religious thought. No longer does any Reform Jew advocate a godless Judaism."[6] Yet in *The Congress Weekly* in 1951, Leslie A. Fiedler wrote, "Like the more debased Protestant Churches, the Temples have tended to substitute 'social service' for religion, felt to belong to the unenlightened past. These conditions do not prevail universally, of course, but in general American Judaism has made everything its centre but God."[7]

In reviewing the book *Basic Judaism*, published in the 1948, Irving Kristol, prominent Jewish social and political commentator, stated, "A great portion of the rabbinate in the American Jewish community as well as the membership has experienced their religion in terms of social (and sociable) principles, the transformation of Messianism into a shallow, if sincere, humanitarianism, plus a thoroughgoing insensitivity to present day spiritual problems."[8] It is not hard to document the fact that after two world wars, most non-Orthodox Jews in the West were stubbornly indifferent to their religious traditions. They had little if any knowledge of biblical or rabbinic teachings. The typical Jew would not speak of himself as an atheist but had no personal experience of dependence on God for aid. No personal prayer. No concept of sin as an inward depravity or even taint. Little appreciation of the ancient Hebrew stories. In 1942 Rabbi Nathan A. Barack declared in *Contemporary Jewish Record* (now *Commentary Magazine*), "I think I do not exaggerate when I say there is nothing in American Jewish literature—and many rabbis have written their autobiographies—that might possibly find a place in any anthology of religious experience...One will find passions engaged by the problems of Zionism, by politics and reform movements, by the conflict of different organizations within Jewish life—but the category of spiritual experience, as ordinarily defined, is absent."[9]

Reform Judaism, from its inception until the middle of the twentieth century, rejected Zionism. Its leaders reacted so strongly to traditional rabbinic Judaism that they showed little concern for their lower-class brothers and sisters of Germany, Eastern Europe, and Russia who were suffering the blows of anti-Semitism. While there were times of liberalization when Jewish life became more secure, those were short-lived. Judeophobia would reappear. In late nineteenth-century Russia, pogroms, which had decreased, then increased after the reign of Alexander II. Jews were gaining cultural status in Germany, but the ones in the lower classes were beset with restrictions and waves of violence while the government looked the other way. In those harassed Jewish communities, the pendulum swung between hope and despair. Yet Reform Judaism, in its more secure settings, rejected any idea of a national home to provide security for their less-fortunate kindred. They had no tolerance for the traditional liturgical emphasis on the Holy Land as being a precious promise and a precious place in the heart. And the story of the biblical Hebrews was doubted as having any real historical basis. Basic elements of Judaism were cast aside as being anachronistic.

In recent years Reform Judaism has followed the predominant thought of liberal Western culture. Jack Wertheimer, professor of American Jewish history at the Jewish Theological Seminary in New York, reporting in the June 2008 issue of *Commentary*, sheds some light on the ethos of Reform Judaism in America:

Their common watchwords are "inclusiveness" and "choice"...The movement incorporated sexual egalitarianism as a cardinal principle...Here the guiding principle has been autonomy and choice. Each individual Jew has the inalienable right to define which aspects of the faith are personally meaningful to him...Only 15 percent of self-identified Reform Jews report any involvement at all in Jewish organizational life...Religious ideology has been replaced by a pragmatic tolerance of pluralism...In 2000, fully 70 percent of Jews saying they were raised Reform were not members of any kind of synagogue, a figure that holds steady across the generational board...[10]

The Reform Jews look here and there. They pick and choose a bit from their tradition and then assess modern culture to see which bits, in the moment, seem to be the desirable norms of decency and correctness. Does the reader believe that this movement is being assessed too severely here, even by its own adherents? We will proceed with other observers.

Leonard Fein, author and professor of political science at Massachusetts Institute of Technology and later Brandeis University, in his book *Where Are We? The Inner Life of America's Jews*, presents a stirring and probing analysis of the Jewish conversation and mind-set in America. The Jews who immigrated to America came because they wanted change of some sort. They were attracted by the open society combined with security. To some, it was also the promise that America gave of freedom from their past—from their Jewishness. Not all were of that mind. Some understood that America was a religious nation and melting pot where they could retain their Judaism and yet be accepted. By dropping this or that part of their tradition, they could easily meld into the American scene. As Fein puts it, "Drop the traditional garb...shift from passion to decorum, focus on the 'Judeo-Christian tradition,' emphasize the brotherhood of man, don't be 'too' Jewish. At one end, the assimilators; at the other, the defenders of the faith; in the vast and disjointed and sometimes disoriented middle, the adapters, a dash of this, a pinch of that, Judaism seasoned to taste."[11]

Fein continues to show the weakening effect that adaptation to American life had on the religion: "We [now] have neither the vocabulary nor the categories for serious conversation, and, besides, we vaguely fear that our expression of interest in such conversation would be taken as evidence that we lack sophistication…So we avoid the subject, which is not hard to do since our friends and neighbors, for the most part, also prefer to avoid it; they are no less intimidated than we by the thought of it."[12]

One facet of this form of Judaism is that it possesses no concept of sin. In 1948, three years following the holocaust, Irving Kristol said, "Judaism, today, and especially liberal Judaism, despite the horrors of modern totalitarianism, seems unable to recognize sin when it sees it. It does see the evil of individual wickedly-minded men (or nations), but it refuses to assign to evil its full and menacing stature."[13] I have found truth in Kristol's observation in conversations with Jewish friends. Not viewing evil as inherent, they seem repulsed by the term *sin*.

Are the modern Reform and Conservative Jews aware of a deficiency in their religious traditions? According to David Klinghoffer, in his article "Anti-Semitism without Anti-Semites" in the April 1998 issue of *First Things*,

We American Jews are not as ignorant as we seem. We know, in our soul, that we have gone astray; but, to borrow a hackneyed phrase of psychological jargon, we are in denial. We have a guilty conscience. We are unhappy about that. What can we do, what defensive strategy can we adopt, to lift the weight of guilt? Fortunately for us, in the 1960s the Cult of Victimhood made its appearance…The Cult of Victimhood performs two valuable services for us Jews with our guilty consciences. First, as it does for everyone else, it assures us that, whatever we know we are doing wrong, we are really angels…. That's quite a relief. But it does something else for us, which it may not do for other groups. We believe that any hostility we can detect on the part of non-Jews is entirely unmerited. We have done nothing to deserve it. God isn't angry with us. And even if He were, He couldn't send dangerous Gentiles against us. Our God is the impotent Harold Kushner.[15] God, if we choose to acknowledge a God at all."[16]

This, then, is what we call here the unbelief of non-Orthodox Judaism. There are degrees and variations in their religiosity, but the lack of substance is telling. Those who reacted to this inanity within Reform Judaism did so by organizing the Conservative movement disdaining the rejection their brothers and sisters had shown to so much of tradition. Their leadership has retained the prescribed liturgy, kept the Hebrew Torah reading, and largely spurned the modern critical view of scripture. From its inception, Zionism has had a firm hold in this Conservative branch of Judaism. Conservative synagogues have supported the immigrants to Palestine and the statehood of Israel with heavy contributions and enthusiastic vocal backing.

In trying to maintain a balance, however, Conservatism has been subject to the charge of being ambivalent on important points. In reacting to Orthodoxy, the Conservative Jews as a whole have not been strict in their observances. Conservative Judaism attracted adherents who didn't want to closely adhere. Because of this, a large gap has appeared between leaders and the membership, the leaders being more conscientious than the majority. Then again, even in the rabbinic leadership, there are some who are more Reformist than Conservative.

Conservative Judaism has produced a body of scholarship and religious literature informed by an admirable attempt to negotiate polarities. "We are the only group," declared Louis Finkelstein, chancellor of the Jewish Theological Seminary (JTS) from 1940 to 1972, "who have a modern mind and a Jewish heart, prophetic passion and Western science." At JTS, Finkelstein famously gathered key exponents of differing—even clashing—schools of thought. He himself, and Talmudists like Louis Ginzberg, represented a traditionalist approach to Jewish law and observance, even as Mordecai Kaplan, perhaps the most radical Jewish religious thinker of his time, sought to persuade rabbinical students of the need to "reconstruct" Judaism thoroughly to suit the American moment.[17]

At the present time, Conservatism, while once a rapidly growing movement, is now losing membership, and the leadership is asking why. As one would suppose, some are advocating a policy of nurturing firm beliefs, while others are seeking to adapt to the modern emphasis on personal autonomy and pluralism. This leaves Conservatism, this middle branch of Judaism, in a state of instability. Again Mr. Wertheimer gives his input:

> It has relied mostly on assertions of what it is not—i.e., it disagrees with the movement on its Right for one reason and the movement on its Left for another—rather than on affirmations of what it is…The prevailing disposition of the movement has been to eliminate discord between culture and Jewish doctrine.[18]

It is safe to say that the majority of the members of Conservative synagogues do not bother themselves too much with these religious issues. Neither do they, according to the above article, adhere nearly as much to tradition as do the few more serious ones within their movement. Dietary and Sabbath laws are not observed by the majority. Frankly, as Wertheimer says, "More than anything else [second-generation Jews in Conservatism] were bound to their synagogue and to each other by the bonds of ethnic solidarity."[19]

Where is the faith? In modern parlance, we use the term *faith* to designate a religion or a branch of one. In that sense, Judaism is one of the world's "faiths." But to use the term *faith* in the biblical sense—from both Old and New Testaments—is to describe an assured confidence in God for His redemption and care. Much of Jewry does not even believe in the veracity of their literature, which offers a documentation of God's saving acts. Arthur Kac observes that "present-day Rabbinic Judaism knows that one of the most important factors in the Jewish religious problem is the loss of faith in the Divine origin of the Law on the part of the vast majority of the Jewish people."[20] Dr. Kac also quotes the "Perplexed Rabbis," an article in *The Jewish Spectator* in 1949: "What is really involved is belief—belief in the Divine origin of the Torah…I have more than twenty years of experience in the practical rabbinate and I have learned that what the average Jew wants is not theorizing and philosophizing but—certainty. If I could really convince my people that God appeared to Moses and gave him the Torah for Israel, I would have no trouble at all turning my congregation into 'shomrey mitzvoth' [observers of the commandments]. But I can't convince them—in fact, I myself am not convinced."[21]

This chapter looks at an empty edifice lacking the furnishings of faith. There is little or no recognized foundation of modern Judaism. Most of the residents are headed out into the culture with little of substance to call their own. "Secular Jewishness" is their name tag for identification in Western society. The sadness of it all is wrenching to those of us who love this people.

To update this analysis of the spiritual crisis in contemporary Judaism, we point to the shocking results of the Pew Research Center's "A Portrait of Jewish Americans," released on October 1, 2013, from which the epigraph at the beginning of this chapter is taken.

Daniel Gordis, well-known author and rabbi who moved from California to Israel, responds to the results with pained words. In the *Jewish Review of Books* he writes,

> Intermarriage rates have climbed from the once-fear-inducing 52 percent of the 1990 National Population Survey to 58 percent among recently married Jews on the whole. (The rate would be about 70 percent if one were to leave out the Orthodox, who very rarely intermarry.) Only 59 percent of American Jews are raising their children as Jews "by religion," and a mere 47 percent of them are giving their children a Jewish education.[22]

In *Commentary* Gordis writes of the Conservative branch:

> Spiritual malnourishment is the malady most afflicting today's liberal Jews. Three generations ago, Conservative Judaism helped traditional Jews make their way into the intellectual world of the West. Today, Jews take that intellectual world for granted. What they have lost are the tools of the spirit—the words and the ways that once sustained and fortified their ancestors.[23]

The Jewish writers quoted here are making their honest appraisal of Judaism's present state of affairs. They are not alone. Historically, many leaders of Judaism have felt and acknowledged the deficiency. The sages of Judaism inserted in their liturgical prayers an acknowledgment of national sins, which they believed resulted in the destruction of the Temple—that event, which destroyed any possibility of the central sacrificial aspect of worship, was in response to the sins of the Jewish people. In the traditional Jewish prayer book, quoted by Arthur Kac, there is the following prayer of confession: "And because of our sins we have been exiled from our country and removed far from our soil, and we are unable to go up and to appear and to worship before Thee in the house of Thy choosing, in the great and holy house which was called by Thy Name, because of the hand which was stretched out [i.e. violence committed] against Thy Sanctuary."[24]

BACK TO THE FIRST CENTURY

So the first- and second-century rabbis didn't fix the problem; they only patched it. And with the onset of the Enlightenment, this became more obvious. Hans Joachim Schoeps, a German Jewish theologian, writing after the Holocaust and the founding of Israel, exposed the rupture that remained:

> We Jews of the mid-20th century live today in what might be called a post-Jewish situation…It is time for us to renounce all fictions of the "as if" kind. We cannot act as if the laws of the Torah still signified

for most of us the rules of conduct; as if fear of God and not self-aggrandizement were the common fact...As the Jews of all previous centuries understood it, the great turning point in Jewish history, the real breach of the historical tradition, was the destruction of the Temple by the Romans under Titus in the year 70 CE...The Temple no longer existed, but Jews the world over bowed in prayer in its direction as if it did. The High Priest no longer made his expiatory sacrifice on the Day of Atonement, but the ritual formula was learned and recited on that day as if he did.[25]

What Rabbi Schoeps is saying is that the Jewish people need to stop living in a "pretend" world—living as if the old system is still in force. And this is why Judaism has been in crisis and remains so today. It has been nearly two thousand years since the great Second Temple was destroyed by the Romans and the sacrificial system was eliminated with it. But in the Jewish religion, it is just as if it happened yesterday. That great crisis remains a crisis. With great emotion, Jesus predicted the time of this great crisis of Israel's faith. Only one generation passed between His prediction and its fulfillment. His words ring throughout history:

> Jerusalem, Jerusalem, the city that kills the prophets and stones those who are sent to it! How often have I desired to gather your children together as a hen gathers her brood under her wings, and you were not willing! *See, your house is left to you, desolate*...His disciples came to point out to him the buildings of the temple. Then he asked them, "You see all these, do you not? Truly I tell you, not one stone will be left here upon another; all will be thrown down." (Matthew 23:37–38; 24:1–2)

The House of Israel—the hugely magnificent temple built by Herod, not yet completely finished until AD 64, and then later desolated—was the center of worship and festivals for the Hebrews of Israel, the Jews of the Diaspora, and many God-fearing Gentiles throughout the Roman world. In it was conducted the most crucial service in the world—reconciliation with the one true God. But after the colossal events of the first century—the appearance, death, and resurrection of Jesus Christ and the destruction of the Temple—Judaism as a religion lost its faith and spiritual power. How could it have been otherwise? It no longer revealed the redemptive work of God. A greater redemptive event had come into the world in Christ, and the Temple was now anachronistic. Throughout this time Judaism has been, as Rabbi Schoepps has said, in an "as if" situation.

Yet in the twenty-first century, in the midst of this unbelief, there is a budding anticipation of spiritual renewal. The very goal of Zionism, in its drive to return to Palestine, was not only the rebuilding of the waste places of Palestine but the remaking of the Jewish character.[26] There are many Jews today who, as they reflect deeply on their history, acknowledge that their very survival in history must be connected to divine providence. That may be as far as their thoughts take them. But in the establishment of the State of Israel and the revival of the Hebrew tongue, there is an intimation of glorious things to come. An Israeli research group reports that a record number of Jews in the State of Israel now profess a belief in God: 80 percent. A growing number believe that Torah is God given, and a modest revival of interest in the Hebrew Bible is reported.[27] Music composed and performed in Israel includes soulful rock, lyrics of prayer, and songs of Zion from the Psalms.[28]

This author was recently surprised when he opened the February 17, 2017 issue of *The International Jerusalem Post* to find an article entitled "Behold the Icon: The Israel Museum puts Jesus in the spotlight, but with a largely local slant, in an exhibition of 150 works by 40 artists, including Reuven Rubin, Marc Chagall and Moshe Castel." Who is put in the spotlight? Yes, Jesus. Yeshua. Dr. Amitai Mendelsohn, senior curator of the David Orgler department of Israeli art commented: "The idea was to take the figure of Jesus as a figure from Jewish art into Israeli art, from the end of the 19th century up to today, through the work of all kinds of artists." Six of these were pictured, including one by Adi Nes with no title but obviously was a portrayal of The Last Supper--Israeli young men seated at a chain of folding tables talking in groups, with the Jesus figure central, looking straight ahead. The ending paragraph of the article sums it up: "The exhibition incorporates an almost bewilderingly expansive array of Jesus-related portrayals and readings across numerous stylistic, genre and cultural divides. It is an enlightening and, aesthetically, richly reward experience." [29]

This represents a change. Classic Zionism has been fervently secular until recently. That hardness is beginning to soften. Into the spiritual vacuum, there is renewed interest here and there in more than vain things. There are some who are being attracted to the holy. It could be that a continuing distaste for the extremes of Talmudic law will manifest itself in an intense focus on scripture and its concentration on the glory of God.

So great is the spiritual vacuum in modern Jewry—it is to be feared that many of them might be deceived by a charismatic politico-religious demagogue. If such a one could bring Israel's enemies to their knees, he might govern uncontested. But I and many others long for Israel to become a people constrained by righteousness and filled with wisdom—a people who will choose spiritually aware leaders of integrity and, most importantly, look with expectation to the glorious appearance of the true Messiah.

In concluding this treatment of historic and contemporary Judaism, it would be helpful to return to the outlook of the Pharisee turned apostle of Christ. In discussing the Jewish people and their position in salvation history, Paul asked, "Have they stumbled so as to fall? By no means. But through their stumbling, salvation has come to the Gentiles, so as to make Israel jealous" (Romans 11:11). Their true identity continues as a sign of divine sovereignty in history. Look at this people and ponder. Again, the Apostle Paul said, "They were broken off because of their *unbelief*...but stand in awe" (Romans

11:20). We are invited to humbly watch and see what wonders God performs in and through His chosen ones.

§

1. Daniel Gordis, "Conservative Judaism: A Requiem," *Jewish Review of Books*, Winter 2014, 9–11.

2. Louis Greenberg, *The Jews in Russia* (New York: Schocken Books, 1976), 12.

   Greenberg quotes Carl L. Becker, *The Heavenly City of the Eighteenth Century Philosophers*, 102–108.

3. Bernard Wasserstein, *On The Eve: The Jews of Europe before the Second World War* (New York: Simon and Schuster, 2012), 13.

4. Paul Johnson, *A History of the Jews* (Harper Perennial, 1987), 333.

5. Frederick Dale Bruner, *The Churchbook: Matthew 13–28* (Grand Rapids: Wm. B. Eerdmans Publishing Co., 2004), 446.

   "In all false and cultic religion it is characteristic to teach that expertise in, and 'knowing' about, a thousand and one details about a thousand and one 'deep' truths of God is the knowledge of God. This is the error of all gnosticism (literally, 'knowing-ism'), which believes and teaches that *knowing* arcane facts about God's truth is equivalent to true religion and superior to simple love of God and neighbor."

6. Arthur Kac, *The Rebirth of the State of Israel* (Chicago: Moody Press, 1958), 101.

   Kac quotes Felix A. Levy, "Reform Judaism in America: Its Problems and Tasks," *Judaism* (New York), October 1952.

7. Ibid., 106.

8. Ibid., 96.

9. Ibid., 106.

10. Jack Wertheimer, "What Does Reform Judaism Stand For?" *Commentary*, June 2008.

11. Leonard Fein, *Where Are We? The Inner Life of America's Jews* (New York: Harper and Row, 1988), 7, 8.

12. Ibid., 25.
13. Arthur Kac, *The Rebirth*, 105.
14. Harold Kushner, author of *When Bad Things Happen to Good People*, is aligned with the Conservative wing of Judaism but is considered a "Progressive" in that branch.
15. David Klinghoffer, "Anti-Semitism without Anti-Semites," *First Things*, April 1998, 12, 13.
16. Ibid., 12, 13.
17. Jack Wertheimer, "The Perplexities of Conservative Judaism," *Commentary*, September 2007, 40.
18. Ibid., 43–44.
19. Ibid., 40.
20. Arthur Kac, *The Rebirth*, 144.
21. Arthur Kac, *The Rebirth*, 144. (Kac quotes T. W. Rosmarin, "Perplexed Rabbis," *The Jewish Spectator*, July–August 1949.)
22. Daniel Gordis, "Conservative Judaism: A Requiem," *Jewish Review of Books*, Winter 2014, 9–11.
23. Daniel Gordis, "Conservative Observance, Then and Now," *Commentary*, March 2014, 26–30.
24. Arthur Kac, *The Rebirth*, 146.
25. Hans Joachim Schoeps, "How Live by Jewish Law Today? A Proposal for Those Who Have Fallen Away," *Commentary*, January 1953.
26. Arthur Kac, *The Rebirth*, 166–168.
27. Nir Hasson, "Survey: Record Number of Israeli Jews Believe in God," January 27, 2012, Haaretz.com., www.haaretz.com/jewish/survey-record-number-of-israeli-jews-believe-in-god-1,409386.

   "Fully 80 percent of Israeli Jews believe that God exists—the highest figure found by the Guttman-Avi Chai survey since this review of Israeli-Jewish beliefs began two decades ago. The latest survey of the 'Beliefs, Observance and Values among Israeli Jews' was conducted in 2009...The two previous surveys were in 1999 and 1991. The study also found that 70 percent of the respondents believe the Jews are the 'Chosen People,' 65 percent believe the Torah and mitzvoth (religious commandments) are God-given, and 56 percent believe in life after death. Overall, the survey found an increase in attachment to Jewish religion and tradition from 1999 to 2009, following a decrease from 1991 to 1999, which was the decade of mass immigration from the former Soviet Union…It found that only 46 percent of Israeli Jews now define themselves as secular, down from 52 percent in 1999, while 22 percent define themselves as either Orthodox or ultra-Orthodox, up from 16 percent in 1999. The remaining 32 percent term themselves traditional, virtually unchanged from 1999…The study also found an upswing in religious practice. For instance, 85 percent of respondents said that 'celebrating the Jewish holidays as prescribed by religious tradition' was 'important' or 'very important,' up from 63 percent in 1999, while 70 percent said they 'always' or 'frequently' refrained from eating hametz (leavened bread) on Passover, up from 67 percent in 1999. Fully 61 percent of respondents said the state should 'ensure that public life is conducted according to Jewish religious tradition,' up dramatically from 44 percent in 1991. But respondents also insisted on preserving their freedom of choice. For instance, between 58 and 68 percent said that shopping centers, public transportation, sporting events, cafes, restaurants and movie theaters should be allowed to operate on Shabbat (exact figures ranged from 58 percent for shopping centers to 68 percent for cafes, restaurants, and movie theaters.)"

28. Yossi Klein Halevi, "Israel's New Spiritual Sound," *The Wall Street Journal*, June 13–14, 2015, C3., www.wsj.com/articles/israeli-rock-musics-spiritual-new-sound-1434122493.

29. Barry Davis, "Behold the Icon," *The International Jerusalem Post*, February 17-23, 2017, 22-23.

CHAPTER 12
Expectation of the Messiah

§

The days are surely coming, says the Lord, when I will raise up for
David a righteous Branch, and he shall reign as king and deal wisely,
and shall execute justice and righteousness in the land. In his days
Judah will be saved and Israel will live in safety. And this is the
name by which he will be called: "The Lord is our righteousness."

—JEREMIAH 23:5–8

I believe with complete faith in the coming of the Messiah
And, even if he should tarry, yet I will wait for him.

—FROM *ANI MAAMIN* (I BELIEVE); BASED ON
MAIMONIDES'S TWELFTH PRINCIPLE OF BELIEF WITH
VARIOUS MUSICAL SETTINGS, ANCIENT AND MODERN

WHEN MY FATHER AND I were in Jerusalem in 1961, our Israeli guide repeated
to us a saying commonly heard there: "The Messiah won't come, and Ben-
Gurion won't go." The first president of the nation, David Ben-Gurion, was
still in that position after decades of having been the leader of the Yishuv and
the subsequent new State of Israel. Were the Israelis only jesting when speaking about their expectation of the Messiah? In an effort to find the answer to
that very question, I took the opportunity in October 2009, while traveling

the land with my wife, to inquire of various Israelis if they were expecting the Messiah. I asked twelve people—taxi drivers, merchants, waitresses, and waiters—nine of whom said "Yes! They were expecting Him." Some expressed this with obvious hope and conviction. Though this questionnaire was small, it would be no surprise to this writer to find widespread expectation and considerable yearning for His coming among the observant Jews of Israel.

The term *Messiah* denotes a long-awaited savior redeemer destined and anointed to usher in a new and glorious kingdom. The word is derived from the Hebrew word *Mashiach*, meaning "anointed one." Maimonides, the great Jewish philosopher of the twelfth century, whose works are still the most widely used and debated in Judaism, included in his "Thirteen Principles of the Jewish Faith" this brief assertion: "The Mashiach will come." That is the twelfth principle, and the thirteenth principle has the same future, supernatural character: "The dead will be resurrected." This indicates that the coming of the Messiah is a fixture in *traditional* Judaism's outlook on the future.

Just as the Jewish people have prayed so consistently throughout two millennia for their return to the land, so have they prayed and waited for the coming of the Messiah. This anticipation was generated by the Tanakh and, in particular, the prophecies. Interwoven with history in the messages of the prophets are prophecies of the Messianic Age, when the righteous ruler will hold sway as justice, peace, and prosperity prevail. The Tenakh was not the only written source for these hopes. A vast sacred literature between the testaments grew up that elaborated on the messianic promise. Altogether, these writings pointed to the coming of a worldwide moral regeneration and the return of the Jews, en masse, to their land. It is known that the messianic hope became an integral part of Jewish belief, as evidenced by its inclusion in the daily liturgy as one of the Eighteen Benedictions, which date to the third century BC and were redacted during the first century AD. This prophetic piece of literature was the seed from which came hopes and rumors in many forms. Time and again in Jewish history, reports circulated in Jewish communities that the Messiah had appeared. On such occasions, many believers would sell their homes and possessions, awaiting the summons to flee to Palestine. Even when there were no such rumors, still every year, at the conclusion of their Passover feast, Jews would declare, "Next year in Jerusalem." The Messianic hope, which included the restoration of the land. was never, never out of mind. (It is said to this day at the conclusion of every Passover Seder.)

Abraham Joshua Heschel said, "The inner history of Israel is a history of waiting for God, of waiting for His arrival. Just as Israel is certain of the reality of the Promised Land, so she is certain of the coming of 'the promised day.' She lives by a promise of 'the day of the Lord,' a day of judgment followed by redemption, when evil will be consumed and an age of glory will ensue."[1]

In the scenario that Jews throughout the ages have envisioned, there was no question about who would lead that return: it would be the righteous, anointed king of the Davidic line—a heaven-sent prince and deliverer. But alas! The modern ingathering of the Jews to Palestine hasn't happened that way. The Zionist leaders, Herzl and Ben-Gurion, though powerful and charismatic, did not conform to the rabbinic ideal of spiritual redeemer. Consequently, many early twentieth-century rabbis discounted and even denounced Zionism. They charged that Zionism was the creation of intellectuals and secular Jews who, in rebellion, turned their backs on rabbinic Judaism. Therefore, these rabbis vigorously opposed the Zionist movement. They pointed out that the Zionists used the language of Judaism for their own purposes, without retaining its meaning. For example, when Ben-Gurion's socialists referred to the purchase of land from the Arabs, they made use of religious terminology by calling these transactions the "redemption of the land."

It is still the case today that many ultraconservative Jews—even in Israel—while awaiting the Messiah and redemption, believe that the present State of Israel has no connection with the redemption they anticipate. Looking at Zionist leadership and seeing the prevalent secularism in Israel today, they cannot conceive of it being so. Simply because half the world's Jews are now in Israel, should this be seen as the beginning of the Age of

Redemption for Israel and the world? They think not. While most of them may have come to terms with the establishment of the state and its administration, they do not consider it to be legitimate, much less a sign of the redemptive activity of God in their midst. When divine redemption comes, it will not evolve under the guidance of human planning and effort but will come when, as the prophet says, "the Lord whom you seek will suddenly come to his temple" (Malachi 3:1).

Yet there are other Jews who believe we may be seeing the small sprouting of the *beginnings* of redemption and the Messianic Age. In most synagogues in Israel and the Diaspora, there is a prayer for the well-being of the State of Israel called the "*reshit geulatenu*"—the "commencement of our redemption." Here is the first verse: "You, The Divine One, Source of our being, we ask your blessing that the State of Israel might become the beginning of the flowering of our Redemption."

Implicit in that prayer for redemption (with an uppercase *R*) is the expectation that redemption will come with the Messiah. In the order of performing "Service for the Second Day of Rosh Hashanah" from a synagogue in Texas, the following poem was inserted:

It's good to live in Tel Aviv
And there to find a home:
To live and patiently to wait
Till the redeemer come...[2]

Even from halfway around the world in Texas, from where few Jewish people have immigrated to Israel, there is some identification with the residents of the land and a yearning for the Messiah. So there are some observant Jews who believe that the restoration of their land as presently seen *is* the "beginning of the flowering" of redemption. Still there are others, just as pious, who believe that only the Messiah, when He comes, will form a legitimate state and government in the Holy Land.

ORIGINS OF THE EXPECTATION

The origins of the expectation of the Messiah are numerous and come from a variety of literary sources. First, as mentioned above, the well-known suggestions and portrayals of a coming savior redeemer are seen in the Tenakh. There are figures such as the Anointed Conqueror in the line of David, the Servant of the Lord in Isaiah, the Son of Man in Daniel, and the exaltation of royalty in some Psalms and other writings. The line of kings in the history of Israel reigned under the national consciousness of the coming ideal monarch who would be *the one* to be anointed the Messiah-king. It would be like a head of state today realizing that his person and record of governance would be vastly bettered by some great future leader that would make his own legacy seem insignificant.

Secondly, the Jewish Apocrypha, a collection of books of doubtful authenticity written in the time between the creation of the Torah and New Testaments (canonized by the Roman Catholic Church but not the rabbis or the Protestant Reformers), has references to a highly anticipated restoration of a Davidic king and redeemer. II Esdras, which has the most Messianic prophecies, provides this sample:

> As for the lion whom you saw rousing up out of the forest and roaring and speaking to the eagle and reproving him for his unrighteousness, and as for all his words that you have heard, this is the Messiah whom the Most High has kept until the end of days, who will arise from the offspring of David, and will come and speak with them. He will denounce them for their ungodliness and for their wickedness, and will display before them their contemptuous dealings...But in mercy he will set free the remnant of my people, those who have been saved throughout my borders, and he will make them joyful until the end comes." (II Esdras 12:31–35)

Thirdly, the Jewish Pseudepigrapha consists of sacred books that were less highly regarded even than the ones in the Apocrypha, and most of them were written under assumed names. They nevertheless reflect what the Jewish people were thinking in that same time period from around 200 BC to AD 200. Some of these themes find an echo in New Testament writings. Many of these books are legendary and literary expansions of the Five Books of Moses that comprise the Torah, with most having themes based on "end of days" and categorized generally as apocalyptic literature. They are valuable for giving us information about the beliefs and longings of people of that period, even though they are not included in any canon or considered truly inspired.

The First Book of Enoch, the most prominent book of that genre, has this prophecy of the Messiah's coming:

> At that place, I saw the One to whom belongs the time before time. And his head was white like wool…His countenance was full of grace like that of one among the holy angels…Who is this?…And he answered me and said, 'This is the Son of Man, to whom belongs righteousness, and with whom righteousness dwells.'
> (I Enoch 46:1ff)

From that same time period, the Dead Sea Scrolls originate. They include books with some references to a coming Messiah. For example, the Aramaic Apocalypse (4Q246) has this prediction:

> He will be called the Son of God, and they will call him the son of the Most High…His kingdom will be an eternal kingdom…The earth will be in truth and all will make peace. The sword will cease in the earth, and all the cities will pay him homage. He is a great god among the gods…His kingdom will be an eternal kingdom."

Such writers were picking up messianic images from the Tanakh, especially from Isaiah, Ezekiel, Daniel, and Zechariah. In those times of political upheaval and Greek influence in Palestine, such literature took the promises of the prophets and projected their fulfillment into the divinely ordained future—a future that would bring justice, peace, and the triumph of pure Judaism.

Finally, there are the *"targums,"* which are Aramaic-language translations of sections of the Tanakh. Most targums expand the text to include the translator's explanation or interpretation—somewhat like today's paraphrased versions of the scriptures, although some targums are hardly recognizable as a translation of the original Hebrew. Here is an example of a targum from Genesis 49:10–12, where Jacob gives the last word from his deathbed to his sons. First, the Genesis passage with the New Revised Version translation—the word of Jacob concerning his son, Judah, who will carry the chosen seed:

> The scepter shall not depart from Judah,
> Nor the ruler's staff from between his feet,
> Until tribute comes to him*;
> And the obedience of the peoples is his.
> Binding his foal to the vine
> And his donkey's colt to the choice vine,
> He washes his garments in wine
> And his robe in the blood of grapes;
> His eyes are darker than wine,
> And his teeth whiter than milk. (Genesis 49:10–12)
> *or "until Shiloh comes" or "until he comes to Shiloh" or
> "until he comes to whom it belongs."

The Hebrew word *Shiloh,* shown in the Genesis passage with asterisk and alternately translated with the pronoun "he" refers to the Messiah. So said the rabbis in the Talmud. So say many biblical interpreters.

And now, the targum on the above passage:

> Kings shall not cease from the house of Judah, nor scribes who teach
> the Torah from his children's children, until the time of the coming

of King Messiah, to whom belongs the Kingdom, and to whom all dominions of the earth shall become subservient...How beautiful is he, King Messiah, who is destined to arise from the house of Judah... How beautiful to behold are they, the eyes of the King Messiah.[3]

Thus, the targum uses the word *Messiah*, explaining to what "Shiloh" refers. The date of this targum's composition is not known. But what matters is that this targum and many like it reveal the messianic expectation prevalent in the Jewish community in ancient times. We do know that some targums were circulating before the time of Christ, because there were some found among the Dead Sea Scrolls at Qumran.

Many of these targums, having their origins in the Torah, are comparable to *some* Christian interpretations of Tenakh passages. They view the Messiah as one who would call the Chosen People back to their land so that they might cease to wander or experience rejection by Gentile nations. They picture Him as one who would rebuild the Temple and reestablish the Torah as law to govern not only the Jewish people but all the world. Thus, He would establish sovereignty over all the nations.

The prophets foretold the coming of this Anointed One, the rabbis elaborated on the prophecies, and the people awaited his coming. Later, when Jesus Christ was rejected by most of the rabbinic leaders of Judaism, the expectation continued among world Jewry. Consequently, during the few centuries following Christ, when persecution was rampant, some of the Jewish communities were duped by some of their own charismatic leaders; however, most of these had brief careers and did not claim Messiahship. Rabbinic Judaism won the day with the fall of the priesthood, and most Jews were faithful to their rabbinic-based religion and their communal traditions. Still, the prayers and yearnings for the Messiah remained.

During this time, as the Talmud grew, the rabbinic writers were adding their own thoughts about the Messiah to it. In it, one can find all types of

Messianic figures foretold with all kinds of characteristics He would have and missions He would fulfill.

Jewish history abounds in claimants to the position of Messiah, but most were of no consequence. One figure to emerge soon after the time of Christ who arguably did make Messianic claims was Simon Bar Kokhba, who rose to prominence as a leader of the Palestinian Jews in AD 132 and led a second rebellion against the Romans. Evidence indicates that he was considered by many to be the expected one. A Jewish state was formed in defiance of the Roman rule, and the coins of the new nation pictured a star set on the top of a temple. (Herod's Temple had been destroyed by the Romans in AD 70.) The star was a symbol of the Messiah, and the rebuilding of a temple was thought to be one feature of his rule. Two years later the outlawed state came to naught when the Romans wrought devastation on Judea, exacting a horrible price by slaughtering hundreds of thousands while others died from starvation and fire.

This was to be the last of the serious pretenders to the position of Messiah for a millennium or more. After Bar Kokhba, the rabbis cautioned the Jewish communities about being taken in by would-be Messiahs. They urged patience in waiting for redemption, for they could not easily forget the consequences of rebellion against Rome. They impressed upon their people the importance of obeying local authorities and giving simple adherence to the everyday teachings of the Torah and Talmud.

SPECULATIONS

The Talmud's greatest surge of expansion came in the centuries following the Roman destruction. With this rise in its importance and its voluminous body of parables, laws, and discussions, there also came a plethora of notions on the Messiah's coming. Every aspect of His person and work was explored. Scores—perhaps hundreds—of differing ideas on the Messianic Age to come poured out of the imaginations of the probing rabbinic minds.

As the rabbis read the ancient literature and dwelled on the possibilities of this great future event, they speculated on the timing of Messiah's arrival. Some believed that the era would be one of great wickedness, when even the Jews would turn their backs on the Torah and collaborate with their enemies. Others were certain that the Messiah would not come until there was a great awakening of righteousness and peace in the world, and Jewry would set an example of strict observance to the Torah. For example, in the Talmud (BT Shabbat 118b) there is this confident assertion: "Rabbi Yohanan said, following Rabbi Simeon bar Yohai: Were Israel to observe two Sabbaths punctiliously, they would be redeemed immediately."[4]

Another view is that He would come when people despaired of redemption, and the Jews would give up on any help for Israel. Still another theory was that it would all depend on when the supply of souls that were to be furnished with earthly bodies would run out! It was thought by some that the Messiah would come on the eve of Passover, since the Passover was the first redemptive event in Israel's history. Others believed that He certainly would never come on the Sabbath, since the day of rest would be violated by all the activity.

Following the catastrophe of the Bar Kokhba era, the rabbis no longer depicted the Messiah as a conquering hero. Christian thinking is said to have influenced rabbinic thought regarding a reduced military role. According to this conception, the Messiah would suddenly bring in the age of redemption with the regeneration of humanity, resulting in a paradisiacal sinless and painless existence. Then, there was the Aramaic Targum, which suggested that there might be two Messiahs—Messiah, son of Ephraim (Joseph) and Messiah, son of David—one to defeat the enemies of Israel and the second to reign as David's descendant.[5] The traditional rabbis believed that humans could do absolutely nothing to hasten this coming; they could only pray and wait in hope. But those who were more mystical were—and remain today—convinced that human effort can bring the day of redemption closer.

The differing portrayals of the Messiah's personality and the role He would play are endless: he would be the beggar at the gates of Rome, the son of Joseph who leads in the battle against Gog and Magog, the arbiter of the world's conflicts, the teacher of the nations from his academy, with all the righteous ones sitting with him, the restorer of glory to Israel. The Talmudic descriptions seem endless and often contradictory. One statement from the Babylonian Talmud asserted that the Messiah's traits would depend on the integrity of the Jews:

> R. Alexandri said, R. Joshua contrasted two verses: It is written, "And behold, one like the son of man came with the clouds of heaven" (Daniel 7:13), and another verse says, "[behold, your king comes to you...] humble and riding on an ass" (Zechariah 9:7). If Israel merits it, [he will come] "with the clouds of heaven"; if not, [he will be] "humble and riding on an ass."[6]

Maimonides specified certain criteria by which one could judge whether or not a great leader was truly the Messiah: He would have to be a fervent student and follower of Torah and all the written and oral law. Further, He would be able to convince all of Israel to follow the Torah, fight the battles of the Lord, rebuild the Temple on the Temple Mount, and gather in the dispersed of Israel. If He displayed these accomplishments, one could be sure He was the Messiah; but if He did not accomplish these tasks, one could be sure he was not the Messiah. Maimonides didn't want the uneducated Jews to be gullible and bring shame upon Jewry, and therefore he set the standards high.

With their wild imaginations, the rabbis did not help bring credibility to the conception of the Messianic Age. Some of their writing on this subject was fanciful: women would give birth painlessly, food and wine would be produced in massive abundance, hens would lay eggs continuously...A few rabbis even taught that man would grow to a height of 160 feet.[7]

The one fairly constant element of messianic teaching to be considered is that this figure would put an end to Israel's suffering and restore her glory. Consequently, in times of great persecution, the Jewish people are apt to return with great longing to their expectation of the Messiah and the age of redemption. One of the sad stories that precipitated such expectation occurred in the Ukraine in the mid-seventeenth century after the Christian Orthodox peasantry there had been exploited by a feudal system run by the Roman Catholic nobility and their Jewish agents. The build-up of peasant anger issued an outbreak of anti-Semitism, resulting in the butchering of some one hundred thousand Jews.

Shabbatai Zevi

Shabbatai Zevi, who was born in 1626 in what is now Turkey, came to believe that he was called to lead his people out of their distress. At age twenty-two he began claiming to be the Messiah and traveled to Palestine to consult with rabbis there. Many of those rabbis belonged to the Kabbalist movement within Judaism, which taught a mysticism they claimed had esoteric ways of discovering the relationship between the mortal and the infinite. For instance, most of the adherents of Kabbalah were convinced that in the Torah, the combination of letters used in the text and all the numbers compiled a code representing hidden meanings that provided access to the divine presence. This Kabbalistic mysticism had great impact on Jewish society throughout Europe. Paul Johnson writes,

> The great historian Gershom Scholem, who spent his life studying the impact of kabbalistic mysticism on Jewish society, stressed the universality of the belief among Jewish communities, around the mid-seventeenth century, that the world was on the brink of great events. The series of catastrophes which overtook Ashkenazi Jewry in eastern Europe from 1648 onwards…constituted a potent factor in raising messianic hopes…[The wave of excitement] swept along rich

and poor, learned and ignorant, communities which were in danger and those which felt themselves safe.[8]

In his early twenties, Zevi began calling himself "Messiah." But it wasn't until many years later, following a Jewish massacre, that he began to command attention. His claims and charm at that point quickly caught on with the help of a talented promoter, Nathan the Prophet, who argued that Zevi had the power to justify sinners. Zevi had all the signs of a manic-depressive, and while he was in his periods of rapture, he was adept in sweeping adoring crowds off their feet. The rabbis were deeply divided over him, and indeed some of them apparently asked the Ottoman authorities to suppress his activities. After being imprisoned and tried, Zevi fell into a deep depression. The authorities gave him the choice of death or conversion to Islam. He chose the latter. The embarrassment for the Jews was deep and forced them, thereafter, to exercise caution regarding messianic expectation. One can feel pity for the Jews of that era: the promise of a bright future was once again beyond their reach. Nothing had changed. They remained scattered, far from their homeland, and, for the most part, despised and dispirited in their host countries.

Chapter 9 set forth the division that ensued within the Jewish communities of Europe upon their emancipation at the onset of the Enlightenment. The Jewish community and its belief system became divided. The modern breakaway Reform movement in Judaism became watered down, thereby scandalizing the Orthodox rabbis. It should not be surprising, then, to find that the expectation of the Messiah and an age of redemption would take on a very different look in this liberal version of Judaism.

THE REFORM VERSION

Orthodoxy remains the religion of the written word. The Orthodox conception of the Messiah and the Age of Redemption is based on the Tanakh and the Talmud: the coming will be climactic and supernatural, a fulfillment of prophecy relating to the end of time. On the other hand, Reform Judaism became rationalistic, and the Reformist concept of the Messiah's coming is a this-worldly, evolutionary process, a phenomenon brought on by human effort as much as by divine action. The 1885 Pittsburgh Platform, a statement at a historic meeting of Reform rabbis, rejected the traditional prayer for the coming of the heir of King David. In its place they substituted the word *geulah* (redemption) for *go-el* (redeemer), indicating that their sights were no longer set on a *personal* Messiah but only on a *process* of bringing about social justice and world peace. The humanism in this change is obvious: the hope is scaled down from a supernatural end-of-days redemption to a radical political change producing a better world.[9] Indeed, the Jewish scholar David S. Ariel, in his book *What Do Jews Believe?*, writes, "Judaism is more comfortable with deferred than attainable messianism…Our sacred myths tell us that the Messiah is always coming and that he might arrive at any moment." And, in the very next paragraph, he declares, "Jews believe that the work of creating a perfect world is more important than the Messiah."[10] How telling! This shows an enormous amount of misplaced confidence, given humanity's record for attempting to create a perfect society. Recall previous attempts: the war to end all wars (World War I); classless societies (Communism); economic equality and freedom from want (Socialism). Is humankind equal to the task of bringing on the Messianic Age, the day of redemption, or the perfecting of society? History shouts *no*! The words of Rabbi Ariel are ones of unbelief and presumption. They remind one of some of those Jewish exiles in Babylon who were too comfortable in their captivity to be interested in any prophetic word about the action of the sovereign God in releasing them from Babylonian captivity. They had become enmeshed in Babylonian culture. They'd become too complacent and unbelieving to take seriously any promise of being led by God's hand back to their Promised Land.

With the Enlightenment and then the emancipation of Jews, European anti-Semitism in the nineteenth century began to subside, and by the twentieth century, the hitherto harassed Jewish communities began to feel more secure. Those who were Reform and nonobservant were basking in their freedom from hide-bound tradition and in their acceptance in society.

> They mingled with the nations
> And learned to do as they did. (Psalms 106:35)

The Orthodox, however, did not welcome this freedom, for they worried that with assimilation and security would come a disregard for the Torah, a breaking from tradition, and the fragmentation of their closely knit communities. To the contrary, Reform and secular Jews were finding a wealth of opportunity in this secular security and politically assured freedom.

GERMAN JEWISH THOUGHT

In Germany this confidence and freedom took the radical form of the Jews' adoption of Germany as their own "fatherland." The Jews felt at home. Their intellectuals were winning Nobel Prizes. Reason, which was lifted up as the apex of the human essence, was honored in Germany, and with reason in control, the old enmity of anti-Semitism was forever gone—or so these educated German Jews believed. Having thrown off the cords of rabbinic Judaism, they gloried in cultural enlightenment. In their view, the vision of Zionism was misguided. The Jewish nation-state was not needed; a geographical center of Judaism, such as Palestine, was obsolete. If they were religious in their ideas, they believed it was Providence that had dispersed the Jews to the ends of the earth so that they might contribute to justice, peace, and the relentless progress of civilization. The expectation of the Messiah was diluted in Germany to a feeling that the age of redemption was upon them in their experience of freedom and cultural assimilation. The "brotherhood of man" was one of the shibboleths of that time, hailed as an indication that their future longing was now being realized and "Germany itself was the new homeland of the Jewish spirit." An essay, "Germanism and Judaism," written in 1919 by Hermann Cohen, foremost Jewish philosopher of his time, makes this consciousness abundantly clear.

> The inner commonality between Germans and Jewishness should now be evident to everyone. The concept of humanity has its origins

in the messianism of the Israelite prophets…*The Messiah is again to be found…within the framework of the German spirit.* The Jews in France, England and Russia are also subject to the duty of loyalty to Germany, because Germany is the motherland of their souls.[11] (emphasis mine)

Though anti-Semitism, accompanied by pogroms and persecution, still abounded in other countries, especially in Russia and Eastern Europe, these leaders of the German Jewish establishment considered Zionism to be foolishness. Walter Laqueur, in *A History of Zionism*, says that Professor Ludwig Geiger, the son of one of the founders of liberal Judaism and one of its representatives on the executive committee of the Berlin Jewish community, suggested, as Laurie Magnus did in Britain, that Zionists should be deprived of their civil rights. It was Geiger's contention that, for German Jews, the future of the German nation "must remain the only one on which German Jews based their hopes." He denounced the "blasphemous prayers" found in the Jewish liturgy that referred to the homeland in Palestine. Europe, and especially Germany, was offering the fulfillment of the ideals of the Hebrew prophets. Rabbi Hermann Vogelstein, one of the most influential leaders of liberal German Jewry, who published books on Jewish history, insisted that Zionism was not compatible with the principles of modern Judaism and that Germany was the true fatherland.[12]

The German spirit was going to provide the framework for the Messiah. Really? In 1933, just eighteen years after the publication of Cohen's essay, Hitler became chancellor of Germany and declared the establishment of the Third Reich! Just a year following Cohen's essay's publication, Karl Barth, German Protestant theologian, was warning Europe about proudly building its pitiable Tower(s) of Babel and—ignoring the righteousness that only God gives—thinking it could manage self-chosen religious philosophy and practice.[13]

Once again, a significant segment of European Jewry was duped. This time the illusions were not from Orthodox Judaism, representing traditional

Jews of the poorer class, but from the most educated Jewish community in the world in the early twentieth century.[14] The messianic idea in liberal Judaism became indistinct and inane. Tanakh had come to take a backseat within the minds of many Jews. The mystical element in Kabbalah was a diversion from the law and the prophets, and the Reform doctrine of Judaism strayed from its scriptural foundation and became humanistic. Thus, Judaism was vulnerable to a wide spectrum of contradictory and confusing ideas about future redemption.

This takes us to the late twentieth century, when an unprecedented claim was made regarding a contemporary rabbi living in Brooklyn, New York.

A sect of Judaism called Hasidism, a significant segment of Jewish Orthodoxy, pious and strict, became the strongest branch of Judaism in much of Europe by the latter part of the nineteenth century. The Hasidim believe that true religious life is not so much one of careful Talmudic study, as per most Judaism, as it is of heartfelt expression. Their emphasis is on the joy of the godly life and is expressed in singing, dancing, fervent prayers, and deeds of kindness. Within the Hasidic sect, we find the Chabad movement, numbering about two hundred thousand people worldwide, which has returned to a more studious approach to Judaism while instilling enthusiasm in worship and service. Added to this is the flavor of Kabbalistic mysticism within Chabad. A sense of mission pervades its adherents' existence: to revitalize the religious life of Judaism. To this end they aggressively implore all Jews to engage in their joyous and prayerful version of active religion. It's a "be joyous" and "get involved" message to all Jews.

The rabbi who encouraged this new worldwide mission of Chabad is the late Rabbi Menachem Mendel Schneerson, who resided near the headquarters of the movement in Brooklyn, New York. This highly educated and winsome leader, called "the *Rebbe*" (Yiddish term for "rabbi") by his people, challenged his congregants to do everything they could to not only gain new followers but also bring the Messiah! Their mission is no less. Before Schneerson's death in 1994, young Chabad married couples went out from Brooklyn to every part of the world just as Christian missionaries have done for centuries. Since his passing, the stream of volunteers has not abated. They go to join existing communities of Chabad or establish new ones, founding new synagogues, day schools, and rehabilitation clinics, working in university student centers, providing language classes, and aiding those in need no matter what their ethnicity. They are responsible for increasing the roles of Chabad Orthodox Judaism all over the world, prodding Jews to become active in joyful religious observance. The institutions and services they organize are highly visible in many major cities throughout the world. Their attendance at services outnumbers their membership. Some rabbis who hold these views hold important posts in the world of Jewish Orthodoxy. Thus, Chabad's influence is far greater than its numbers would indicate.

The expectation of the coming Messiah was a key part of the Rebbe's message, and he believed that coming to be imminent. He encouraged his followers to pray and work fervently for the time of redemption, teaching them that every good deed would hasten the Messiah's advent. Rabbi David Berger, professor of history at Brooklyn College, reports on the Rebbe's message:

> He himself unqualifiedly proclaimed the imminence of the redemption; encouraged the cry, 'We want mashiach [messiah] now!'; *and strongly implied that he would be the redeemer.* Among such statements were these: that the metaphysical process of separating the sparks of holiness from the domain of evil had been completed…that the messiah had already been revealed, and all that remained was to greet him…that the final Temple would descend from heaven to a spot in Crown Heights adjoining Lubavitch headquarters, and that only then would the two buildings be transferred to Jerusalem. That the messiah's name was Menachem.[15] (emphasis added)

Berger proceeds to explain that the Rebbe "refrained from any open, explicit proclamation of his own messianic identity…though in his last years the

Rebbe tolerated and even appears to have encouraged the singing of the formula declaring his messiahship—'may our Master, Teacher, and Rabbi the King Messiah live forever.'"[16]

The Rebbe's ambivalence about declaring his messiahship was not reflected in the attitude of his followers. A large portion of them now proclaim him to be the Messiah, some saying he will rise from the dead and others that his death never occurred. This is odious to many Orthodox rabbis and rejected by many adherents, but a surprising number of them have taken one of these two positions: he died but will rise in due time, or he did not die and will be seen again. Thus, a variety of beliefs exist today within the Chabad-Lubavitch movement concerning his messiahship.

One thing about this latest Jewish messianic figure is notable: he was the first that some believed would rise from the dead. Up until this time, no leader of rabbinic Judaism of any time or in any place ever suggested that the Messiah would experience death, burial, and resurrection, after which He would rule as the successor to the biblical King David. That proposition resembles the Christian belief in Jesus Christ too much, and so it would, in the past, have precluded any branch of Judaism from adopting this belief in a resurrected messiah. Yet this belief about the Rebbe persists! Furthermore, in their admiration for the good works, fervor, and positive spirit of the Chabad-Lubavitch movement, and in the interest of unity, the rabbis who disagree with this claim of messiahship have been largely silent on this issue. They quietly assess the direction and fruit of this lively sect and remain silent on the obvious doctrinal issue of whether it might be idolatry to give the late Rebbe such adulation.

Whim and Fantasy

The variety of beliefs about the Messiah taxes the imagination. I have yet to discover two Jewish writers who give the same portrayal of the coming

Messiah. Very few quote the Tanakh in their description. As we have seen, vast difference in portrayals extend to things like the time of His coming, the nature of the Messiah, whether or not man's efforts make a difference in the time of His coming, whether His coming will portend the end of the world, and even whether there will be a personal Messiah or only an Age of Redemption or progress. I see two reasons for these many and bizarre reckonings. First, observant Jews have a plethora of sacred literature to which they can refer. They are presented with a veritable flood of rabbinic opinions in the Talmud, consisting of the ruminations from centuries of confusing and often contradictory teachings. Second, those who are mystical can find quite an assortment of fanciful conceptions.

The Hebrew prophets, which the rabbis typically neglect, issued sharp criticisms of invalid prophecy, and the same would apply to false teaching and glibness of the rabbis. "Messiah was born on the day the Temple was destroyed," declares one rabbinic promise in the Talmud.[17] One would think that the fear of God would keep them from making such declarations and compiling one dissertation upon another that their followers will spend hours a day studying. "Thus says the Lord God," cries Ezekiel, "Alas for the senseless prophets who follow their own spirit, and have seen nothing. They have envisioned falsehood and lying divination; they say, 'Says the Lord,' when the Lord has not sent them, and yet they wait for the fulfillment of their word!" (Ezekiel 13:3, 6) The word of the Lord is the greatest need of the people. Yet they are offered a flood of rabbinic opinions, centuries of confusing and contradictory words of legalism, as well as mystical and cryptic conjecture from the Hasidim.[17]

Another reason I posit for the confused reckonings about the Messiah in Jewish literature outside the Tanakh is the following: the scriptures tell us— and experience bears it out—that when people neglect the gift of God, their minds become clouded. The truth becomes less important than the human *search* for it. And the search for it becomes not really a search for the truth but a diversion from it. That detour leads to confusion.

We mortals get detoured from truth because an acknowledgment of the truth often demands leaving the past, and the past holds loyalties and institutions that have provided for us an identity and sometimes bestowed power and position on us. First-century Judaism certainly did offer a solid sense of identity and *attempted* to provide justification by the keeping of the rabbinical version of the law. But, the heart of the law and the perspective of God's graciousness was largely absent. That was the assessment of Yeshua, placing the Jewish Sanhedrin and its establishment on the defensive. Very soon after the public ministry of Jesus began, they began discussing what they could do with Him. A generation or so later, with the destruction of the Temple and the disappearance of the priesthood, they were given increased authority. They gloried in that new spotlight. A minority of them did repent in humility, believe, and join the new Yeshua community, but the institution of rabbinical Judaism became ever stronger following the demise of the priesthood. With that centralization of religious power, the rabbis possessed renewed vigor to add to their sacred literature and make *their* law their religion.

§

"Then Yeshua said to the Jews who had believed in him: 'If you continue in my word, you are truly my disciples; and you will know the truth, and the truth will make you free'" (John 8:31, 32). In speaking to the religious establishment in the temple, Yeshua said confidently but humbly: "When you have lifted up the Son of Man, then you will realize that I am he (or simply "I am"), and that I do nothing on my own, but I speak these things as the Father has instructed me. And the one who sent me is with me; he has not left me alone, for I always do what is pleasing to him." (John 8:28-30)

When I observe older American Jews whose life ambitions have been nearly lived out and who face the end of their earthly lives, I think I see that emptiness of which Karl Barth speaks when he says, "Necessarily, therefore, the Jew who is uniquely blessed offers the picture of an existence which, characterized by the rejection of its Messiah and therefore of its salvation and mission, is dreadfully empty of grace and blessing."[18] They have not believed in the Messiah who said, "Let not your hearts be troubled. Believe in God; believe also in me. In my Father's house are many rooms." Or the Messiah who said, "Peace be with you, my peace I give unto you." Who said, "I am the light of the world. Anyone who follows me will not walk in darkness but will have the light of life." Who said, "I am the resurrection and the life; those who believe in me, even though they die, will live." Unbelievers do not know this promise and this outlook. They think of immortality only as their progeny. Yet they know that before long they will be forgotten. Therefore, their lives are like a shadow that will soon pass. One can only earnestly pray that our Jewish friends will believe, as some indeed have, and open their eyes to the Light of Life.

1. Abraham Joshua Heschel, *Israel: An Echo of Eternity* (New York: Farrar, Straus, and Giroux, 1969), 160.
2. "Service for the Second Day of Rosh Hashana," Congregation Agudas Achim, September 2003.
3. Glen Miller, "Messianic Expectations in 1st Century Judaism," Christian Think-Tank, August 6, 1996, christianthinktank.com/messiah.html.

    Source for website: S. H. Levey, "The Messiah: An Aramaic Interpretation, Monograph of the Hebrew Union College" Cincinnati, 1974.
4. Rabbi David S. Ariel, "Modern Jewish Messianism," My Jewish Learning, www.myjewishlearning.com.

    http://www.myjewishlearning.com/beliefs/Theology/Afterlife_and_Messiah/Messianism/Th...
5. Rabbi David S. Ariel, *What Do Jews Believe?* (New York: Schocken Books, 1995), 226–227.
6. Jeffrey Spitzer, "Who is the Messiah?" My Jewish Learning, http://www.myjewishlearning.com/beliefs/Theology/Afterlife_and_Messiah/Messianism/W...

7. Rabbi David S. Ariel, "Modern Jewish Messianism," My Jewish Learning, http://www.myjewishlearning.com/beliefs/Theology/Afterlife_and_Messiah/Messianism/Th...

8. Paul Johnson, *The History of the Jews* (New York: Harper Perennial, 1987), 267.

9. We recognize, in the modern era of universal culture of heart and intellect, the approaching of the realization of Israel's great Messianic hope for the establishment of the kingdom of truth, justice, and peace among all men. We consider ourselves no longer a nation, but a religious community, and therefore expect neither a return to Palestine, nor a sacrificial worship under the sons of Aaron, nor the restoration of any of the laws concerning the Jewish state. ccarnet.org. (Central Conference of American Rabbis, Declaration of Principles, The Pittsburgh Platform)

10. Rabbi David S. Ariel, *What Do Jews Believe?* (New York: Schocken Books, 1995), 246.

11. David Hazony, Yoram Hazony, and Michael B. Oren, eds., *New Essays on Zionism* (New York and Jerusalem: Shalem Press, 2006), 44–45.

12. Walter Laqueur, *A History of Zionism* (New York: Schocken Books, 1972, 2003), 393–396.

13. Karl Barth, *The Word of God and the Word of Man* (New York: Harper and Row, 1956, 1957), 9–27.

14. This type of philosophy also infected the thought of non-German Jews in Europe and America. For instance, in Amsterdam, the educated Jews called the city "Mokum" (Hebrew for "place"), indicating the affection they had for this place of Jewish culture. In their minds, Jerusalem took second place to Amsterdam. Judaism was weakening, the Jewish birthrate was on the decline, and the population was aging. So though life was good in Amsterdam for the Jewish community, the survival of that community, as in other such European areas, looked bleak.

    See Bernard Wasserstein, *On the Eve: The Jews of Europe before the Second World War* (New York: Simon and Schuster, 2012), 99.

15. David Berger, "The Rebbe, the Jews, and the Messiah," *Commentary*, January 1, 2001.

16. Ibid.

17. Milton Viorst, *What Shall I Do with this People?* (New York: The Free Press, 2002), 172.

18. Karl Barth, *Church Dogmatics*, IV, pt. 3.2 (Edinburgh: T & T Clark, 1962), 877

CHAPTER 13

The Servants

§

Here is my servant, whom I uphold,
My chosen, in whom my soul delights.

—Isaiah 42:1

You are my witnesses, says the Lord,
And my servant whom I have chosen,
So that you may know and believe me
And understand that I am he.

—Isaiah 43:10

In this book's treatment of the Chosen People, Israel, there has been discussion of the concept of the Messiah. In the biblical history of the Chosen People, there are hints and prophecies of the coming of the Chosen Person, who will arise from their midst. The Chosen People, therefore, will be the kinsmen of the Messiah. Out of the Chosen People will emerge the Chosen Person.

To shed light on the concept of "the chosen," we turn to Isaiah, the best loved of the Hebrew prophets. According to *The Jewish Study Bible*, the book of Isaiah is cited more than any other prophetic text in rabbinic literature.[1] In its beauty of form and substance, it is second to none in the prophetic canon.

Adobe Stock/byjeng
The Dead Sea Scrolls on display at the caves of Qumran, Israel. One scroll among the many found (not the one pictured) is called "The Great Isaiah Scroll," the best preserved of all the scrolls, which contains the entire "Prophecy of Isaiah."

One of the recurring themes running through Isaiah's prophecy is messianic hope. The "Christmas texts" familiar to Christians are located in the first part of Isaiah, in which the Messiah is seen as being in the line of David. There His righteous rule as king is emphasized. What stands out, however, in this text are the passages in which not the king but the servant of the Lord is highlighted. These references are in the second major division of Isaiah, what is often called Deutero-Isaiah.[2]

The questions that have engaged biblical interpreters as they've studied this servant of the Lord are these: Who is this? Is it an individual or a group? And what is this servant's mission? These are the questions this chapter will engage.

Again, this Chosen One is highlighted in the later part of Isaiah's prophecy, beginning with chapter forty, where the historical setting is the exiled Israel in Babylonian captivity. At this point they were sorely in need of assurance that God, the Lord who chose them, still delighted in them, was able to save them, and had a bright future planned for them. Here we find words of confirmation about Israel's role in history. We also find three chosen beings that were placed on Isaiah's stage, all of whom were to carry forward the Lord's good purposes: first is Israel, as the servant of the Lord, second is Cyrus, the anointed king who extends liberty to the Jewish expatriates, and third is the Suffering Servant of the Lord. We can ignore, for this discussion's purposes, the second chosen servant, Cyrus of Persia, who was to release the Jewish people from their captivity. His mission was decisive but temporary. We will focus on the two chosen figures that are fixtures in the divine plan to bless the whole world: Israel the servant of the Lord and the Suffering Servant. The question is, is the Suffering Servant simply a personification of the nation of Israel?

Inserted in the elegantly written later section of Isaiah are four identifiable passages of verse that, for the last century, scholars have called "the Servant Songs": the first is 42:1–9; the second is 49:1–13; the third is 50:4–9; and the fourth is 52:13–53:12. In addition, there are other references to be noted of a servant of the Lord not included in "The Servant Songs." The identity of the servant in these others is clearly, as will be seen, the nation of Israel. Thus, Israel is named as the servant in 41:8–20, 42:18–25 and 43:1–10. The question remaining is, if Israel is the figure Isaiah was pointing to in these latter three sections (those in the following list with no asterisks), to whom do the four with asterisks refer? Do they not also refer to Israel, the chosen nation-servant? Is it possible that Isaiah was referring to Israel in *all seven* of these "servant" references? More discussion will proceed.

THE SERVANT SONGS AND SECTIONS

Isaiah 41:8–20
Isaiah 42:1–9*
Isaiah 42:18–25

Isaiah 43:1–10
Isaiah 49:1–7*
Isaiah 50:4–9*
Isaiah 52:13–53:12*

* Designates passages commonly known as "Servant Songs"

The idea of servanthood in Isaiah is not that of brutal, forced slavery. Depicted here is a precious relationship in which the Master protects and honors the servant, while the servant is at His disposal to represent His interests. Mosaic legislation provided a model for slavery: it included a variety of protections, Sabbath rest, sabbatical-year releases, and masters' dispositions of mercy and kindness. It provided a process for a freed slave to remain with the master. Implicit in this law was the expectation of a relationship built on mutual trust, respect, and dignity, though it continued to be a hierarchical arrangement.

The servant in Isaiah was one who was respectfully called a close associate and indispensable agent of the Lord. The author of this prophecy emphasized many aspects and features of the servant's character and conduct. One would expect, then, that this scripture would immediately identify this servant beyond all doubt, but such is not the case. As this figure is introduced on Isaiah's stage, the light increases and the lens focuses on the figure only gradually and incompletely.

SECTION ON SERVANT ISRAEL: ISAIAH 41:8–20
Before the four Servant Songs, the first text in Isaiah that points to "the servant" clearly refers to a group instead of an individual.

But you, Israel, my servant, Jacob whom I have chosen,
The offspring of Abraham, my friend;
You whom I took from the ends of the earth,
And called from the farthest corners,

Saying to you, "You are my servant,
I have chosen you and not cast you off." (41:8–9)

Here the servant is clearly the whole nation whose patriarch is Abraham and whose reason for being is the call of the Lord. At numerous points in Israel's history, God called his people from distant places—Abraham from Chaldea, the new nation from Egypt, the rebuked nation from Babylonia ending the exile. Later, after the Jews became scattered abroad, they still journeyed back from those "farthest corners" to their joyful feasts in Jerusalem to celebrate God's blessings on His Chosen People. They have always been returning from scattered points or dreaming of the day they could.

At this point, is it possible not to reference the return to the land within the past century of this modern era? The Jews of the Diaspora have come "from the farthest corners." They have made the aliyah. (the Hebrew term meaning "to go up" to the Land). The call came, however it might be explained. It was intuition, yearning, and necessity, and it was reinforced by liturgical repetition: "Next year in Jerusalem!" All of that was grounded in the call of the Lord God: "You whom I took from the ends of the earth, and called from the farthest corners." This is a statement of divine sovereignty in the history of the world and of the right of the Creator to choose, to take, appoint, and gather this people.[3]

The Jews in Babylon, to which this message of Isaiah was given, were doubtful about God and dubious about their future. They needed assurance that this God of their forebears was truly sovereign in human history. Isaiah asks who it is who acts as prompter on the world stage. Is it the gods of the nations? That is a subject for the Lord's ridicule: their gods are idols made by wood carvers. What about the rulers themselves? Is final sovereignty in *their* hands? Isaiah's answer is this:

It is he who…brings princes to naught,
And makes the rulers of the earth as nothing.

Scarcely are they planted, scarcely sown,
Scarcely has their stem taken root in the earth,
When he blows upon them, and they wither. (40:23, 24)

An example is given. Proud Babylon, the instrument of the Lord for taking Israel into captivity, was succeeded by the Persian Empire. The rise of the Persian King Cyrus, said the Lord, was a development He brought about. This more benevolent emperor of Persia was nothing less than the anointed of the Lord who would show favor to the Jews and invite them to return and repopulate the land.

Who has roused a victor from the east,
Summoned him to his service? (Isaiah 41:2)

It is He, the Almighty, who has raised up King Cyrus that this king of Persia might declare the Jewish exile to be over and done.

But the Lord planned to reveal much more to Israel than the actual political deliverance from Babylon; there was *spiritual* restoration and re-demption in their future. These two were revealed side by side, yet they were distinct. The political deliverance would come through the agency of Cyrus of Persia, and the spiritual deliverance and renewal would come through the servant. Cyrus would soon be taken off the stage of Isaiah's prophecy so the servant could be the focal point of the promised redemp-tion. Cyrus's role would be short-lived, while the servant's would be of indefinite duration.

So now there comes an introduction to this servant who had a special relationship to the Lord. As if for a stage, Isaiah's text presents a whole com-pany of actors at first, but this eventually narrows to a single individual. The identity of that single personage has been the object of intense controversy throughout the history of Jewish-Christian relations.

THE FIRST SERVANT SONG: ISAIAH 42:1–7

In this first of the four Servant Songs, the servant was introduced in very personal terms. Because the text comes so close on the heels of the passage just cited in chapter 41, it is easy to suppose that this figure still represents Israel. Some scholars do take this position—that this is still the nation-servant described in chapter 41. But some careful readers of the text and of Israel's condition see a more idealized personage. Read and ponder:

> Here is my servant, whom I uphold,
> My chosen, in whom my soul delights;
> I have put my spirit upon him;
> He will bring forth justice to the nations.
> He will not cry or lift up his voice,
> Or make it heard in the street;
> A bruised reed he will not break,
> And a dimly burning wick he will not quench;
> He will faithfully bring forth justice.
> He will not grow faint or be crushed
> Until he has established justice in the earth...
> I am the Lord, I have called you in righteousness,
> I have taken you by the hand and kept you;
> I have given you as a covenant to the people,
> A light to the nations, to open the eyes that are blind,
> To bring out the prisoners from the dungeon,
> From the prison those who sit in darkness. (42:1–3, 6–7)

First, note that the identity of this servant was not raised. He was simply introduced: "Here is my servant." (The King James Version states, "Behold my servant.") The nation-servant in 41:8 was *spoken to*. This servant in 42:1 was *pointed to*. Furthermore, there are features here similar to that of the Messiah-as-King portrayed in Isaiah chapter 11, a well-known and accepted messianic prophecy: "A shoot shall come out from the stump of Jesse, And a branch shall grow out of his roots. The spirit of the Lord shall rest on him" (11:1–2a).

In both the earlier and the later Isaiah prophecies, the servant will be endowed with the Spirit. It would seem, then, that the chapter 11 and chapter 42 prophecies could refer to the same coming figure. But we should not draw conclusions too quickly. This first Servant Song follows, by just a half chapter, the description of *Israel*-as-servant. Could it be that the identity of the servant would change so quickly?

The servant is described as gentle—showing tenderness to the weak—but at the same time strong and effective. "He will not cry or lift up his voice, or make it heard in the street," and "a bruised reed he will not break." He will not be overbearing, will not "cry" (the Hebrew word is *yis-aq*, meaning "to cry out or shriek"), and will not "lift up his voice," which perhaps means he will not "shout others down." (Motyer) He will not "make it heard in the street," which perhaps refers to hawking one's wares in a market, or to politicians' self-advertisement.

The perfect counterbalance to this gentleness, in rounding out his sublime character, is his strength. He will establish justice (or righteousness) while not exhausting his energy in doing so, and he'll establish it not only for Israel but for the nations. The Hebrew word translated as "justice" is *mishpat*. It is a versatile word, and its meaning depends somewhat on the context. It could denote "justice," "the righting of wrongs," or connote "the right way." "The true way" is how the *Jewish Study Bible* translates it.[4]

It is an ideal image portrayed here—a sensitive, gentle, unpretentious personage, yet strong and enduring, who will be successful in bringing the right and true way to the nations. It is the supreme example of a servant. The servant was called by the Lord and taken by the hand, revealing an intimate relationship. His mission was not only to Israel but to the entire world.

I have given you as a covenant to the people
A light to the nations,
To open the eyes that are blind. (vss. 6c)

The servant here is described not as being in covenant with the Lord but as *being himself* a covenant, bringing the people, Israel, into a proper relation to God in a covenant based on mercy and truth. The implementation of that covenant is meant to bring healing and release from bondage.

This chapter cites representative interpretations of Jewish scholars both ancient and modern. The *Jewish Study Bible* states that the nation of Israel is the servant who will *be* the covenant. It says, "The term 'servant' in most other passages in chapters 40–66 clearly refers to the nation Israel or to the faithful within Israel, and that is the most likely explanation here as well."[5] Other modern Jewish scholars and leaders have insisted on this same application.

Zionist leaders, such as David Ben-Gurion, have used this portion of Isaiah to sanctify their designs and rouse the interest of their people; they have lifted the phrase "light to the nations" from this Servant Song for their idealistic purposes. They maintain that it refers to Israel. Are they right in doing so? Does that comport with this text from which they draw this sense of calling?

Is it exemplary, or is it presumptuous? Israel is God's Chosen People. But to go further and consider them as "light to the nations" is another question. Historically, have they desired to be a "light to the nations"? Do they think they have been that? Do they want to be that in this era?

In Dan Kurzman's biography of David Ben-Gurion (the Zionist leader and first prime minister of the State of Israel), Kurzman states, "Ben-Gurion wanted not simply a state but an exemplary one that would ultimately lead to universal redemption...His vision was rooted in the Bible." In the Arab uprising of 1936, in which the harvest of three decades of Jewish toil was threatened, Ben-Gurion still ordered restraint in fighting, insisting that any violence be only defensive, stating that Jewish troops must be guided by one word: *havlagah*—self-restraint. "The Jew was to be the purest fighter in the world, for he was defending a people destined to purify the human spirit."[6] Time after time, using the phrase from the servant passage presented in this book, he preached to the Israelis that they were to be a "light to the nations." The phrase "light unto the nations" has been used as a designation for Israel in official matters ever since.

Can and do the Israelis live up to such an extraordinarily noble motto? Today, the majority of Jewish people worldwide are secular and unbelieving. The State of Israel is beset by corrupt politics and loose moral behavior, with a high rate of divorce and fragmented families and a low rate of synagogue participation. Israel does strive for high standards of social justice, but the cultural decline of the West has infused Israeli culture. There is an increase in religious interest, but in facing the threats and turmoil around them, the majority of Israeli Jews live with no reference to the Lord as their helper.

Nevertheless, should we keep this an open question? Could it possibly be that *both* the chosen nation, Israel, *and* the chosen individual Messiah fulfill the description of this phrase—"light to the nations"? Do they not both have a mission to the nations? The Lord announced to Abraham that "in you all the nations of the earth would be blessed." The blessing of Abraham lives on in Israel (Isaiah 51:1–3). From her beginnings, Israel was the servant on display. Israel was an international spectacle, judged and protected by God.

All of this is true, but after looking at the entirety of this first Servant Song, in which the servant is the delight of the Lord (verse 1) and *he is in himself the covenant* (verse 6), it is easy to have grave doubts about identifying this servant as Israel.

A Section on Servant Israel: Isaiah 42:18–25
Proceeding shortly after the first Servant Song, the prophet, speaking for the Lord, urgently demands attention: "Listen…look up." Whom did he demand? The very people he was writing to. It is startling as he points to the servant— "my servant"—as deaf and blind!

> Listen, you that are deaf;
> And you that are blind, look up and see!
> Who is blind but my servant
> Or deaf like my messenger whom I send?
> Who is blind like my dedicated one,
> Or blind like the servant of the Lord?
> He sees many things, but does not observe them;
> His ears are open, but he does not hear. (42:18–20)

In spite of being chosen by the Lord, this servant was stubbornly insensible. The servant here saw and heard without perceiving the truth. He was termed a "servant," a "messenger," and "my dedicated one" but, nevertheless, was incompetent! The first Servant Song in the first part of the chapter describes the servant opening the eyes of the blind, whereas in this section, the servant *himself* is four times identified as blind and then also as deaf! This is appalling, and the mood here is one of urgency and immediacy: "Listen…look up and see!" This stands in bitter contrast to the portrayal of the faithful servant figure in the first part of the chapter.

We know who this insensible servant was. It was Israel. The succeeding verses attest to this. But how useful was this servant Israel? How could the blind and deaf be aided by a servant who had this condition? Israel was to be an example to the nations—a hearer and doer of the word. Her ministry in the world was needed for the nations around her that were in darkness. But she was unable to fulfill the role. Like the prophet Jonah, she had no inclination for it. In Isaiah 2:2–4, that role is envisaged; it is announced that the Lord would display the beauty of His ways through Israel, and the world would be guided by her: "All the nations shall stream to it…and say, 'Come, let us go up to the mountain of the Lord…For out of Zion shall go forth instruction.'" But after having lived in the culture of Babylon, she suffered from the same moral disabilities of other peoples, and therefore the world went on in ignorance. Who would be in the forefront of influencing the world for righteousness?

Not the Greeks or Persians or any others who were pagan polytheists. Not as witnesses to the revelation of the Lord! What people had such a history as the Hebrews, with their succession of stalwarts such as Abraham, Moses, and David? None but Israel. Yet the Lord lamented their spiritual blindness.

Bringing this sad situation to a climax, when the servant Israel is punished, the prophet continues:

Who gave up Jacob to the spoiler,
And Israel to the robbers?
Was it not the Lord, against whom we have sinned...
Whose law they would not obey?
So he poured upon him the heat of his anger
And the fury of war;
It set him on fire all around,
But he did not understand;
It burned him, but he did not take it to heart. (42:24–25)

Servant Israel did not recognize that divine wrath was at work in the destruction of their homeland and the Temple in Jerusalem. They were too stiff-necked to acknowledge that war and destruction were the outworking of the terrible chastisement of their Lord and Father-God. They would rather conclude that the God of their history was, after all, an impotent deity and really no god at all. Living in Babylon and seeing its power and glory, they became agnostic and turned off by the pronouncements of their prophets.

We can breathe a sigh of relief when the tenor of the prophecy changes in chapter 43. There the promise of God the Lord is that He will redeem Israel. However, before turning to that brighter prospect, I suggest that it is becoming increasingly difficult to look at the nation of Israel as the faithful servant. Though Israel is identified as the servant, another servant figure is also slowly unveiled in Isaiah, one who would bring salvation to the ends of the earth.

It must be considered that there was more than one servant in the revelation given to Isaiah. One servant listened closely to the Lord, was faithful, and was strong to bring forth justice (the right way) to the world. The other had become oblivious to the Lord's voice and command, yet despite that, remained the Lord's servant. Two figures stand before us.

Before focusing on the faithful servant, we must proceed to the next section on the stubborn servant and the Lord's relationship with him.

ANOTHER SECTION ON SERVANT ISRAEL: ISAIAH 43:1–10

But now thus says the Lord,
He who created you, O Jacob,
He who formed you, O Israel:
Do not fear, for I have redeemed you;
I have called you by name, you are mine.
When you pass through the waters,
I will be with you,
And through the rivers,
They shall not overwhelm you;
When you walk through fire
You shall not be burned,
And the flame shall not consume you.
For I am the Lord your God,
The Holy One of Israel, your Savior...
Because you are precious in my sight and honored
And I love you.
I give people in return for you,
Nations in exchange for your life. (43:1–4)

The fire of chastisement is not the last word, because Israel remains the beloved of Hashem, chosen and precious. The covenant between the Lord and his bride is in disrepair but is not broken. Israel is bound to Him by the ties listed: Hashem "created you...formed you...redeemed you," and named you (verse 1). It is in the Lord's sovereign purpose to keep Israel for His service. In fact, His very identification as "the Holy One of Israel" is used to prove that the covenant still exists and is permanent. Even when they are living under His wrath, they are assured that He Himself is called by their name and will redeem them. Other nations may be born and come to naught, but Israel will not be destroyed. In an exchange, the Lord is willing to give up peoples and nations in return for Israel (verse 4). This is the Sovereign God who determines to act according to His wisdom, and thus, the world may ponder the miracle of this small nation's survival from time immemorial.

This pledge of protection to servant Israel is accompanied by the promise to gather them from the nations:

> I will bring your offspring from the east,
> And from the west I will gather you:
> I will say to the north, "Give them up,"
> And to the south, "Do not withhold;
> Bring my sons from far away
> And my daughters from the end of the earth."

From Babylon, yes, but also from the earth's farthest regions. Mark that worldwide perspective where the promise of ingathering is highlighted—first, that of Israel, and secondly, that of all peoples. In the Genesis story of the Tower of Babel, the people were *scattered* to prevent them from establishing a unity independent of God. In Israel's history of rebellion against the Lord, there was civil strife resulting in division into two separate nations. Then there was the eviction from their own Promised Land, leaving them as expatriates in other countries. Division and eventual dispersion. But now there is this promise of *ingathering*. The prophecies now soar, holding a vision not only of Israel's return from Babylonian exile but also of the far future, a vision of universal ingathering in which peoples and nations stream to the mountain of the Lord (Isaiah 2:1–4).

Let all the nations gather together,
And let the peoples assemble. (43:9)

Many peoples shall come and say,
"Come, let us go up to the mountain of the Lord,
To the house of the God of Jacob;
That he may teach us his ways." (2:3)

At the culmination of days, people of the world are moved by a righteous impulse to hear the teaching—the Torah. They are drawn together, formed into a "united nations" of hearing, not speaking—finally and eagerly listening for the word of the Lord. And there, in that gathering, servant Israel is a witness that the Lord is a saving God.

However, in the following chapters, Israel is still pictured in her present condition as obstinate, burdening Him with her sins and wearying Him with her iniquities. So in this time before the culmination of days, the Lord turns again to His other servant, gradually unlocking the secret of that servant's identity and mission. Here we have the second Servant Song.

THE SECOND SERVANT SONG: ISAIAH 49:1–7

Listen to me, O coastlands,
Pay attention, you peoples from far away!
The Lord called me before I was born,
While I was in my mother's womb he named me.
He made my mouth like a sharp sword,
In the shadow of his hand he hid me;
He made me a polished arrow,
In his quiver he hid me away.

And he said to me, "You are my servant,
Israel, in whom I will be glorified." (49:1–3)

This second song enlarges our view of the servant. He is not spoken of; he himself speaks, beginning with a command to the peoples of the whole world: "Listen!" (verse 1)

He gives his credentials and the reasons his words are to be accepted as credible. First, his call, his naming, and his birth: "While I was in my mother's womb, he named me." The reference to his prebirth calling hints at some very significant person, and the reader may think here of Jeremiah. "Before I formed you in the womb, I knew you, and before you were born, I consecrated you" (Jeremiah 1:5). But I proceed in order to let the text sharpen the picture, and it will become clear that this figure is one far more significant than a prophet.

One might expect, as J. Alec Motyer says, that this figure would be political—one who would, like Moses, lead Israel out of their exile with great display. But instead, says Motyer, we find that the servant's task has more of a spiritual nature.[7] The warfare is that of the spoken word—his mouth a sharp sword. Further, not limited to the battle close at hand, he has sharp arrows in his quiver, signifying the effectiveness of his words at a distance from his standing location.

The servant reveals what the Lord has commissioned him to do: "You are my servant, *Israel*, in whom I will be glorified." Could it be Israel the nation? Probably not. This is one place where the name used is not verified, since it was left out in the Septuagint (the pre-Christian Greek version of the Old Testament). But even if it was used by Isaiah, one must consider that this name, Israel, was one originally given to the individual patriarch, Jacob. Jacob was given the task of living out the covenant and producing many sons and, through them, tribes. During the centuries to follow, the nation that came out of Jacob's loins forfeited the right to the name. The following indictment is seen only a few paragraphs back, in the passage in which the Lord insinuated that the nation was *undeserving of her name*:

Hear this, O house of Jacob,
Who are called by the name of Israel,
And who came forth from the loins of Judah;
Who swear by the name of the Lord,
And invoke the God of Israel,
But not in truth or right...
You have never heard, you have never known,
From of old your ear has not been opened,
For I knew that you would deal very treacherously,
And that from birth you were called a rebel. (48:1, 8)

Israel's perennial treachery and stubborn ignorance left her unworthy of her name. By contrast, the faithful servant speaks, saying that the Lord would be glorified through *him*—glorified, not resisted and ignored! He, the servant, would be like a sharp sword and "polished arrow" (49:2), free from imperfections and prepared to wound and to fly with the warfare of the word that purges—thus a personification of the *true* Israel.

This poem brings further evidence that this figure, though perhaps called Israel, is not to be identified with the nation:

And now, the Lord says,
Who formed me in the womb to be his servant,
To bring Jacob back to him,
And that Israel might be gathered to him,
For I am honored in the sight of the Lord,
And my God has become my strength—
He says,
"It is too light a thing that you should be my servant
To raise up the tribes of Jacob
And to restore the survivors of Israel;
I will give you as a light to the nations,

That my salvation may reach to the end of the earth." [or, better translated in the New King James Version: "That you may be my salvation to the end of the earth."] (49:4–6)

This servant figure surely could not be the nation of Israel if his mission was to "bring Jacob back" to the Lord and revive this recalcitrant people! Israel the nation, herself, needed a revivalist! But that task, daunting though it was, was too small for the servant; his calling would extend to the end of the earth! That wider work is to *be* the salvation the Lord designed for the world. Note the better translation given for the last clause: the Hebrew word for "reach" is not in the original, but the infinitive "to be" *is* there, so then, we read with amazement, "that you may *be* my salvation to the end of the earth." So in verse 6, the dignity of his person and vocation is underscored in a parallelism: "be my servant" and "be my salvation." The servant is, in his own person, what Israel and the nations have need of. The servant is the Savior!

One deeply despised, abhorred by the nations…
Kings shall see and stand up,
Princes and they shall prostrate themselves. (49:7)

Scorned by the world yet honored by nobility—how can this be? As we are here only briefly introduced to the idea that he will encounter rejection, we can expect that the prophet will later elaborate.

The servant's outline appears with ever-growing clarity as Isaiah continues. It becomes evident to us that the servant is an individual messianic figure. In fact, the two preceding quoted passages of Isaiah seem to be a perfect description not of Israel (at any point in her history) but of the manner in which Jesus of Nazareth conducted Himself in His ministry. The separate missions of the nation servant and the messianic servant are related, but their extent is vastly disproportionate.

I do acknowledge that not all interpreters would agree, so I will move on to the two remaining Servant Songs and lay out the arguments.

THE THIRD SERVANT SONG: ISAIAH 50:4–9

The Lord God has given me the tongue of a teacher,
That I may know how to sustain the weary with a word.
Morning by morning he wakens—wakens my ear
To listen as those who are taught.
The Lord God has opened my ear,
And I was not rebellious,
I did not turn backward.
I gave my back to those who struck me,
And my cheeks to those who pulled out the beard;
I did not hide my face from insult and spitting.
The Lord God helps me; therefore I have not been disgraced.
There I have set my face like flint,
And I know that I shall not be put to shame;
He who vindicates me is near.
Who will contend with me?
Let us stand up together.
Who are my adversaries?
Let them confront me.
It is the Lord God who helps me;
Who will declare me guilty?
All of them will wear out like a garment;
The moth will eat them up. (50:4–9)

The fidelity of the Suffering Servant is shown here. He listened to the Lord God, to whose will he was ready to submit. He suffered from torture inflicted by his enemies, but that failed to deter him from his mission. He did not hide his face from shame but set his face like flint, determined to complete his work. With every successive Servant Song, more about his humiliation and suffering is revealed. Here it has the features of a judicial scene in which his accusers confront him and the Lord God is his defender: "He who vindicates me is near" (verse 7).

Each of the four sections of this song is introduced by the divine name "the Lord God." In every case, the Lord God acts on behalf of the servant; and in turn, the servant has full confidence in Him and obeys in spite of undeserved enemy repercussions.

What provoked his accusers is not any wrongdoing but rather his teachings. They tried to entangle him in his talk, and for his talk he was brought to trial. The Lord God made his mouth like a sharp sword to be used for righteous warfare, though his tongue was the "tongue of a teacher," which he used "to sustain the weary." Leaping ahead to Palestine in the first century, we think of Yeshua of Nazareth, who began his teaching ministry with the blessing of the multitudes of Galilean common folk: "Then he began to speak, and taught them, saying: Blessed are the poor in spirit, for theirs is the kingdom of heaven. Blessed are those who mourn, for they will be comforted. Blessed are the meek; for they will inherit the earth" (Matthew 5:2–5).

THE CHARACTERS OF THE TWO SERVANTS FURTHER CONTRASTED

To sum up, Israel, the nation servant, was disheartened from the trials of its exile. The people, feeling they had been abandoned by the Lord, were tempted to adopt the gods of Babylon. This Isaiah prophecy comes with encouragement, assurance, and the promise of defense against other nations: "Do not fear, I will help you. Do not fear, you worm Jacob, you insect Israel! I will help you, says the Lord." Israel was helpless and without hope, passive and unconvinced of the Lord's covenant love. She was called a worm and an insect to emphasize the vast difference between the Lord God's greatness and her poor, inadequate self. Quite a way for the prophet to provide perspective! She was not only small but incorrigible and so would be reprimanded, yet she would not be cast off, for she was chosen and loved. She was vulnerable to temptation and oppression yet remained upheld by the Lord.

On the other hand, in the Suffering Servant, there is a beauty of character that draws universal attention. And there is much to admire. Every feature of the servant's conduct—meekness, gentleness, patient listening, skill in teaching, endurance under assaults, and much more—qualified him for being in himself the covenant between the Lord and the people. He was fitted to be the provision for the deepest needs of mortals. His weapons seemed to be not earthly, but spiritual. He operated not from cleverness or with trumpet sounds of loud promotion but simply with gracious initiative. Israel suffered for iniquity and rebellion, whereas the servant suffered because he was obedient to Hashem. He can be seen as dear and submissive—the shining star of the Lord, who, in turn, showed the utmost confidence in him. Indeed, he and the Lord are the two figures of preeminence in this section of Isaiah's prophecy.

How will insensible and stubborn Israel respond to the Suffering Servant, who is full of grace and truth? We find clues to this in the final Servant Song of Isaiah 53.

1. Berlin and Brettler, *The Jewish Study Bible* (New York: Oxford University Press, 1985), 780.
2. Isaiah chapters 40–66 are considered by many modern scholars to be a separate writing from chapters 1–39. To this second half they then give the title Deutero-Isaiah because of what they see to be its distinctive style and vocabulary. But in recent time, the unity of the whole of Isaiah is receiving new emphasis. It has always been recognized that alongside the differences, there are, for instance, many terms that

are common to both "First Isaiah" and "Deutero-Isaiah," including some that rarely or never occur in other Old Testament writings. The differences between the two halves can be explained by the undoubted differences in the prophet's age at the time of writing these two sections and the radically different situations he was addressing. In this author's view, the theory of multiple authorship creates as many problems as it purports to solve. It should be noted that in the Great Isaiah Scroll found among the Dead Sea Scrolls, there is no division whatsoever.

3. J. Alec Motyer, *The Prophecy of Isaiah: An Introduction and Commentary* (Downers Grove: IVP Academic, 1993), 312.

   Motyer, in his commentary on this passage, says, "This election carries with it a guarantee of perpetuity."

4. Adele Berlin, Marc Zvi Brettler, *The Jewish Study Bible* (New York: Oxford University Press, 1999), 867.

5. Ibid., 867, 883.

6. Dan Kurzman, *Ben-Gurion: Prophet of Fire* (New York: Simon and Schuster, 1983), 177, 210.

7. J. Alec Motyer, *The Prophecy of Isaiah*, 383.

CHAPTER 14

The Suffering Servant

§

He was despised and rejected by others;
A man of suffering and acquainted with infirmity.

—ISAIAH 53:3

THE FOURTH SERVANT SONG: ISAIAH 52:12–13

IN THE FOURTH SERVANT SONG, the Servant's work is seen as coming to its fulfillment. The suffering glimpsed in the second and third songs is held up for a closer examination in the fourth song, making it clear that suffering is the key vocation of the Servant and that it is vicarious suffering of the one for the many. The Christian Isaiah scholar, J. Alec Motyer says, "It is typical in the Isaianic literature that a hint made in one section becomes the theme of the next."[1] Here in the fourth song, this theme becomes so vivid that, as the text itself says, we would turn our faces from it. He was more than a martyr; he willingly took up the task of sin bearing, as the Lord God gave him this work.

The song begins with the introduction to this person: "Here." Here he is. Behold him. Preceding this song, in chapters 51 and 52, the Lord repeatedly called Israel to attention: "Listen to me" and "Awake, awake" and "Rouse yourself." *Do not remain oblivious to what I am about to do!* He shook His people from their listlessness. And once they were awake, then, and only then, He, Hashem/the Lord, made the introduction:

See, [or "here"] my servant shall prosper;
He shall be exalted and lifted up,
And shall be very high.
Just as there were many who were astonished at him—
So marred was his appearance,
Beyond human semblance,
And his form beyond that of mortals—
So he shall startle many nations;
Kings shall shut their mouths because of him;
For that which had not been told them
They shall see,
And that which they had not heard
They shall contemplate. (52:13–15)

Kings and people gazed upon him and pondered. Many were astonished. Viewing him was a life-changing experience. He was exalted and lifted up, a personage with great dignity, just as God Himself was seen by Isaiah as "the high and lofty one" (57:15). But in contrast, another reaction to this servant immediately follows his exaltation: astonishment at his disfigurement, so much so that people stepped back in horror, even questioning whether or not he was human, "so marred was his appearance." They were shocked into silence. Isaiah here gets into unfamiliar territory—to think that the Lord's servant, who was to help Israel, would have a repulsive appearance. The nation was being roused from her lethargy to be introduced to *this*?

Then the *prophet* speaks, and this is the pattern we see in this song: the Lord and the prophet share the telling of this story; both God and man view this servant and report what they see. Here is the prophet speaking:

Who has believed what we have heard?
And to whom has the arm of the Lord been revealed?
For he grew up before him like a young plant,

And like a root out of dry ground;
He had no form or majesty that we should look at him,
Nothing in his appearance that we should desire him.
He was despised and rejected by others;
A man of suffering and acquainted with infirmity;
And as one from whom others hide their faces
He was despised, and we held him of no account. (53:1–3)

The portrayal of the Servant in 52:15, though startling, was contemplated even by kings. But now the prophet asks who would believe what is being revealed. Possibly it is a rhetorical question indicating that *no one* believes what the prophet heard. But the Lord will act, and "the arm of the Lord" refers to not someone other than the Lord but to the Lord Himself, who is present in power, and His actions will reveal the salvation event.

We have two enigmas here, says Motyer in his commentary: first, how could such a repulsive-looking person in his suffering become so exalted; and furthermore, how could one so obviously human be the arm of the Lord?[2] I would add another: being so rejected, how could he be an effective leader? He could not be a king. Could this be a prophet?

One thing does stand out: the masculine, personal pronouns come one after the other, in contrast to plural nouns and pronouns referring to people affected by his person and mission. There is counterpoint between the one and the many. Thus, it is difficult to see the Suffering Servant figure as a group or nation. The hypothesis so far has been that the Suffering Servant is the Chosen *One*, and this has been supported so far. We move forward to find yet more clarity.

Surely he has borne our infirmities and carried our diseases;
Yet we accounted him stricken,
Struck down by God and afflicted.
But he was wounded for our transgressions,
Crushed for our iniquities;

Upon him was the punishment that made us whole,
And by his bruises we are healed.
All we like sheep have gone astray;
We have all turned to our own way,
And the Lord has laid on him the iniquity of us all. (53:4–6)

We have come to the climax of the Servant Songs. The essential mission of the Servant is graphically portrayed here: he was to bear the sins of others. He was a man of sorrows, not out of a natural inclination to be sullen but because he was carrying the burdens of a broken humanity.

In the Biblical Hebrew language, future events are foretold in what is defined as "the prophetic perfect." They are viewed as having happened, conforming to the conviction that what God has promised is as good as already fulfilled. Isaiah is speaking from within the new order of things brought about by the Servant. The guilt and punishment of Israel has had its final day, the salvation provided by the Lord being seen as accomplished. When the prophet is through speaking of the atonement made by the Servant, he will break out in exuberant shouts and singing, welcoming Israel and the nations into a vastly enlarged gathering of the redeemed (see Isaiah 54, 55). So the prophet sits in a futuristic position where he sees the fulfillment of God's promises.

But in this song in chapter 53, he emphasizes the great gap in understanding between the Servant and the people: *we* the people thought he was being punished by God for his own presumptuousness, while *he* was enduring pain for *us*. *He* was alone in his sorrow and suffering, bearing our sin and shame, while *we* wandered like sheep without a shepherd. *He* was performing a service on our behalf, while *we* remained aloof. What *he* accomplished was done in splendid isolation, working to meet the deep need of *us all* even as we were oblivious to what he was accomplishing. Furthermore, adding the word *all* to the plural pronouns suggesting the universal benefits of his service; verse 6 begins with "all we" and ends with "us all." Therefore, we know that the servant was involved in this suffering not only for the Jews in exile but for all people in their sin, since all collectively went astray.

God the Lord Himself is the emphatic subject of the final phrase in verse 6. It was His good pleasure to offer up the servant. The servant was the provision and plan of the Lord, who Himself "superintends the priestly task (Lev. 16:21) of transferring the guilt of the guilty to the head of the Servant, giving notice that this is indeed his [the Lord's] considered and acceptable satisfaction for sin."[3] The servant thus resembles, in his service, the sacrificial lamb or the scapegoat on which the High Priest in the system of the Old Covenant liturgically placed all the sins of the individual worshipper or the congregation of Israel.

> He was oppressed, and he was afflicted,
> Yet he did not open his mouth;
> Like a lamb led to the slaughter,
> And like a sheep that before its shearers is silent,
> So he did not open his mouth;
> By a perversion of justice, he was taken away.
> Who could have imagined his future?
> For he was cut off from the land of the living,
> Stricken for the transgression of my people.
> They made his grave with the wicked
> And his tomb with the rich,
> Although he had done no violence,
> And there was no deceit in his mouth. (53:7–9)

The Servant is pictured as being brought to trial before his accusers and there submitting to unjust charges in silence. He was then put to death with transgressors but buried with the rich. The specificity here is remarkable, even while the description to the Israelite reader would have been a great mystery: how could such a passive, suffering victim be the one that has been described as "the arm of the Lord," an expression always indicating the strong action of God? How could one so despised be the one who would bring redemption to Israel? No wonder, then, that Isaiah cried out in the middle of this song: "Who has believed what we have heard?" (53:1)

But Isaiah's perspective was much wider than his readers', and the Spirit of God revealed to him the great need not only of rebellious, wayward, and disheartened Israel but also of the primal burdens of mankind. This servant was to be not only a leader but also a savior from sin and guilt—a profoundly heavier burden. The task of suffering vicariously is born of love—a love that stoops to bear the reproach and cost of others' sins. This is the utmost in servanthood.

> Yet it was the will of the Lord to crush him with pain.
> When you make his life an offering for sin,
> He shall see his offspring and shall prolong his days;
> Through him the will of the Lord shall proper...
> The righteous one, my servant, shall make many righteous,
> And he shall bear their iniquities...
> He poured out himself to death,
> And was numbered with the transgressors;
> Yet he bore the sin of many
> And made intercession for the transgressors. (53:10–12)

The servant was a vicarious sufferer: he identified with sinners, freely bearing their guilt, even while he himself was blameless; he was the Chosen One of God to perform this service; and he was willing to accept and wholly take the substitute's role for this incomparable saving purpose. Though he was "cut off from the land of the living," still the prophet says that he "shall prolong his days," which surely indicates a resurrection.

On the other hand, "we" are described as straying like dumb sheep but, through the Servant's work, becoming his children (offspring) and being made righteous. The prophecy leaped far ahead of the situation of the exiles. Such a future redemption being presented to them is material for deep contemplation.

THE INTERPRETATION OF JEWISH SCHOLARS

The question now is how the Jewish people have received this "report." What do they do with it? How have the rabbis received it in both ancient and modern times? Have they received it as the glorious, saving declaration that it is obviously meant to be? If they put all four of these grand Servant Songs together, what vision do they see? Surely, surely, they see God's chosen and beloved personage—a light to the nations and a sin bearer for all people—as the Messiah whom they have expected from the time of the prophets. Indeed, this passage must be one chief literary source of their expectation of future messianic redemption. Is it not?

The answer is yes and no. The division between the two answers was generally drawn between the pre-Enlightenment and post-Enlightenment times. That is to say, in the modern and postmodern eras, most rabbis and Jewish scholars categorically deny that the Servant Songs are pointing to a Messiah figure. As discussed previously, the expectation of a personal Messiah declined when human reason became the measure of all things and Reform Judaism was the outworking of rationalism within European Jewry. The majority of Jewish people shed their regular observance of religious traditions and became skeptics and secularists. Expectation of the Messiah and knowledge of the sacred texts that prophesied His coming were largely dismissed. This stands in stark contrast to medieval and ancient rabbinic interpretations; literature suggests that most of them identified the servant with the coming Messiah. But let us first examine some contemporary Jewish scholars.

MODERN JEWISH SCHOLARS INTERPRET THE FOURTH SERVANT SONG

The Jewish Study Bible is a popular Oxford University Press publication of 2004, boasting nearly forty scholars worldwide who contributed to the translation and commentary of the Tanakh (Old Testament). The publisher represents them as being the best of Jewish biblical scholarship worldwide from Orthodox, Conservative, and Reform Judaism.

In its treatment of the fourth Servant Song, after pointing out that there has been much dispute about the identity of the servant, this Jewish commentary states,

> Many argue that the servant symbolizes the entire Jewish people... The passage, then, describes the nation's unjust tribulations at the hands of the Babylonians...as well as the nation's salvific [saving] role for the world at large...Targum and various midrashim identify the servant as the Messiah, but this suggestion is unlikely, since nowhere else does Deutero-Isaiah refer to the Messiah, and the absence of belief in an individual Messiah is one of the hallmarks of Deutero-Isaiah's outlook (in contrast to that of First Isaiah).["]4

It goes on to state that some commentators identify the servant with a prophet or a small group of faithful Jews. It also notes in passing that Christians have argued that it predicts the coming of Jesus, with no other comment except, "Medieval rabbinic commentators devoted considerable attention to refuting this interpretation."[5] So the study Bible throws its weight behind the argument that the Servant was the nation Israel, that it was probably the kings and nations of the world that were "stunned that such an insignificant and lowly group turns out to have been so important to the divine plan."[6] Israel was the Suffering Servant, the innocent one that took upon itself the sins and guilt of the world. Israel was the righteous one that will make others righteous. Through Israel's suffering, the world will be made whole. Here there is no prophecy of a Messiah—the Anointed One—but rather a reference to the Jewish people.

Susan Ackerman, who is listed in the Jewish Women's Archive, is a professor of religion and women's and gender studies at Dartmouth College.

She is the contributor commentator on Isaiah for *The New Interpreter's Study Bible*, published by Abingdon Press, a publishing arm of the United Methodist Church. Her argument comes to the same conclusion as *The Jewish Study Bible*, and it is unequivocal: the Suffering Servant was the Israelite people.

> These verses offer them [the Israelites] a revolutionary theology that explains the hardships of exile: The people had to endure the exile and the suffering it engendered because that suffering was done in service to God so that God, through their atoning sacrifice, could redeem the nations…Israel's suffering during the exile was something God willed in order that the sins of the nations might be forgiven. Now, having endured these agonies on behalf of the nations, Israel will be rewarded."[7]

In Ackerman's comments there are no references to a Messiah who might fulfill this role of servant, except in an excursus that explains how the Servant Songs are interpreted by Christian scholars. But in the explanatory notes, there is nothing to indicate that this could point to a Messiah. However, there is a substantial amount of ancient and medieval Jewish literature that does interpret this passage as messianic. It seems that she wants to elude all reference to this possibility. Again, as in the *Jewish Study Bible*, the Suffering Servant is interpreted as Israel, according to the author. Israel paid the penalty for the sins of the world. This is set forth in the study Bible mentioned above, which is issued by an American mainline Protestant publisher. Are we to believe, then, that Israel is the Savior? Are the Gentiles, therefore, to give thanks to Israel for removing the guilt of their sins? Is there no individual chosen Savior—only Israel? Are the Jewish People, then, the chosen, not just to bring in monotheism and the law of God but to be the redeemer saviors of this sinful world?

Rabbi David S. Ariel is the director of the Oxford Centre for Hebrew and Jewish Studies. He states emphatically that "the 'suffering servant' passage was a memorial ode to King Josiah, a Davidic descendant, who was killed in a battle at Megiddo (2 Kings 23:29)." He offers no supporting evidence for his argument. (He states that the heart of the passage is in Isaiah 53:1–5, which is strange, since verse 6 is laden with meaning about a vicarious death and the line of thought then continues uninterrupted through verse 12.) Rabbi Ariel says, "In the Christian tradition…it [the Suffering Servant Song] was taken to mean that Christ had died for the sins of the people. Not knowing the original intent of the passage, Christians read their prediction into the text after the fact." Then he asks, "Why do Jews and Christians read these passages so differently? Jews read them in the historical context in which they were written. The passages refer to the sufferings and hope for restoration of the Jewish kingdom in all its moral and religious glory. Jews understand the metaphors in these passages in the context of Jewish historical events, which refer to real persons and kings. Christians take them out of their historical context and read them as predictions."[8]

The rabbi would have his readers believe that Christian scholars are unschooled in hermeneutics and exegesis—in the historical settings of scriptures. If only Christian theologians had better training in biblical texts, he implies, then they would understand that this passage has nothing to do with a Messiah.

But it should be understood that placing a prophecy in historical context certainly does not mean that future redemptive acts of God are absent from view. On the contrary, the prophet was a seer who wrote at a stressful time in history but beckoned his hearers look into the future to get a glimpse of the Lord's saving activity. The historical setting is important for seeing the situation of the hearers, but quite obviously, the time of fulfillment for God's plan could be some time in the future. Prophecy is designed to show how that situation fits into the overall divine plan. In fact, the foundation of Israel's sense of history is *promise*. It was so from the beginning, when God promised Abraham to make of him a great nation. It was so when God promised David that his kingdom would be perpetual. Because Israel's true sense of history is built on promise, they are a future-oriented people. The Suffering Servant

Song is no exception: it was composed during a period of international crisis, but its fulfillment was in the future

These noted Jewish religious authors seem to be representative of modern rabbinical opinion on the fourth Servant Song. Those rabbis who are willing to speak about this issue are divided between those who apply it to a historical leader, as Rabbi Ariel does, and those who point to the nation of Israel as the Suffering Servant, as Ms. Ackerman does. Supporters of both conclusions brush off ancient and medieval Jewish interpretations of this passage.

However, there were rabbis both before and after Christ who considered the fourth Servant Song to be a messianic prophecy.

ANCIENT AND MEDIEVAL RABBINICAL INTERPRETATIONS

From the first century on, there were teachings—some that made it into the Talmud—that interpreted at least a portion of the fourth Servant Song as pointing to a coming Messiah.

The Targum of Yonatan (Jonathan) is well known. In a monograph published by the Hebrew Union College of Cincinnati, the Jewish scholar Samuel H. Levey says that this targum is dated to the first century AD. But such targums, though not written down until the first century, typically represent even more ancient understandings of Old Testament passages. The Targum of Yonatan was an official and authoritative version of the prophets used in the synagogues. It might be surprising to some that targums were used in the synagogues at all, since they are interpretative expansions of the biblical translation similar to expanded Bible translations that are on the market today.

Let's make a comparison: the New Revised Standard Version of Isaiah 52:13 reads, "See, my servant shall prosper; he shall be exalted and lifted up and shall be very high." That is a strict translation of the first verse of the fourth Servant Song. The Targum of Yonatan, to this same verse, adds to the sentence subject "the Messiah": "Behold my servant, the Messiah, shall prosper; he shall be exalted and great and very powerful." A rabbi of the first century respected enough to be a translator and interpreter made that insertion.

The Targum of Yonatan is startling as it proceeds in this Servant Song, for although it is close in its translation of 52:13, it takes the usual targumic liberties with the text as it continues. In chapter 53 it assigns to the Messiah only those references that portray the servant in his glory and power. Those many references to the servant, in the same chapter, that portray *the servant as suffering and dying* are then applied to Israel or to the Gentile nations![9] This is a clear distortion of the text, since it is evident that the same person endured the sufferings as well as victoriously provided salvation for the many. Nevertheless, in contrast to the interpretations of modern Jewish scholars, this Servant Song does refer to the promised Messiah in this ancient expanded translation.

The Isaiah Targum is an expanded translation of the Isaiah prophecy. It probably originated in the first or second century AD, though most scholars agree that changes were made to it through perhaps the eighth century. In it, the fourth Servant Song of Isaiah is interpreted as referring to a Messiah figure and the regathering of the Jewish people. For example, from verse 5, this targum affirms that the Messiah would build the sanctuary, and, from verse 10, God would establish His kingdom. These interpretations stretch the meaning of the text almost beyond recognition, but the point is that to these ancient authors, the Suffering Servant represented the coming Messiah.[10]

These writings indicate that a Messiah both suffering and triumphant was incompatible with the views of some Jews. Therefore, Isaiah 53 was difficult for them to interpret in relation to the Messiah. Nonetheless, there was a way around this, and that was to posit two Messiah figures—one who would die, perhaps in battle, and the other who would reign triumphant and never see suffering and death. Others took another way around this, saying that the Servant would simply have a *readiness* to suffer and die. Still others stretched the interpretation to the point that when death was mentioned, it referred to Moses.[11]

Looking to a later time, the Babylonian Talmud—probably put into writing in about AD 200—includes this speculative conversation in the Bavli Sanhedrin chapter:

Said Rab, "The world was created only for David."
And Samuel said, "For Moses."
And R. Yohanan said, "For the Messiah."
What is his name?
The house of R. Shila said, "His name is Shiloh, as it is said, 'Until Shiloh come.'..."
[Three more names are here suggested.]
Rabbis said, "His name is 'the leper of the school house,' as it is written, 'Surely he has borne our griefs and carried our sorrows, yet we did esteem him a leper, smitten of God and afflicted.' (Isaiah 53:4)[12]

The Babylonian Talmud is the most widely accepted version of the Talmud. In it we find the Suffering Servant identified as a leper and the Messiah. The descriptive words *stricken* and *afflicted* in 53:4, and the mention of his being marred in appearance "beyond human semblance" in 52:14, suggests the disease of leprosy. Above that reference is the question, "What is his name?" and the answer "His name is Shiloh." Shiloh was a place name designating the town where, during the conquest, Israel put up her Tent of Meeting. The text quoted by R. Shila has four possible readings in the cryptic text, one of which is, "until Shiloh comes" and another, "until he comes to Shiloh." Most scholars, both Jewish and Christian, believe it possible that this has a messianic meaning or at least acknowledge that this has traditionally been viewed as a messianic prophecy. The tent of meeting was where Moses and the Lord spoke to each other. In the Messiah, God and mortal man would meet.

Yephet ben Ali was a distinguished tenth-century commentator on the Tanakh whose theological position was Karaite, a sect of the Jews that did not acknowledge the authority of the Talmud but adhered strictly to the Tanakh. He says of the Servant Song of Isaiah in 52:13–53:12.

> I am inclined, with Benjamin of Nehawend, to regard it as alluding to the Messiah, and as opening with a description of his condition in exile, from the time of his birth to his accession to the throne: for the prophet begins by speaking of his being seated in a position of great honour, and then goes back to relate all that will happen to him during the captivity. He thus gives us to understand two things: In the first instance, that the Messiah will only reach his highest degree of honour after long and severe trials; and secondly, that these trials will be sent upon him as a kind of sign, so that, if he finds himself under the yoke of misfortunes whilst remaining pure in his actions, he may know that he is the desired one.

I'll list here a few more of his thoughts, selected from his commentary. In commenting on 53:4, he explains, "God appoints his servant to carry their sins, and by doing so lighten their punishment in order that Israel might not be completely exterminated."

Explaining verses 7 and 8, he says, "In these two verses seven things are enumerated which God brought upon the Messiah."

About verse 10 he says that Israel will be the beneficiary of the Servant's suffering: "The prophet next says, 'When his soul makes a trespass-offering,' indicating thereby that his soul was compelled to take Israel's guilt upon itself, 'And he bare the sin of many' (ver. 12)."[13]

For Yephet ben Ali, it was none other than the Messiah who, in Isaiah's view, suffered vicariously, and it was Israel for whose sins atonement was being made. He was bold to insist that the Messiah would be one who would be a sacrifice for sin.

Isaac ben Judah Abrabanel, a fifteenth-century Portuguese statesman, philosopher, and scripture commentator, is commonly known as simply Arbabanel. He himself believed that the Suffering Servant figure represented the coming Messiah, but more importantly, he reports that this was the majority opinion among the rabbis: "Jonathan ben Uzziel interprets it in the Targum of the future Messiah; and this is also the opinion of our learned men in the majority of their Midrashim."[14]

With this in mind, how can modern Jewish scholarship reject, out-of-hand, the consensus of its own revered rabbis and argue that the Jewish *nation* is the meaning and fulfillment of this prophecy? We must continue probing for the reason the modern Jewish intellectual community reacts so strongly to the messianic interpretation of the fourth Servant Song.

As noted above, many adherents of Judaism, especially those of the Reform branch, have discarded the miraculous, supernatural elements of the faith. The same goes for the high percentage of secular Jews in both the Diaspora and Israel—they are skeptical or simply disinterested. Their mind-sets will not allow the idea that some Tanakh prophecy might be predictive—that God, if there is a god, would give to their prophets a vision of future redemption.

But there is another reason that Jewish scholarship rejects the four Servant Songs as messianic. I leave it to the evangelical writer the late Arthur Kac, a Jewish scholar himself who came to believe in Yeshua as the Messiah, to help the discussion here. He argues that Jewish scholarship's resistance to a messianic interpretation of the Servant Songs is partially explained by Judaism's push-back against Christianity's expansion. He writes concerning Judaism's approach to this scripture during the whole two-thousand-year period since Jesus Christ:

The rise and growth of the Christian movement has, in due course of time, brought about a definite change in the attitude of Rabbinic

Judaism to the Messianic teachings of the Old Testament…The national rejection of Jesus by the Jewish people induced the Rabbis to exercise greater caution in their interpretation of these Messianic teachings…The manner in which Christian theologians applied to Jesus the Messianic predictions of the Old Testament often colored Jewish understanding and interpretation of these portions of Scripture. This was especially true with reference to the mediatorial function and the vicarious sufferings of the Messiah.[15]

Kac continues, saying that the Christian theologians' use of the Tanakh in confirming the messiahship of Jesus "proved quite embarrassing to Jewish theology," prompting the rabbis to "downgrade the whole doctrine of a personal Messiah."[16] According to Kac, it was a defensive reaction to Christian interpretation. The portrayal of the Suffering Servant provides a vivid picture of Jesus of Nazareth, who came centuries after the writing of Isaiah. Therefore, the passages from Isaiah must be kept from being a prophecy of salvation for all people for all time.

God had a greater gift to offer the world than His recalcitrant servant, Israel. As we pointed out in chapter 1, Israel was and is a gift to our world and our history. But within and through Israel, there was to come a gift far greater than Israel—the Chosen *One* who would bring salvation. Abraham, father of many nations, was willing to offer his son on the sacrificial altar, and every Hebrew knew that story. Now there appears in this Isaianic prophecy a person who would be a sacrifice for all. Take one more look at this text:

When you make his life an offering for sin,
He shall see his offspring, and shall prolong his days;
Through him the will of the Lord shall prosper. (verse 10bcd)

"Offering for sin" is literally "a guilt offering," the sacrifice that spoke of satisfaction. "He shall make many righteous" (verse 11). The death of the servant satisfied the needs of the sinful people who stood guilty before God. It also satisfied the requirements of God in relation to His broken law and offended holiness. Then the will of the Lord was completed, and those recipients of the servant's work became his "offspring." His family was gathered under his authority, and the servant lives on and prays for them (verse 12).

Chapter 13, under the title "Two Servants," looked at both Israel and the Messiah as I and others believe they are presented in the prophecy of Isaiah. Each entity has sections devoted to it. Each has a distinctive relationship to the Lord and a unique mission to the world. But here in chapter 14, I contend that the Servant Songs are directed to the individual figure, the Anointed One, the Mashiach (Messiah). So, then, both are chosen servants, but the one who emerges as the Suffering Servant is the perfectly faithful One who effectuates the work of redemption for both Israel and the Gentiles—Jesus Christ.[17]

He becomes the salvation of the world for those who believe. *He* is the Lamb of God, who was silent in the face of verbal and physical abuse—the One who bore our sins. No one else could do it. No other individual. No nation. No special group. *He* was and is *the One*, the chosen, whom the Father upholds.

See—here is the Servant of the Lord. Here is our redemption.

The prophet seer saw beyond Israel, beyond the eighth century BC, and beyond the exile. He could naturally see Israel; he did see her chosen role and her suffering. But he saw something greater and more exalted that only the Spirit of God could have shown Him.

The prophecy is a glimpse of the Messiah—a portrait of pathos and beauty.

1. J. Alec Motyer, *The Prophecy of Isaiah* (Downers Grove: Inter Varsity Press, 1993), 289.
2. Ibid., 427–428.
3. Ibid., 431.
4. Berlin and Brettler, *The Jewish Study Bible* (New York: Oxford University Press, 1999), 891.
5. Ibid., 891.
6. Ibid., 891.
7. *The New Interpreter's Study Bible*, (Nashville: Abingdon Press), 1031, 1032.
8. David S. Ariel, *What Do Jews Believe?* (New York: Schocken Books, 1995), 235–236.

   An example is 53:4, where the NRSV reads, "Surely he has borne our infirmities and carried our sorrows; yet we accounted him stricken, struck down by God and afflicted." The Targum of Jonathan has the same verse 4 reading this way: "Then he shall seek pardon for our sins, and our iniquities shall be forgiven for his sake; though *we* are considered stricken, smitten by God, and afflicted." Samson H. Levey, *The Messiah: An Aramaic Interpretation: The Messianic Exegesis of the Targum* (Cincinnati: Hebrew Union College-Jewish Institute of Religion, 1974), 33, 63.
9. Craig A. Evans, *Noncanonical Writings and New Testament Interpretation* (Peabody: Hendrickson Publishers, Inc., 1995), 103.
10. Ibid., 103.
11. Driver and Neubauer, *The "Suffering Servant" of Isaiah According to the Jewish Interpreters* (New York: Hermon Press, 1969), xliv.
12. *The Talmud of Babylonia: An American Translation, XXIIIC: Tractate Sanhedrin*, Chapters 9–11. (Chico: Scholars Press, 1985), 139.
13. Driver and Neubauer, *The "Suffering Servant,"* 19–31.
14. Arthur W. Kac, *The Rebirth of the State of Israel* (Chicago: Moody Press, 1958), 220–221.
15. Ibid., 215.
16. Ibid., 222.
17. Ibid., 222.

CHAPTER 15

The Denouement

§

He is the Lord, our God;
His judgments are in all the earth.
He is mindful of his covenant forever,
Of the word that he commanded,
For a thousand generations,
The covenant that he made with Abraham,
His sworn *promise* (emphasis mine) to Isaac,
Which he confirmed to Jacob as a statute,
To Israel as an everlasting covenant,
Saying, "To you I will give the land of Canaan
As your portion for an inheritance."

—PSALMS 104:7–11

They are Israelites, and to them belong the adoption, the glory,
the covenants, the giving of the law, the worship, and the promises;
to them belong the patriarchs, and from them according to the flesh,
comes the Messiah, who is over all, God blessed forever. Amen.

—ROMANS 9:4–5

As regards the gospel they are enemies of God
For your sake; but as regards election they are beloved,

For the sake of their ancestors;
For the gifts and the calling of God are irrevocable.

—Romans 11:28–29

How is the Middle East conflict going to be resolved? That is the question people pose after conversing awhile about the seemingly endless wars and skirmishes in the Holy Land. Who will the winners be, and who the losers? They are wondering what the resolution will be of all the historical and present-day intricacies of the plot concerning the Chosen people. Some assume that when one party or the other finally prevails, it will emerge as conqueror and ruler. Others, who think in terms of biblical prophecy, have some idea about what they consider will be the end time. We will look at Israel's history and then at promises in the scriptures concerning the outlook for this people.

In the scripture epigraph at the head of this chapter, I quote from the Apostle Paul's writing. Implicit in it is a truth relevant to the denouement of the ages-long conflict. Where is Israel in this plot—now, since the life, death, and resurrection of Jesus Christ?

The door of salvation for the Gentiles has been opened wide. This open-door gospel, obtained by faith, replaced Judaism's core teaching that righteousness (justification) is obtained by keeping the Law of Moses. So the primitive church, composed of both Jews and Gentiles, was confronted with this issue: Do the Jewish people still have a *special role* in the divine purpose? Or have they now lost their distinctive place in the Kingdom of God?

The Apostle Paul, himself a Jew, insists that he is not separating himself from the Jews and that the ancient promises to them have not been annulled. He startles readers by stating solidarity with the Jews, calling them "my brothers" (verse 3, translated "my people" in the NRSV)—the same title he uses for his beloved Christian friends in Rome! "My brothers"—kin to him even though they spit on his ministry from the very beginning!

JEWISH BELONGINGS

The apostle further argues that the Chosen People have not lost what was granted them. He declares, "To them belong" these listed privileges:

1. "the adoption" (They are called the "sons of God" in the Old Testament.)
2. "the glory" (God's glory revealed to them at Sinai, on their march to Canaan, and at other places)
3. "the covenants, the giving of the law, the worship, and the promises" (The promises will be highlighted in this chapter.)
4. "To them belong the patriarchs, and from them according to the flesh, comes the Messiah, who is over all, God blessed forever. Amen."

These are, in a special way, the belongings of the Jews.[1]

Toward the end of the letter to the Romans, Paul inserts the following to underscore what he wrote further up in the letter: "For I tell you that Christ has become a servant of the circumcised on behalf of the truth of God in order that he might confirm the promises given to the patriarchs" (Romans 15:8a). Christ, the servant—the servant of Judaism's adherents! Would this pertain even to the promises of the land made to Judaism's adherents? What scholar of the New Testament would answer no—and why?

The point is that despite Israel's stubbornness, *she remains the recipient of God's gifts and promises.* They are her belongings—this people whose lineage has continued from Abraham and Sarah. In the Chapter One, I discussed the question of Jewish identity and whether or not modern Jews are the descendants of ancient Jewry (with some small proportion of them being Gentile converts). Supporting evidence indicated that their identity has been maintained throughout the ages—that there is a vital continuity between ancient and modern Jewry—and I have proceeded on this premise.

And now these points come together, giving us perspective on modern Israel—the people we know and the state that is situated in today's Middle East.

In the course of the Jews' long history, God has chosen to bless and judge them according to His purpose. And so it seems credible to maintain that it is God who has interested Himself so mysteriously in the destiny of His people and who has given land to them in the midst of other nations. Further, when He judged them and permitted them to be spewed out of the land and scattered to the ends of the earth, He did not utterly forsake them. He preserved their identity throughout their worldwide wanderings and persecutions. Lately, through His own providential action and their own catastrophic circumstances in tandem with world wars and regional conflicts, they are experiencing an unparalleled return to the Promised Land. Therefore, one might ask, is He not behind the return of His people? Is not the whole history of this people an anomaly of history wrapped up in the fulfillment of His promises, illustrating the faithfulness of their God and ours? Is that history not as consequential—or more consequential—than the history of any other people, though not acknowledged as such in academic discussions? Christopher Dawson, a twentieth-century historian, writes, "The world-transforming events which changed the whole course of human history have occurred as if it were under the surface of history unnoticed by the historians and the philosophers."[2] The crucial events in Israel's experience fit Dawson's thesis.

This ancient set of promises with which this discussion is concerned was first given to Abraham: God would make of him a great nation; the nation would be a blessing to all peoples; and all the land shown to him, then inhabited by the Canaanites, would belong to his descendants. That these claims should have such relevance in today's Middle East conflict is absurd to secularists and debatable to some Christian theologians, but these promises should not be overlooked in the study of world history. The promises stand in the Tanakh, where they are repeatedly enunciated. Therefore, those who take the scriptures seriously surely should contemplate these promises as they judge the legitimacy of the modern State of Israel.

The Apostle Paul is speaking to Europeans residing in Rome when he says, "To them belong the promises." The promises include that little parcel of land in the Middle East. Yet some Christian scholars contend that this Promised Land is not recognized as a gift in the New Testament, under the New Covenant; therefore, for that reason, individuals should not support Israelis in their claim to the land of Palestine. Such is the case with one biblical theologian who has said,

> The New Testament goes a long way toward spiritualizing the nature of these promises. That is, the Israelite endeavor to acquire land and forge a nation takes on a different shape in the new covenant of Christ. God's people [Israel] are no longer called to build an empire based on the books of Genesis or Joshua. The Israeli attempt to take land and forge a nation is religiously misdirected.[3]

But one then might ask, is the land no longer a concern to the Lord of history? Does God now only deal with the church and with individuals and not with nations and peoples and their position in the world? Was not the land one of those promises made to Abraham and his posterity? Again I quote the Apostle Paul:

> As regards the gospel they are enemies of God
> For your sake; but as regards election they are beloved,
> For the sake of their ancestors;
> For the gifts and the calling of God are irrevocable. (Romans 11:28–29)

The author quoted above says, "The Israeli attempt to take land, " speaking as if it were all absconded, stolen, bought cheaply, or taken in battle. How did the early Zionists who settled Palestine acquire the land? By purchasing it, much of it from rich Arabs, or effendis, some of whom were absentee landowners living in Jerusalem, Paris, Damascus, Amman, and Beirut—and who extracted every bit of wealth possible out of the poor peasants who lived on and worked the land. Those rich Arabs were delighted to make such deals with the immigrating Jews, especially at the exorbitant prices they demanded. Then those pioneering Jews had to spend years draining the swamps and clearing the land for agricultural use. Additionally, a large portion of the land was public land held by the Turks under the Ottoman Empire. Later, following the reordering of nations after World War I, the British held the land under the Palestinian Mandate of the League of Nations, with the proviso of it becoming a homeland for the Jewish people. It took that radical disruption in international boundaries following a world war to give the persecuted Jewish Diaspora hope—hope to once again possess their ancient land for security and for a renewal of their culture and religious life.

> Do not remember the former things,
> Or consider the things of old.
> I am about to do a new thing;
> Now it springs forth, do you not perceive it? (Isaiah 43:18–19a)

God's will was that Israel would be scattered when they became unfaithful. That was made clear by Moses, the prophets, and Jesus. Is it not just as clear that the Jewish people are to be regathered? Would it not be incongruous to see Israel as a nation that has been preserved for thousands of years and that has received the prophetic promise of an ingathering? Is it logical to think they will never return, never see their culture revived, never experience reunion with their kin, never again be close to the great holy places and landmarks of their history—the Mediterranean coastline, the Jordan Valley, the Negev desert, Hebron, the historic heartland, the plains of Sharon and Megiddo,

Mount Carmel, and most of all, the city of Jerusalem? If the Hebrew people were formed to be the chosen, and if they remain such today, it is certainly fitting that the Lord of history would take them back to the land that represents His care and love. They are His vine and the apple of His eye. And though they have been absent from the land for almost two thousand years, He remains their God, and their yearning for a return to that gift of land has never faltered.

After the 1967 Six-Day War, Dr. Abraham Joshua Heschel wrote,

> The Jewish people has never ceased to be passionate about Zion… Exile from the land was conceived as an interruption, as a prelude to return, never as an abandonment or detachment. Bonds of hope tied us to the land. To abandon these bonds was to deny our identity.[4]

This attachment is more than just the patriotism or nationalism that other peoples experience. It is the Chosen People's tie to their past patriarchs, law, kings, and prophets and to their own future in the hoped-for Messiah—the One who they believe will bring redemption to their people and eventually to the world. They were scattered, with no power to return and resettle, for a seemingly never-ending length of time. Those who assimilated into the societies of their adopted nations may not have realized the intensity of longing that other Jews who kept the Torah and prophets had. But it was there, in the heart of that nation. This future—the longed-for Messiah—was secularized by modern, liberal Judaism, as we have pointed out. But liberal Judaism is now weakening because of both assimilation with Gentiles and disinterest; and the world is watching a modern Orthodox Judaism come to life—more serious and substantive. In fact, the compiler of *The Zionist Idea*, Arthur Hertzberg, says in his introduction that "from the Jewish perspective messianism, and not nationalism, is the primary element in Zionism."[5] Thus, the attachment to the land involves more than land; it involves the blossoming of renewed interest in the tradition, religion, and perennial hope of Israel for the Messianic Age. Israel's past, her embrace of Zionism, and her future must all be considered as we ponder Paul's statements: "To them belong the promises," (Romans 9:4) and, a few paragraphs later, "The gifts and the calling of God are irrevocable" (Romans 11:29).

THE PROMISES

God, who interests Himself in the destiny of His People and who has overseen the maintenance of their identity, issues promises for a bright future. What I am calling a denouement, or the outlook of vindication and hope, is not defined in terms of years and months. It is a vision of hope for the ending of the Babylonian exile, but it is also much more. It foresees a worldwide dispersion of the chosen and their ingathering from all those far-off places. The near term is a paradigm that will precede the final and complete one. But can we believe that we could be living in the era when the ultimate fulfillment of the prophets takes place? Without answering that, let's proceed to the promises couched in the word of the faithful God of Israel.

Isaiah contains a notable prophetic promise of return:

Because you are precious in my sight,
And honored, and I love you,
I give people in return for you,
Nations in exchange for your life.
Do not fear, for I am with you;
I will bring your offspring from the east,
And from the west I will gather you;
I will say to the north, "Give them up,"
And to the south, "Do not withhold;
Bring my sons from far away
And my daughters from the end of the earth—
Everyone who is called by my name,
Whom I created for my glory,
Whom I formed and made." (Isaiah 43:4–7)

Israel is addressed here in endearing terms. She is precious, honored, and loved. Could this prophecy refer to all who call on the name of the Lord, both Jew and Gentile? Isaiah does indeed take the reader into the universal realm when he tells of salvation to the whole earth. However, this poetic section *refers only to the Jewish people*. That is clear when the word of the Lord says, "I give people in return for you, nations in exchange for your life." Other peoples may have to lose their national identities and be forgotten, but Israel will retain hers because of the Lord's covenantal love and promises.

Later, Isaiah refers to the return from Babylon, but in this passage he sees something else, and that is a worldwide ingathering of the Chosen People. He is speaking *to* the Jewish nation *about* the Jewish nation as he portrays not the foreseeable but what lies beyond the usual, ordinary, and predictable in history. Isaiah's prophecy encourages the Jews with the assurance that in the near term—and the long term as well—they are the Lord's, and He will bring them back for the day of redemption; they'll return from the east, the west, the north, and the south.

The Partial Restoration

The first return from exile was incomplete. Not all Jews returned from Babylon. Paul Johnson says that "between 734 and 581 B. C. there were six distinct deportations of the Israelites, and more fled voluntarily to Egypt and other parts of the Near East. *From this time onwards, a majority of Jews would always live outside the Promise Land.*"(emphasis mine)[6] That was the beginning of the Jewish Diaspora that would last for twenty-five hundred years—and still counting. Only a minority returned from Babylonia; others stayed, and still others who engaged in trade and commerce settled in far-off lands. Louis Greenberg, in his book *The Jews in Russia*, says that "records left by historians of Armenia and Georgia tell us that Jewish settlements appeared in the Caucasus and in Transcaucasia soon after the destruction of Jerusalem in 586 BCE and that at the end of the fourth century BCE cities in Armenia had large Jewish populations. From the ruins of tombstones, synagogue inscriptions, and Greek sources, we learn that in the Crimea more than two thousand years ago there were well-organized Jewish communities whose origin undoubtedly dates back many centuries more."[7] Joan Peters writes that a Jewish community in Egypt dates back to before the Babylonian captivity, and Jewish communities in Morocco and Yemen date back to about the same time—586 B.C.E.[8] Yet back in Palestine, the land was a vassal nation of the empire in power.

So was this return from Babylon the glorious worldwide return to the land, and was it followed by the era of prosperity and holiness of which the prophets so eloquently spoke? It would seem not. That more complete worldwide return would happen later, after the great empires of history had had their day. This prophecy was an encouragement to those in Babylonian exile, but the homecoming was incomplete. Furthermore, it became evident that the restoration of the monarchy was not going to usher in the great time of redemption, since Jerusalem became corrupted and influenced by Greek culture. "Eschatology (latter days) is interwoven with history," says J. Alec Motyer in his Isaiah commentary, and "Isaiah realized that his ministry was significant beyond his own times and that its immediate relevance did not exhaust its meaning." The immediate purposes of God "are blended with a vision of the eschatological fulfilment of all He ever promised."[9]

PROPHETIC PROMISE IN JEREMIAH AND EZEKIEL

Now therefore thus says the Lord, the God of Israel...See, I am going to gather [the people of Israel] from all the lands to which I drove them in my anger and my wrath and in great indignation; I will bring them back to this place, and I will settle them in safety. They shall be my people, and I will be their God. I will give them one heart and one way, that they may fear me for all time for their own good and the good of their children after them…Fields shall be bought in this land of which you are saying, It is a desolation, without human beings or animals; it has been given into the hands of the Chaldeans. Fields shall be bought for money, and deeds shall be signed and sealed and witnessed, in the land of Benjamin, the places around Jerusalem, and in the cities of Judah, of the hill country, of the Shephelah, and of the Negeb, for I will restore their fortunes, says the Lord. (Jeremiah 32:36–39, 43–44)

Heschel says, "Pagans have idols, Israel has a promise. We have no image, all we have is hope. Israel reborn is a verification of the promise." (10)

The prophecies of the destruction of Jerusalem were so drastic that even the prophets who uttered them could hardly believe the tragedy that was in store for their People and land. After hearing the word of the Lord pronounce judgment on the wicked nation, the prophet Ezekiel fell down on his face and cried out with a loud voice: "Ah Lord God! will you make a full end of the remnant of Israel?" (Ezekiel 11:13) It is at that point that the Lord gives him the promise of return, not on Israel's terms, but according to His determination:

Though I removed them far away among the nations, and though I scattered them among the countries, yet I have been a sanctuary to them for a little while in the countries where they have gone. Therefore say: Thus says the Lord God: I will gather you from the peoples, and assemble you out of the countries where you have been scattered, and I will give you the land of Israel…I will give them one heart, and put a new spirit within them; I will remove the heart of stone from their flesh and give them a heart of flesh… (Ezekiel 11:16–17, 19)

Later in Ezekiel's prophecy, we hear the Lord, in a figure of speech, speaking to the land, specifically the hill country west of the Jordan. He, as judge, will make the slander and offenses of the nations turn back on them.

And you, mortal, prophesy to the mountains of Israel, and say, O mountains of Israel, hear the word of the Lord. Thus says the Lord God: Because the enemy said of you, 'Aha!' and, 'the ancient heights have become our possession,' therefore prophesy, and say: Thus says the Lord God: Because *they made you desolate* indeed, and crushed you from all sides, so that you became the *possession of the rest of the nations*, and *you became an object of gossip and slander among the people;* therefore, O mountains of Israel, hear the word of the Lord God: Thus says the Lord God to the mountains and the hills, the watercourse and the valleys, *the desolate wastes and the deserted towns, which have become a source of plunder and an object of derision to the rest of the nations all around*; therefore thus says the Lord God: I am speaking in my hot jealousy against the rest of the nations, and against all Edom, who, *with wholehearted joy and utter contempt, took my land as their possession*…I swear that the nations that are all around you shall themselves suffer insults. (Ezekiel 36:1–5, 7b) (emphasis mine)

Ezekiel's apt personification of the mountains is utilized to denounce the wars of words and actions that the nations waged against Israel. When God used these nations to militarily punish Israel, they were not content with normal aggressive action; they conspired to crush Israel and annihilate the Jews in order to make the land their own. So God will punish them.

From Desolation to Gladness

In chapter 3 we pointed out that Palestine was once largely a wasteland, the British consul in Palestine reporting in 1857 that "the country is in a considerable degree empty of inhabitants and therefore its great need is that of a body of population," and that the effendi families who had been dispossessing and exploiting the peasant migrants in Palestine were resentful of the few immigrant Jews who were working the land.

The prophet Jeremiah speaks of the restoration in terms of first the land—its desolation and recovery—and then the Messiah's coming:

> Thus says the Lord: In this place of which you say ["it is" or "it will be"] a waste without human beings or animals,' in the towns of Judah and the streets of Jerusalem that are desolate, without inhabitants, human or animal, there shall once more be heard the voice of gladness, the voice of the bridegroom and the voice of the bride, the voices of those who sing, as they bring thank offerings to the house of the Lord. (Jeremiah 33:10–11)

In the Hebrew language, the preposition *without* is used five times in Jeremiah's statement above, indicating the abject desolation and hopelessness of the land. Bruggeman says,

> The cessation of wedding joy signifies a crushing judgment in which conventional social relations are impossible and the entire infrastructure of the community has failed...In this massive assertion of judgment, there is no will for celebration, not enough security or trust or buoyancy or confidence to undertake a wedding which always constitutes some investment in the future...It is in this place of desolate silence that a new sound will be heard...Israel will resume the social practice of mirth.[11]

Then, following the statement about land restoration, Jeremiah continues with messianic prophecy:

> The days are surely coming, says the Lord, when I will fulfill the promise I made to the house of Israel and the house of Judah. In those days and at that time I will cause a righteous Branch to spring up for David, and he will execute justice and righteousness in the land. (33:14)

THE MUSLIM UNDERVALUATION OF THE LAND

Joan Peters, the well-known researcher of Palestine, states, "For centuries the non-Jewish, particularly the Muslim, people who did inhabit the land had been largely composed of a revolving immigrant population of diverse ethnic origins…migrants and peasants originating from other lands."[12] Under the rule of the Ottomans and other empires previous, the land was desolate. Most of the peasants were poverty-stricken, and much of the population was migratory. Furthermore, Palestine never existed as a separate country under any of the several Islamic administrations. The claims made today by Palestinians about their roots being in that land are suspect, and according to some researchers, such as Joan Peters, they are absolutely false. Her conclusions, noted above, came after her tracing of those claims.

The land did not hold any historical significance for them, except as a means of subverting the narrative of the Hebrew people. The legends the Islamic people recited and the edifices they erected there were meant to *erase the credibility of the Bible.* It may be difficult to believe, but Palestine had very little significance in the religion of Islam. It was not considered a gift of Allah. Jerusalem has had significance for Muslims only since the legend circulated following Mohammed's death and ascent to the seventh heaven on his horse (which had a woman's face and a peacock's tail). The heavenly journey was said to have begun at the "uttermost mosque," with no mention of its location. However, at a later time and in an effort to usurp the holy meaning of the Jewish Temple area, the composers of the legend deemed the lift-off point to have been the location of the Temple Mount in Jerusalem.[13]

Arabs themselves have underscored this proposition that Palestine was never designated a separate country.

When the First Congress of Muslim-Christian Associations met in Jerusalem in February 1919…the following resolution was adopted:

"We consider Palestine as part of Arab Syria, as it has never been separated from it any time."...The representative of the Arab Higher Committee to the United Nations submitted a statement to the General Assembly in May 1947 that said, "Palestine was part of the Province of Syria" and that, "politically, the Arabs of Palestine were not independent in the sense of forming a separate political entity."... Later Ahmed Shuqeiri, later the chairman of the Palestine Liberation Organization (PLO), told the United Nations Security Council, "It is common knowledge that Palestine is nothing but southern Syria."[14]

But the Hebrew prophets convey the message of the Lord that the dream of the Chosen People will be realized. They shall return to the land of promise. And they will return at the behest of their God and in no way except that. He will make it possible. His judgments and His compassion will bring forth the amazing actions of His Providence, making the nations and Israel herself come to terms with His call to His people.

But you, O mountains of Israel, shall shoot out your branches, and yield your fruit to my people Israel; for they shall soon come home [or literally, "for they draw near to come]. See now, I am for you; I will turn to you; and you shall be tilled and sown; and I will multiply your population, the whole house of Israel, all of it; the towns shall be inhabited and the waste places rebuilt; and I will multiply human beings and animals upon you...[I] will do more good to you than ever before. Then you shall know that I am the Lord...and no longer will I let you hear the insults of the nations, no longer shall you bear the disgrace of the peoples; and no longer shall you cause your nation to stumble," says the Lord. (Ezekiel 36:8–11, 15)

This is the faithful God of Israel comforting His exiled people. It is the Lord God of Israel, who is claiming the land for the purpose of resettling His people in it. Other nations have wasted it; now it is time for Israel to recover it.

The world's family of nations has been home to the Jewish people, but their habitation has been in a place of victimization. Therefore, God is acting.

Ezekiel's prophecy correlates with modern history. Theodore Herzl, a European journalist and head of the Zionist movement, reported on the insults that the Jews have suffered. In his pamphlet "The Jewish State," he confronted the Jewish question. This was 1896, when Europe prided itself on offering liberty and the widespread belief among the intelligentsia was that human mortals were approaching perfection. But for the Jewish people, the black clouds had already formed and were visible. Herzl put them on notice:

> No one can deny the gravity of the Jewish situation. Wherever they live in appreciable number, Jews are persecuted in greater or lesser measure. Their equality before the law, granted by statute, has become practically a dead letter…Attacks in parliaments, in assemblies, in the press, in the pulpit, in the street, on journeys—for example, their exclusion from certain hotels—even in places of recreation are increasing from day to day. The forms of persecutions vary according to country and social circle…Is it not true that the Jewish middle classes are seriously threatened? Is it not true that the passions of the mob are incited against our wealthy? Is it not true that our poor endure greater suffering than any other proletariat? I think that this pressure is everywhere present. In our upper economic classes it causes discomfort, in our middle classes utter despair.
>
> The fact of the matter is, everything tends to one and the same conclusion, which is expressed in the classic Berlin cry: *"Juden raus!"* ("Out with the Jews.")
>
> I shall now pose the question in the briefest possible form: Shouldn't we "get out" at once, and if so, whither?[15]

Franz Kafka (1883–1924), German Jewish writer, was conflicted about his Jewishness and wrote in 1923 to his lover, Milena Jesenska:

> I've spent all afternoon in the streets, wallowing in the Jew-baiting. "Prasive Plemeno"—"filthy rabble" I heard someone call the Jews the other day. Isn't it the natural thing to leave the place where one is hated so much? The heroism which consists of staying on in spite of it all is that of cockroaches which also can't be exterminated from the bathroom.[16]

In fact, in Eastern Europe, it was common in those days to compare the Jews to giant insects!

So consider God's voice, through Ezekiel, speaking of anti-Semitism as it correlates precisely with the situation in Europe. "No longer will I let you hear the insults of the nations." And, "they made you desolate indeed, and crushed you from all sides, so that you became the possession of the rest of the nations, and you became an object of gossip and slander among the people."

It was time for the Lord to act, and the promise is reiterated in chapter 37 of Ezekiel:

> Thus says the Lord God: I will take the people of Israel from the nations among which they have gone, and will gather them from every quarter, and bring them to their own land. I will make them one nation in the land, on the mountains of Israel; and one king shall be king over them all...My servant David shall be king over them; and they shall all have one shepherd. (Ezekiel 37:21–22, 24)

What about this? We are now pushing the limits of historical paradigms and comprehensible developments. Secular people will scoff at the biblical outlook. They, with their limitations, will quickly cast aside scriptural portrayals of Israel's future. These limitations include the inability to see beyond physical laws and historical paradigms. Secular people reject out of hand the future view of the prophets. But to those who believe, these prophecies hold the key to unlocking the mystery of the whole Jewish drama since before the time of Jesus. *It must be affirmed that the prophetic promise of a return to the homeland is so bound up with the literal, historical scattering of Israel that this promise must surely be that of a real physical return.* Along with that return, on the horizon is a spiritual awakening. Together they constitute a veritable "resurrection" of Israel—a quickening of interest, a homecoming of her people, a reclaiming of her portion, a sprouting of faith. Her God, who humiliated her before the nations, now lifts her up—in real life and reportable happening. Eventually, Israel's people shall have one king—he who comes from the house of David and, at the same time, one who will be their true high priest. The peoples who once insulted the Jews in their scattered places will now look in awe.

Today those Jews who are in the holy land can hardly escape their identity and history. Archeological finds corroborate biblical history, bringing to light revelatory events. They are living with ancestral infrastructure, real estate, and tombs right beneath their feet. They are awakening as from a sleep that has lasted for generations, and now they see, albeit dimly, that their very environment speaks of the covenant with their God. The land is important in the future spiritual rebirth of the nation. Jewish skeptics from around the globe are moving to the place where God revealed Himself to their ancestors. They will be enticed, convinced, convicted, and drawn into the circle of their people's history and God's mercy. Many observant Jews have lived by promise and hope. Their anticipation varies but is often high in these days. Their hearts overflow. Israel reborn is a vindication of their historical longing and expectation.

JESUS ON ISRAEL'S IDENTITY AND FUTURE

What can we say about Yeshua? First, He was a prophet, as His audiences recognized. The little that He said about Israel's future is notable. Secondly,

He was specific about the Israelite identity and calling. The concentration in His ministry was the House of Israel, and he instructed His disciples on their special mission to "go only to the lost sheep of the House of Israel" (Matthew 10:5–6). While conversing with the woman at Jacob's well in Samaria, He plainly told her that the Samaritans' worship was ignorant of the truth but that Jewish worship was authentic (John 4:22). It is true that He came to break down barriers, *yet He did not nullify Israel's special identity and calling.*

Further, He made it very clear that His teaching did not nullify the law and the prophets. His coming would put the prophetic word in greater perspective and fulfill the scriptures. He opened a window to the future when He spoke of the destruction of Jerusalem and the Jewish worldwide dispersion. "When you see Jerusalem surrounded by armies, then know that its desolation has come near...For there will be great distress on the earth and wrath against this people; they will fall by the edge of the sword and be taken away as captives among all nations; and Jerusalem will be trampled on by the Gentiles, until the times of the Gentiles are fulfilled" (Luke 21:20, 23b–24). Gentile rule would not last forever: Jesus said there would be an ending to it!

All that was predicted has happened! Jerusalem was destroyed by the Romans and then trampled on—by the Byzantines, Arabs, Seljuk Turks, Crusaders, Mamluks, and Ottoman Turks. These Gentile peoples stomped their heels on Jerusalem, inflicting repressive policies and massacres on the Jews. That scenario is over, or nearly so. Now, since the times of the Gentiles are nearly fulfilled—since the empires no longer control Palestine and the Middle East, and since the Jewish nation has governmental control over Jerusalem, though she is still somewhat subject to the bidding of the United Nations and the United States—the prophecy of Jesus looms large in the contemporary Middle East sequence of events.

God is calling the descendants of the Hebrews back. The fulfillment of the prophecies is in progress. How can one think differently if he or she believes in this God of faithfulness, justice, and steadfast love? He is lifting out and placing in—lifting out his people from the ends of the earth and placing them in the land. Not all who immigrate to Israel like it there: some are unenthusiastic, some in fact are anti-Zionists, and some originally did want to go but, after being there a while, became discouraged with the hardships or change of culture. Some left to return to their countries of origin or went elsewhere, to assimilate. But the Jewish population in the land keeps growing. The birth rates are among the world's highest, and the immigrants are still arriving. There is more. Increasing anti-Semitism in the developed countries of the West has the potential of creating additional major waves of Jewish immigrants.

ZECHARIAH'S PROPHECY

We will look in the Tanakh at one more prophecy about the return and restoration. Martin Luther did not act kindly to the Jews, yet he called Zechariah's prophecy "the quintessence of the prophets." In it the reader senses first the divine zeal for the restoration of Zion. Secondly, the messianic theme is very strong and is typified by a consecrated, perfect high priest who is later called "the branch"—a metaphor used also by Jeremiah. Thirdly, God expresses His attitude toward the nations. When Zechariah wrote these words, he was living in Palestine *following* the termination of the Babylonian exile. Therefore, we can conclude that he was speaking of another exile and ingathering.

> Thus says the Lord of hosts: 'Even though it seems impossible to the remnant of this people in these days, should it also seem impossible to me, says the Lord of hosts? Thus says the Lord of hosts, I will save my people from the east country and from the west country; and I will bring them to live in Jerusalem. They shall be my people and I will be their God, in faithfulness and in righteousness...Just as you have been a cursing among the nations, O house of Judah and house of Israel, so I will save you and you shall be a blessing. Do not be afraid, but let your hands be strong.' (Zechariah 8:6–8, 13)

Hashem speaks and repeatedly calls Himself by name in this chapter. The name "the Lord of hosts" signifies that He who speaks has all the heavenly powers at His disposal. It is He who guarantees that this restoration will come, and therefore they should not doubt the fulfillment despite the unlikeliness of its occurrence from a natural point of view. It is as if He says, "Don't doubt me."

The beginning of this oracle sets the tone:

The word of the Lord of hosts came to me, saying: "Thus says the Lord of hosts: I am jealous for Zion with great jealousy, and I am jealous for her with great wrath." (8:1–2)

Why the wrath? Because of the oppression and cruelty of the nations directed toward His chosen and beloved people. He used these nations to punish His people, and He warned those nations not to "make a full end" (Jeremiah 5:10) of His beloved. But they showed no mercy. The Gentile nations up to the modern era, even many so-called Christian nations, have collaborated to demonize, torment, banish, and attempt to vanquish the Jews. So now, too, in our time, history is replicating itself.[17]

The United Nations General Assembly, now dominated by Arab and Muslim states, has repeatedly convened emergency sessions to rail against the State of Israel. The UN Human Rights Council has passed more resolutions and decisions condemning Israel than all other UN member nations combined. The Human Rights Council's privileged membership has included China, Libya, Cuba, Saudi Arabia, Pakistan, Algeria, and even Sudan (when they were engaged in genocide in Darfur). Yet their own shameful human rights records receive minimal attention, whereas Israel is continually viewed with contempt.

Worldwide, the sentiment against Israel is coming to the boiling point, even as many nations are finding it advantageous to trade with Israel. Meanwhile,

Iran, which is one of the most brazen in its vow to destroy the Zionist entity, is gaining influence with the family of nations. Furthermore, Russia and Iran have combined to gain predominant influence in the Middle East, since the United States has pulled back its place as the dominant superpower.

A Climactic World War in Jerusalem

The Jewish destiny of suffering would reach its climax when all the nations united to descend upon Israel with the intent to finally rid the world of Jewish influence—yes, even of its population. Here is a prophecy that would have been doubted in past ages but that is much easier to find credible in today's world. In the wars against the new state of Israel, the Arabs were frank in announcing that this was a war of annihilation. Arab influence in the United Nations; Arab investments in United States assets and institutions of higher learning; the world's media bias toward the Palestinian viewpoint; the secularism blanketing Europe; and global lawlessness and moral decay have all resulted in increasing anger throughout the world toward Israel the Chosen. The hatred nurtured in the heart of Arab peoples has spread worldwide. The Chosen People have increasingly become the worldwide object of extreme enmity.

But as promised, the Lord of Hosts will take things in hand, will show compassion to the House of Israel, and will strengthen and save her. He is jealous, and He is determined.

> The word of the Lord concerning Israel: Thus says the Lord who stretched out the heavens and founded the earth and formed the human spirit within: See, I am about to make Jerusalem a cup of reeling for all the surrounding peoples; it will be against Judah also in the siege against Jerusalem. On that day I will make Jerusalem a heavy stone for all the peoples; all who lift it shall grievously hurt themselves. And all the nations of the earth shall come together against it. (Zechariah 12:1–3)

The Denouement

The Lord is seen here as both the God of creation who made heaven and earth, and the God of human history. The surrounding peoples will initially be the object of God's action. They will have to drink the cup of wine, causing them to stagger. Then Jerusalem, the center of the Chosen People, will become a heavy stone. Because of the fierce animosity of many nations, those "nations of the earth" will join Israel's neighbors to annihilate the Jews. But even with all the power of the international community, the weight of the resources at Israel's disposal will be too much for the enemy. Israel's time of utmost desperation will be the opportunity for the Lord to display His power on their behalf.

"ON THAT DAY…"

This phrase, repeatedly used by Zechariah, describes the day of the Messiah—not the day of His coming in humiliation and being subject to the hostility of the authorities but the day of His second coming in power. It describes the day of vengeance, as Isaiah puts it (Isaiah 61:2; see also Zechariah 14).

At another crucial time in Israel's military history, the army of the Assyrian Empire came and besieged Jerusalem with a mighty host. Isaiah assured the king of Judah that the city would not be taken. Accordingly, Hezekiah spoke encouragingly to the people: "Be strong and of good courage. Do not be afraid or dismayed before the king of Assyria and all the horde that is with him; for there is one greater with us than with him. With him is an arm of flesh; but with us is the Lord our God, to help us and to fight our battles. The people were encouraged" (II Chronicles 32:7–8). Then the Lord sent an angel, who cut down all the warriors, commanders, and officers of the Assyrian army, and Sennacherib, the Assyrian king, returned home in disgrace. The *Archeological Study Bible* states that the data support the biblical accounts of Sennacherib's military campaigns in what is now known as Palestine.[18] The Assyrian Empire could not strike back.

That event was a precursor to the final "day of the Lord." On that day, when the confederate anti-God powers descend upon Jerusalem, the Lord Himself will act, vindicating His sovereignty in choosing Israel. For Israel, it will be the final struggle with the nations that have despised her. The Lord will display His majesty and righteousness in some mysterious manner, defeating the Gentile powers.

> On that day the Lord will shield the inhabitants of Jerusalem so that the feeblest among them on that day shall be like David, and the house of David shall be like God, like the angel of the Lord, at their head. And on that day I will seek to destroy all the nations that come against Jerusalem. (Zechariah 12:8–9)

This is, I think, an easier scenario to imagine now than it was for previous generations because of current events taking place in the Middle East. Increasingly, the attention of the world is drawn there, where ages-old religious and political disputes and anti-Semitism have boiled into a cauldron of rage.

The Chosen People See the Chosen One

The Hebrew prophets and most of the Jewish sages recognized that their nation would never experience religious awakening while its people were scattered to the ends of the earth. They knew it would be in the land where Israel would experience a spiritual rebirth. In their homeland, as a people gathered from the ends of the earth, they will experience their redemption. Thus, the ingathering will take place *before* the Lord pours out His spirit upon them. They will come to Jerusalem from the ends of the earth. Then, on that great day, the appearance of an unnamed person will throw the house of David and the inhabitants of Jerusalem into an outpouring of grief.

> And I will pour out a spirit of compassion and supplication on the house of David and the inhabitants of Jerusalem, so that, when they look [Hebrew "on me"] on the one whom they have pierced, they

shall mourn for him, as one mourns for an only child, and weep bitterly over him, as one weeps over a firstborn. (Zechariah 12:10)

In Zechariah's dramatic prophecy, the one who had been pierced presents Himself as the unmistakable Savior. He appears to them in the city of peace—Jerusalem. And the hearts of gathered Israel are won over in the very city where He was arrested—the city of their pride.

Note that their preparation for this appearance was an outpouring of a "spirit of compassion and supplication." In this astounding prophecy, God first gives the Jewish nation a spectacular deliverance from all their enemies that have surrounded them in their land and city. But what comes next is just as amazing: the Jewish people are filled with a new spirit—that of compassion and supplication. The word translated "compassion" might also be translated "grace" as it is in the New American Standard Bible and the New International Version. "Supplication" is a prayer from a supplicant—one who pours out his or her heart in earnest and with passion.

This compassion and supplication is not readily apparent in much of Jewry today. As discussed in chapter 11, "The Crisis in Judaism," many of their rabbis show an awareness of this deficiency in the religious life of modern-day Jewry. Long ago, Moses charged them with being stiff-necked. The prophets said their hearts were adamant and stubborn. More polite modern rabbis, concerned about their constituencies, charge modern Jews (notably of the Reform and Conservative branches) in America with having abandoned a commitment to any substance of religion—which is to say that they too turn a deaf ear and lay bare a hard heart.

But now, this lack of depth is converted in this portrayal of the Jews who gather as one in Jerusalem—converted to a beautifully fervent and grace-filled spirit. Now, in this spirit, they are given a vision—a vision that they all, as one body, see.

Anyone who has tried to talk to Jewish people about Yeshua can testify that he or she was stopped cold. There are exceptions, but the rule is there. Neither openness nor tolerance is shown. As Michael Medved, the Jewish film critic and political commentator (not a Messianic Jew), has so plainly put it,

> The chief distinguishing characteristic of most American Jews is not what they do believe, but what they do not believe. They do not believe in Jesus as the Messiah. Period. End of sentence, end of story. Tragically, for all too many members of today's Jewish community, this rejection marks the sum total of their theological commitment, the beginning and end of their ideological identity as adherents to what is still misleadingly described as "the Jewish faith."...Acceptance of Jesus is the one theological permutation that Jews of all persuasions find unacceptable, the only issue on which Jewish Americans from the militantly secular to the militantly Hasidic are ready to draw a common line.[19]

Historians use the term *rejectionism* to describe how Israel's neighbors (especially Arab Muslims) regard the Jews. Just as neighboring nations and peoples have totally rejected the Israeli Jews, so too do most Israeli Jews exhibit an absolute rejection of Yeshua. The parallel is uncanny. The emotions accompanying both these positions are deeply set.

One incident in the early history of the Chosen People is suggestive of the many rejecting the one. Joseph was hated by his brothers. This rejection within the brotherhood foreshadowed the enmity of the Jewish establishment toward Yeshua. As Joseph gained favor with his father, the brothers' hatred was sown and then increased by Joseph's dreams of rulership. During the unlikely reign of Joseph over Egypt, when he was second only to Pharaoh in authority, Joseph confronted the needy brothers. In that encounter they did not recognize him, though they were intimidated by his position and his treatment of them. When at last he identified himself, they were overcome with fear and astonishment. The brother they rejected, almost murdered, and then sold into slavery was now in authority over them. Happily, the denouement of this story showed Joseph forgiving and providing for their needs—a dramatic reconciliation.

So in the great denouement at the end of days, as seen by Zechariah the prophet, Israel, having rejected her Savior, gathers in Jerusalem, unwittingly doing so to meet Him. The people gaze upon Him, who was born an Israelite and brought up in a Torah-observant family. He is their brother.

"When they look on the one whom they have pierced..." This is no casual look. The Hebrew word for "look" is *nabat*, which means "to look, look intently at, gaze, or regard." His appearance is there for all to see and contemplate. They who have rejected Him are confronted with His image.

> When they look on the one whom they have pierced, they shall mourn
> for him, as one mourns for an only child, and weep bitterly over him,
> as one weeps over a firstborn. (12:10)

This experience of all Israel is reminiscent of Saul of Tarsus, who was stopped dead in his tracks on the road to Damascus. As Saul was, this people is transfixed. In this moment, they see the one they pierced. In Saul's experience, he heard Jesus say to him, "I am Jesus whom you are persecuting" (Acts 9:5). In fighting against the Christians, Saul was fighting the Lord. Likewise, the Jewish nation has fiercely resisted Immanuel ("God with us").

We must now note a translation issue of great significance in the middle of verse ten: the Hebrew text uses the first-person singular "me," not "the one." A most amazing variation in translation is here: "When they look on me whom they have pierced" (12:10).

Not "look on the *one* whom they have pierced" but "on *me* whom they have pierced" (emphasis mine). The Lord was speaking. It was the Lord in human flesh whose body was pierced—a phenomenon that the prophet Zechariah was inspired to write. The New Bible Commentary says that "all the ancient Versions and the best Hebrew MSS [manuscripts] read the first person singular."[20] Here is Messiah/Christ, who appears to those in Jerusalem whose hearts have been filled with grace. They are made ready to receive. They see that He is Savior. "Then the eyes of the blind shall be opened" (Isaiah 35:5). On this day, there is no veil to hide His glory.

Just as discussed in Isaiah's prophecy in the chapter "The Suffering Servant," the Suffering Servant is a messianic figure; here we see again the one who came down to save and was smitten by God to atone for sins. This alludes to the mystery of the Godhead, as it is the Lord speaking who is the pierced one.

In the days of Jesus's earthly ministry, when Jesus was approaching this very city of Jerusalem, the very city of which Zechariah was speaking, He stopped and wept over it. He longed to minister to Jerusalem, its religious establishment, and throngs of Jewish worshippers who came to the Temple, but they, their leaders, and many others conspired to do away with Him. As He and His followers approached the city where He would make what is called the Triumphal Entry, "he wept over it, saying, 'If you, even you, had only recognized on this day the things that make for peace! But now they are hidden from your eyes'" (Luke 19:42).

In Zechariah's vision of the last days, it is not the Messiah who weeps but the house of David and the people of Jerusalem: "The land shall mourn, each family by itself…and their wives by themselves" (12:12).

The whole land shall mourn, not (only) as a gathered people but as families, humbling themselves before the Lord and their family members. The children will see their parents humbled. Their pride will dissipate—their stubbornness also—as they are stunned and shaken to the depths as they gaze upon the one they rejected, the one who came to save Israel. Their hearts of stone will be changed into hearts of flesh. The one who came conquering their enemies will come also to transform their spirits.

It is fascinating that some rabbinical scholars whose works are in the Talmud agree that this section of Zechariah's prophecy refers to the Messiah. In Sukkah 52a in the Babylonian Talmud, it reads,

> It's well according to him who explains that the cause (of the mourning) is the slaying of the Messiah the son of Joseph, since that well agrees with the Scripture verse: "And they shall look upon me, whom they have pierced; and shall mourn for him, as one mourneth for his only son."[21]

The day when Israel views the one they pierced and then humbles themselves, recognizing Him as the Lord of all peoples and nations—that will be the decisive and final day of national atonement. The nation, on that day, will receive forgiveness and justification, be purified from its sin, be reconciled with God the Lord, and be restored to her covenant position as a nation of priests and servants.

But the Jewish heart of stone is not the only heart to be humbled: the church too will be humbled at the homecoming and cleansing of the Jews. Dietrich Bonhoeffer, Christian martyr in Nazi Germany, saw this vision of Israel's future and the church's humble position.

> That is to be the end of the people's suffering. From here the Christian Church sees the history of the people of Israel with trembling as God's own, free, fearful way with his people. It knows that no nation in the world can be finished with this mysterious people, because God is not yet finished with it...As it [the Church] looks at the rejected people, it humbly recognizes itself as a church continually unfaithful to its Lord and looks full of hope to those of the people of Israel who have come home, to those who have come to believe in the one true God in Christ, and knows itself to be bound to them in brotherhood.[22]

The church will rejoice as it sees, welcomes, cherishes, and admires Israel. John's vision of the New Jerusalem in the Book of Revelation (21:9–14) includes the names of the twelve tribes of Israel on the twelve gates of the Temple, and then he sees the names of the twelve apostles of the Lamb on the foundations of the city wall. The cleansing of Israel and the renewal of the church makes possible the positioning of these names together on the same temple structure—unified in their acclamation of the one Lamb of God.

REDEMPTION

The denouement, when all things come together, is the Day of Redemption— the coming of the Messiah, world peace, prosperity, and the dissemination of wisdom—a radical transformation of man, beast, and the whole of creation, when God's glory will be revealed. It is written and underscored in the scriptural doctrine of the end of days that it will be the day of the coming of the Son of Man. He will come the second time, and we will see Him in His glory. Then the church of Jesus Christ and its brothers and sisters among the Jewish people will shine in their oneness.

> For Zion's sake I will not keep silent,
> And for Jerusalem's sake I will not rest
> Until her vindication shines out like the dawn,
> And her salvation like a burning torch.
> The nations shall see your vindication,
> And all the kings your glory;
> And you shall be called by a new name
> That the mouth of the Lord will give.
> You shall be a crown of beauty in the hand of the Lord
> And a royal diadem in the hand of your God. (Isaiah 62:1–3)

1. We can also find this affirmation of the original promises (presumably including the land) to Abraham in Galatians 3:17–18, where Paul says, "My point is this: the law, which came four hundred thirty years later [than Abraham], does not annul a covenant previously ratified by God, so as to nullify the promise. For if the inheritance comes from the law, it no longer comes from the promise; but God granted it to Abraham through the promise."

2. Christopher Dawson, *Dynamics of World History* (Wilmington: ISI Books, 2002), 249.

3. Gary M. Burge, *Whose Land? Whose Promise?* (Cleveland: The Pilgrim Press, 2003), 189.

4. Abraham Joshua Heschel, *Israel: An Echo of Eternity* (New York: Farrar, Straus, and Giroux, 1969), 59.

5. Arthur Hertzberg, *The Zionist Idea* (Philadelphia: The Jewish Publication Society, 1997), 16.

6. Paul Johnson, *A History of the Jews* (New York: Harper and Row, 1987), 82.

7. Louis Greenberg, *The Jews in Russia* (New York: Schocken Books, 1976), 1.

8. Joan Peters, *From Time Immemorial* (Chicago: JKAP Publications, 1984), 38–50.

9. J. Alec Motyer, *The Prophecy of Isaiah* (Downers Grove: IVP Academic, 1993), 244, 247.

10. Abraham Joshua Heschel, *Israel: An Echo of Eternity*, 101.

11. Walter Brueggemann, *A Commentary on Jeremiah: Exile and Homecoming* (Grand Rapids: Eerdmans Publishing Company, 1998), 315–316.

12. Joan Peters, *From Time Immemorial* (Chicago: JKAP Publications, 1984), 196.

13. Samuel Katz, *Battleground: Fact and Fantasy in Palestine* (New York: Taylor Productions, 2002), 132.

14. Mitchell Bard, *The Complete Idiot's Guide to Middle East Conflict* (Indianapolis: Alpha Books, 1999), 89.

15. Arthur Hertzberg, *The Zionist Idea* (Philadelphia: The Jewish Publication Society, 1997), 215–216.

16. Bernard Wasserstein, *On the Eve: The Jews of Europe before the Second World War* (New York: Simon and Schuster, 2012), 280.

17. Europe, once again, is becoming a place where synagogues are burned, Jews are struck down, and justice is slow.

18. *The Archeological Study Bible* (Grand Rapids: Zondervan Publishing, 2005), 659, 1118.

19. Milton Himmelfarb, "What Do American Jews Believe?: A Symposium,"Michael Medved, *Commentary*, August 1996, 68-69.

20. Guthrie and Motyer, *The New Bible Commentary*, 3rd ed. (Grand Rapids: Wm. B. Eerdmans, 1970), 800.

21. Sukkah 52a in the *Babylonian Talmud*.

22. Dietrich Bonhoeffer, *Selected Writings* (London: Fount [Harper Collins], 1995), 50.

GLOSSARY

aliyah. A Hebrew term meaning "to ascend," "to go up." It is applied in modern times to a Jew who immigrates to Israel.

Ashkenazim. Jews of European descent; one of two Jewish groups that spoke Yiddish. The name derives from the rabbinical term for Germany.

demigod. A minor deity in mythology; a highly regarded leader who is celebrated as a god or as godlike.

dhimmi. A Christian or Jew whose life is protected by Muslim authorities because of being part of the "people of the book," meaning those who are guided by their scriptures.

dhimmitude. Muslim treatment of Jews and Christians, placing them one step higher than infidels, thus giving them status as protected people or "dhimmis." Because dhimmis are not Muslim, dhimmitude usually requires an extra head tax, denial of many rights such as legal status in the courts, and being subject to many forms of humiliation.

Diaspora. from the Greek *diasperein* to scatter. The aggregate of Jewish people who live in lands other than Israel.

Emancipation (used with "The") Refers to the emancipation of the Jews in various countries of Europe between the latter part of the 18th century and the early 20th century. Jews had been subjected to various restrictive laws such as the requirement to wear specific types of clothing and/or badges, reside in isolated areas, swear special oaths and wear distinctive clothing. The rights of full citizenship were withheld, such as voting and unrestricted travel. Gradually, the Jewish people were given official recognition as citizens with its attendant opportunities along with full integration into society.

Enlightenment (used with "The") An eighteenth-century movement based on the primacy of human reasoning, tending to undermine at least some of traditional religious and social thought. It was the foundational thinking for the political revolutions of 18th and 19th century Europe, neutralizing the control of the Church and the monarchy. It advanced the ideals of liberty, progress and tolerance. The Enlightenment has since been opposed by competing intellectual movements.

fellah. Plural **fellahin.** An Arab peasant or common laborer.

Gemara. An analysis and commentary on the Mishna composed during the third, fourth, and fifth centuries.

Hamas. An Arabic acronym for the Islamic Resistance Movement. It was inaugurated in 1987 at the formation of the first Palestinian Intifada.

Hashem. A Hebrew term literally meaning "the Name." Out of reverence, it is used for "God" in order to avoid speaking the divine name.

intifada. An Arabic term literally meaning "shaking off" that is used in a metaphorical sense to mean "uprising." When capitalized, used to describe a period of Palestinian violent attacks that were made to shake off the Israeli presence in Samaria and Galilee.

jihad. Means "exerted"; the act of striving or struggling to maintain and advance the Muslim religion, commonly rendered as "holy war." Most Muslim jurists consider jihad to refer at least partly to military action as well as a personal effort to live the religion.

Judaism. The religion, nationality, and culture of the Jews. The religion, though, is the element that forms the nationality and culture. Its main elements go back to the beginnings of the Hebrew religion, when God revealed Himself to Abraham, Isaac, and Jacob, giving them the promises for Israel's future. But strictly speaking, "Judaism" is the name given to the rabbinical formulations of the second or third century before Christ. It designates certain foods as kosher or nonkosher and sets certain days of the Jewish year as holy days. It was highly institutionalized by the rabbis in the time between the Babylonian exile and the coming of Christ. Its focus was on the interpretation and elaboration of the law and its promulgation in the synagogues. It was this system that issued in the composition of the Midrash and Mishna and later the Talmud. Reform Jewish (liberal) definitions are much weaker, defining Judaism as being built on sacred myths and rituals that attempt to give meaning and purpose to life.

kehillah. Plural **Kehillot.** A Jewish community in any city, organized for charity and other work.

mandate. A system created and commission given by the League of Nations to a member nation to administer conquered territory. Near the end of World War I, Great Britain was awarded a mandate to temporarily govern Palestine, Transjordan, and Iraq—lands that had been ruled by the Ottoman Empire.

Mashiach. Hebrew name for "the Anointed One." The English translation is "Messiah."

Middle East. A region, primarily in western Asia, consisting of such nations as Syria, Lebanon, Israel, Jordan, Iraq, Iran, Saudi Arabia, Kuwait, Bahrain, Qatar, Yemen, United Arab Emirates, Oman, Egypt, and Turkey. Formerly identified as the Near East.

Midrash. Literally, "probing." A compilation of rabbinical writings seeking meanings and explanations not readily apparent on a surface reading of the Torah; the commentary reaches back to the second century in its written form, and it is much older in oral-discourse form.

Mishna. Compilation of Jewish oral law—they memorized it!—passed from generation to generation. Still called the "oral Torah," it was put into writing at the end of the second century.

mitzvah. Plural **mitzvoth.** A commandment of the law, especially Jewish law; a charitable act.

Mizrahim. Jews who never left the Middle East and North Africa after the Babylonian captivity—those who chose not to return to their native land. Large, old Jewish communities of Mizrahim were found, especially in Iran and Iraq, until the mid-1940s.

mufti. A Muslim leader responsible for interpreting Islamic law, usually held in high esteem by the adherents of Islam.

Palestine. This term was originally applied to the territory of the Philistines. Later, the Romans used it for the land of Israel in the form of *Palaestina*. Under the Ottoman rule, the land was just the south subprovince of southern Syria. Under the British Mandate, the area between the Mediterranean Sea and the Jordan River became known as Palestine, and the name was applied to Jewish institutions such as the Palestine National Orchestra. Today it is thought of as distinct from Israel.

Palestine Liberation Organization (PLO). An umbrella organization that includes subsidiary groups like Fatah, the more militant Marxist Popular Front for the Liberation of Palestine, and others. It was organized in 1964 by Arab nations, but after the Six-Day War of 1967, it became autonomous. It is strongly anti-Zionist and has always used terrorist methods to harass Israel, even though it professed to delete its nonrecognition of Israel in its covenant.

perestroika. This Russian word literally means "restructuring." It refers to a policy of economic reform that loosened control of the output of state enterprises under secretary of the Communist Party Mikhail Gorbachev. This, with the new policy of "glasnost" (openness), loosened the grip of the Communist Party in the 1980s.

pogrom. An organized attack on Jewish towns and villages, often demolishing homes and synagogues and inflicting massacres. The term is most commonly used to refer to Russian anti-Semitism in the latter part of the nineteenth19th century.

Rejectionism The persistent rejection by the Arab people of the Jews and the State of Israel. Resistance to any reasonable and coherent plan for the co-existence of Arabs and Jews.

Sabra The term is used of a desert plant which is prickly to the touch but sweet to the taste on the inside. The Jews who have lived in Israel since their birth are known by this name because of their supposed personal characteristics of being prickly in their exterior but kindly when known well.

Salvific Having the power and authority to save.

Sephardim A group of European Jews who settled in Spain and Portugal, later to be expelled. They then scattered to various parts of the Ottoman Empire and North Africa.

Septuagint The Hebrew translation of the Tenakh into Greek.

Siddur Jewish book of daily prayers. The word itself means "order."

Six-Day War The war of June, 1967 as Egypt and Syria were calling for the elimination of Israel and quickly building up their armies, closing off the Suez Canal to Israel's shipping.

Talmud The discussions and commentaries on the Mishnah (see below) were compiled, interpreted and organized along with the Mishna itself, producing the Talmud. This mammoth work then became the authoritative work of law and tradition for Judaism. The Jerusalem version of this work was completed in the 4th century, and the more authoritative version in the 5th.

Temple Mount A 40-acre plot of land on what is thought to be Mount Moriah in Jerusalem on which Solomon's temple was built in the middle of the tenth century B.C. It was destroyed by the Babylonians in 586 B.C. and rebuilt 70 years later after the exile. It was renovated and expanded by Herod the Great, then razed by the Romans in 70 A.D. The Muslims later constructed the Dome of the Rock and the Al Aqsa Mosque on it.

Tenakh The Hebrew Bible, made up of twenty books. The Christian Old Testament includes the same books but combines some in such a way that it numbers thirty-nine books. For instance, I and II Kings in the Tenakh are only one book, and all of the Minor Prophets are considered one unit. In the first century A. D, Jewish scholars decided on the canon—the books that should be included.

Torah. In Hebrew this terms means "instruction" or "teaching." It usually refers to the first five books of the Old Testament/Tenakh, or the Five Books of Moses. However, it is sometimes used to describe all the Hebrew sacred writings, including interpretations of them. It can also refer to the scroll on which the Five Books of Moses are written. The *Pentateuch* is another term for the first five books.

West Bank. The standard name for the area west of the Jordan River. The Israelis and many Christians refer to it as Judea and Samaria—the biblical name.

Yahweh The commonly used English transliteration from the four Latin letters *YHWH*, which is called the "tetragrammaton," meaning "God." Placing vowels in it gives us "Yahweh." Its derivation may be from a verb meaning "to be." Many Jewish people believe it to be too sacred to utter or put into writing, and so this book uses "the Lord" or "Hashem"instead.

Yiddish. The language used by the Jews of Central and Eastern Europe until the Holocaust. It combined a medieval German dialect with Hebrew language elements.

Yishuv. The organized Jewish community in Palestine before it became a nation.

Yeshiva. A Jewish school, whether for the study of the Talmud in particular or a day school teaching both secular and religious subjects. Also refers to a Jewish rabbinical seminary.

Yeshua. Hebrew name for "Jesus."

Zionism. Zion was the name of the Jebusite stronghold in what was later, in King David's time, to become the city of Jerusalem. Zion thus became an alternate name for Jerusalem. In modern times, *Zionism* is the term used for a philosophy of return and the resulting movement of the Jews to immigrate to Israel. Zionist thinkers challenged the European and Russian Jews to escape the persecution there and join the spiritual and political movement to what was then called Palestine.

BIBLIOGRAPHY

Albright, William Foxwell. *From the Stone Age to Christianity.* New York: DoubledayAnchor, 1957.

Albright, William Foxwell. *Archaeology and the Religion of Israel.* Baltimore: Johns Hopkins Press, 1942.

Ariel, David S. *What Do Jews Believe? The Spiritual Foundations of Judaism.* NewYork: Schocken Books, 1995.

Bard, Michael. *The Complete Idiot's Guide to the Middle East Conflict.* Indianapolis: Alpha Books/Macmillan, 1999.

Bard, Michael. *Myths and Facts: A Guide to the Arab-Israeli Conflict.* Chevy Chase: American-Israeli Cooperative Enterprise, 2006.

Barth, Karl. *Church Dogmatics*, II, 2. Edinburgh: T & T Clark, 1957.

Bellow, Saul. *To Jerusalem and Back: A Personal Account.* New York: Penguin Books, 1977.

Bergen, Doris L. *Twisted Cross: The German Christian Movement.* Chapel Hill and London: The University of North Carolina Press, 1996.

Berman, Joshua A. *Created Equal: How the Bible Broke with Ancient Political Thought*. New York: Oxford, 2008.

Bokser, Ben Zion. *The Wisdom of the Talmud*. New York: Philosophical Library, 1951.

Braaten, Carl E., and Robert W. Jenson. *Jews and Christians: People of God*. Grand Rapids: William B. Eerdmans Publishing Company, 2003.

Brueggemann, Walter. *The Land*. Philadelphia: Fortress Press, 1977.

Dawson, Christopher. *Dynamics of World History*. Wilmington: ISI Books, 2002.

Dershowitz, Alan. *The Case for Israel*. Hoboken: John Wiley and Sons, 2003.

Dimont, Max. *Jews, God, and History*. New York: Penguin/Mentor, 1994.

Entine, Jon. *Abraham's Children: Race, Identity, and the DNA of the Chosen People*. New York: Grand Central Publishing, 2007.

Fein, Leonard. *Where Are We? The Inner Life of America's Jews*. New York: Harper and Row, 1988.

Frank, Anne. *The Diary of a Young Girl*. New York: Bantam Books, 1993.

Fromkin, David. *A Peace to End All Peace: The Fall of the Ottoman Empire and the Creation of the Modern Middle East*. New York: Henry Holt and Company, 1989.

Gidal, Nachum T. *Jews in Germany: From Roman Times to the Weimar Republic*. Köln: Konemann, 1998. English Language Edition.

Gilbert, Martin. *Jerusalem in the Twentieth Century.* New York: John Wiley and Sons, Inc., 1996.

Gilder, George. *The Israel Test.* Richard Vigilante Books, 2009.

Gordis, Daniel. *Home to Stay.* New York: Three Rivers Press, 2002.

Gordis, Daniel. *Israel: A Concise History of a Nation Reborn.* New York: Harper Collins, 2016.

Gordis, Daniel. *Saving Israel.* Hoboken: John Wiley and Sons, Inc., 2009.

Gorenberg, Gershom. *The Accidental Empire: Israel and the Birth of the Settlements, 1967–1977.* New York: Times Books (Henry Holt and Company), 2006.

Greenberg, Louis. *The Jews in Russia.* New York: Schocken Books, 1976.

Harkabi, Y. *The Palestinian Covenant and Its Meaning.* London: Valentine, Mitchell and Company, 1979.

Harrelson, Walter, and Randall M. Falk. *Jews and Christians: A Troubled Family.* Nashville: Abingdon Press, 1990.

Hazony, David, Yoram Hazony, and Michael B. Oren. *New Essays on Zionism.* New York and Jerusalem: Shalem Press, 2006.

Hazony, Yoram. *The Jewish State: The Struggle for Israel's Soul.* New York: Basic Books, 2001.

Herzog, Chaim. *The Arab-Israeli Wars: War and Peace in the Middle East.* New York: Vintage Books, 1984.

Heschel, Abraham Joshua. *Israel: An Echo of Eternity*. New York: Farrar, Straus, and Giroux, 1969.

Himmelfarb, Gertrude. *The People of the Book: Philosemitism in England, from Cromwell to Churchill*. New York: Encounter Books, 2011.

Hoffman, Joel M. *In the Beginning: A Short History of the Hebrew Language*. New York and London: New York University Press, 2004.

Hurewitz, J. C. *The Struggle for Palestine*. New York: W. W. Norton and Company, Inc., 1950.

Jenson, Robert W. *Ezekiel*. Grand Rapids: Brazos Press, 2009.

Johnson, Paul. *A History of the Jews*. New York: Harper Perennial, 1987.

Kac, Arthur W. *The Rebirth of the State of Israel*. Chicago: Moody Press, 1958.

Karsh, Efraim, and Inari Karsh. *Empires of the Sand*. Cambridge and London: Harvard University Press, 1999.

Karsh, Efraim. *Fabricating Israeli History: The "New Historians."* London and Portland: Frank Cass, 2000.

Karsh, Efraim. *Palestine Betrayed*. New Haven and London: Yale University Press, 2010.

Karsh, Efraim. *The Arab-Israeli Conflict: The Palestine War 1948*. Wellingborough: Osprey Publishing, 2002.

Kass, Leon R. *The Beginning of Wisdom: Reading Genesis*. New York: Free Press, 2003.

Katz, Samuel. *Battleground: Fact and Fantasy in Palestine.* Taylor Productions, Ltd., 2002. Revised.

Kleiman, Yaakov. *DNA and Tradition: The Genetic Link to the Ancient Hebrews.* Devora Publishing, 2004.

Kozodoy, Neal, ed. *The Mideast Peace Process.* San Francisco: Encounter Books, 2002.

Kurzman, Dan. *Ben-Gurion: Prophet of Fire.* New York: Simon and Schuster, 1983.

Laqueur, Walter. *A History of Zionism.* New York: Schocken Books, 2003.

Laqueur, Walter and Rubin, Barry, ed. *The Israel-Arab Reader.* New York: Penguin Books, 1976.

Levin, Kenneth. *The Oslo Syndrome: Delusions of a People under Siege.* Hanover: Smith and Kraus, 2005.

Lewis, Bernard. *Islam and the West.* New York: Oxford University Press, 1993.

Lewis, Bernard. *The Middle East: A Brief History of the Last 2,000 Years.* New York: Simon and Schuster, 1995.

Lozowick, Yaacov. *Right to Exist: A Moral Defense of Israel's Wars.* New York: Doubleday, 2004.

Mackey, Sandra. *Passion and Politics: The Turbulent World of the Arabs.* New York: Penguin/Plume, 1994.

Makovsky, Michael. *Churchill's Promised Land: Zionism and Statecraft.* New Haven: Yale University Press, 2007.

Mamet, David. *The Wicked Son: Anti-Semitism, Self-Hatred, and the Jews.* New York: Schocken Books, 2006.

Meir, Golda. *My Life.* London: Futura Publications, 1976.

Merkley, Paul Charles. *Christian Attitudes towards the State of Israel.* Montreal and Kingston: McGill-Queen's University Press, 2001.

Meyer, Michael A.: *Judaism within Modernity.* Detroit: Wayne State University Press, 2001

Miller, Aaron David. *The Much Too Promised Land: America's Elusive Search for Arab- Israeli Peace.* New York: Bantam Dell, 2008.

Morris, Benny. *Righteous Victims: A History of the Zionist-Arab Conflict, 1881–1999.* New York: Alfred A. Knopf, 1999.

Motyer, J. Alec. *The Prophecy of Isaiah.* Downers Grove: Inter-Varsity Press, 1993.

Neill, Stephen. *Christian Faith and Other Faiths: The Christian Dialogue with Other Religions.* London: Oxford, 1970.

Niebuhr, Reinhold. *Love and Justice: Selections from the Shorter Writings of Reinhold Niebuhr.* Louisville: Westminster/John Knox Press, 1957.

Novak, David. *The Election of Israel: The Idea of the Chosen People.* New York: Cambridge, 1995.

Oren, Michael B. *Six Days of War: June 1967 and the Making of the Modern Middle East.* New York: Ballantine Books, 2003.

Parkes, James. *End of an Exile: Israel, the Jews and the Gentile World.* New York: Library Publishers, 1954.

Parkes, James. *Whose Land? A History of the Peoples of Palestine.* Baltimore: Penguin Books, 1970.

Peters, Joan. *From Time Immemorial.* Chicago: JKAP Publications, 1984.

Pipes, Daniel. *Militant Islam Reaches America.* New York: W. W. Norton and Company, 2002.

Prager and Telushkin. *Why the Jews? The Reason for Antisemitism.* 2nd ed. New York: Simon and Schuster, 2003.

Prior, Michael, ed. *Speaking the Truth: Zionism, Israel, and Occupation.* Northampton: Olive Branch Press, 2005.

Rabinovich, Abraham. *The Yom Kippur War: The Epic Encounter That Transformed the Middle East.* New York: Schocken Books, 2004.

Rabkin, Yakov M. *A Threat from Within: A Century of Jewish Opposition to Zionism.* Black Point: Fernwood Publishing, 2006.

Remennick, Larissa. *Russian Jews on Three Continents.* New Brunswick: Transaction Publishers, 2007.

Robins, Philip. *A History of Jordan.* Cambridge: Cambridge Press, 2004.

Rosenbaum, Ron, ed. *Those Who Forget the Past: The Question of Anti-Semitism.* New York: Random House, 2004.

Rosenthal, Donna. *The Israelis: Ordinary People in an Extraordinary Land.* New York: Free Press, 2003

Sachar, Howard M. *A History of Israel: From the Rise of Zionism to Our Time.* Second Edition, Revised and Updated. New York: Alfred A. Knopf, 2003. Third Edition, Revised and Updated. New York: Alfred A. Knopf, 2007.

Said, Edward W. *The End of the Peace Process.* New York: Vintage Books, 2001.

Sarna, Nahum M. *Exploring Exodus: The Heritage of Biblical Israel.* New York: Schocken Books, 1986.

Schechtman, Joseph B. *On Wings of Eagles: The Plight, Exodus, and Homecoming of Oriental Jewry.* New York: Thomas Yoseloff, 1961.

Simon, Reeva Spector; Laskier, Michael Menachem; and Reguer, Sara, Editors. *The Jews of the Middle East and North Africa in Modern Times.* New York: Columbia University Press, 2003.

Steinsaltz, Adin. *The Essential Talmud.* New York: Basic Books, 1976.

Teveth, Shabtai. *Ben-Gurion and the Palestinian Arabs: From Peace to War.* New York: Oxford University Press, 1985.

Tillich, Paul. *Against the Third Reich: Paul Tillich's Wartime Radio Broadcasts into Nazi Germany.* Louisville: Westminster John Knox Press, 1998.

Tuchman, Barbara W. *The Proud Tower.* New York: The Macmillan Company, 1962.

Twain, Mark. *The Innocents Abroad*. Mineola: Dover Publications, Inc., 2003.

Viorst, Milton. *What Shall I Do with This People? Jews and the Fractious Politics of Judaism*. New York: The Free Press, 2002.

Wasserstein, Bernard. *On The Eve: The Jews of Europe before the Second World War*. New York: Simon and Schuster, 2012.

Wind, Renate. Dietrich Bonhoeffer: *A Spoke in the Wheel*. Grand Rapids: William B. Eerdmans, 1992.

Wisse, Ruth R. *If I Am Not for Myself…The Liberal Betrayal of the Jews*. New York: The Free Press, 1992.

Wright, Christopher. *New International Biblical Commentary: Deuteronomy*. Peabody: Hendrickson Publishers, 1996.

Yaari, Abraham. *The Goodly Heritage*. Jerusalem: Youth and Hechalutz Department of the Zionist Organization, 1958.

Ye'or, Bat. *Islam and Dhimmitude: Where Civilizations Collide*. Madison: Fairleigh Dickinson University Press, 2002.

Ziff, William B. *The Rape of Palestine*. Mansfield Centre, CT: Martino Publishing, 2009. Originally Published: New York: Longman's, Green and Co., 1938.

INDEX

Abbas, Mahmoud, 119, 149, 167, 187

Abd al-Rahman Azzam, 111

Abdulhamid II, 106

Abrabanel, Isaac ben Judah, 290

Abraham, 27-28, 30, 39, 41-42, 46, 55, 64-68, 70-71, 74, 78, 100-102, 159, 202-203, 205, 207, 208, 213, 232, 257-258, 263, 265, 285, 291, 294, 296-298, 300.

Ackerman, Susan, 283

Adoption, 294

Aelia Capitolina, 22

Age of Redemption, 232, 239, 241-242, 244, 249

A History of Israel: From the Rise of Zionism to Our Time, 185

Albright, Secretary of State Madeline, 165

Albright, William Foxwell, 27

Algeria, xvii

Al-Haram al-Sharif, 109

Aliyah (or Alijah), 41, 93, 106-107, 181, 258

Allah, 17, 71, 122, 307

America, 22, 57, 59, 92, 94, 98, 118, 122, 158-170; America chastened, 158-170.

American State Department, 170

Amman Jordan, 16, 299

Amorites, 31, 78

Anti-Semitic, 90, 99. 107, 114, 121, 145-146

Anti-Semitism, 217, 219, 241, 243-245, 310, 313, 317

Apocrypha, 234

Arab League, 111, 115, 117, 143, 182

Arab Palestinians, 12, 112, 114, 188

Arabia, 16, 95, 98, 100, 117, 314

Arabian Desert, 68

Arab Muslims, 104

Arabs, ix, xxi, 13, 71, 78, 87, 98, 99; Arab rejectionism, 101-114

Arafat, Yassir, 15, 141-145, 148-161, 165-167, 186

Aramaic Apocalypse (4Q246), 235

Archeological Study Bible, 316

Ashkenazi Jews, 241

QUINTON EVEREST, JR. HOLDS A bachelor of arts from Bethel College in Indiana and a master of divinity from Asbury Theological Seminary in Kentucky, but he's studied everything from biblical and English literature to European history, political science, and choral conducting.

Everest has pastored three Presbyterian Church (USA) congregations.

Made in the USA
Columbia, SC
06 December 2021